Cricketers' Who's Who

DEBRETT'S

Cricketers' Who's Who

Compiled and edited by
Iain Sproat, M.P.

With an introduction by
Colin Cowdrey, C.B.E.

DEBRETT'S PEERAGE LIMITED

© Iain Sproat 1980

Published by Debrett's Peerage Limited
73/77 Britannia Road, London SW6

ISBN 0 905649 26 5

Printed in Great Britain by
Ebernezer Baylis & Son Limited
The Trinity Press, Worcester, and London

Preface

THE CRICKETERS listed in this volume are all those who played one first-class game, or more, in the 1979 season in England.

The statistics are accurate up to the end of the 1979 season in England. The following abbreviations apply: * is an abbreviation for not out; f/class for first-class; jpl for John Player League; and b&h for Benson & Hedges.

Readers will notice certain occasional differences in the way the same kind of information about different cricketers is presented. This is because I have usually tried to follow the way in which the cricketers themselves provided the relevant information. Some cricketers, for example, are prepared to give both their address and telephone number, others prefer to give one but not the other; others again prefer to give neither. I have respected their individual wishes. Where a comment in one of the biographies appears in quotation marks, it is, with a very few exceptions obvious from the context, in the words of the cricketer himself.

I should like to acknowledge with sincere gratitude the great help I have received from Mr. Robert Brooke. I should also like to thank Mr. Leslie Hatton and Mr. Victor Isaacs for putting so much of their wide-ranging research at my disposal; Mr. Bill Smith, F.R.P.S., who personally took most of the photographs; Mr. Alan Lee for his most valuable assistance on many important aspects; and Mr. David Frith for his much appreciated encouragement and advice. Above all, I should like to thank the cricketers themselves, without whose generous support this volume could not have been compiled.

Iain Sproat

Introduction

CRICKET IS A SUBJECT on which there are already a huge number of books, although no player or spectator could ever feel there are too many. This book however covers untouched ground by giving a complete biography on each first class cricketer. All sportsmen have their idiosyncracies, and cricketers are no exception. It is the many varied personalities of the people who play the sport who make the game, and until now there has been no publication which gives details about the sportsmen themselves, rather than just their cricketing prowess. Cricketers are often regarded as a species set apart from the rest of mankind, but happily this book shows them to be mortal. I am sure the thousands of cricket supporters in this country will welcome the publication of this book, and will find it an invaluable and amusing guide. I hope it will become an annual fixture in the cricketing world.

Colin Cowdrey

ABBERLEY, Robert Neal.
County: Warwickshire.
Role: Right-hand bat, off-break bowler.
Date and place of birth: 22 April 1944, Birmingham.
Height: 5′ 8″. *Weight:* 10 st 7 lbs.
Parents: Arthur and Winifred Abberley.
Wife: Christine Mary.
Married: 15 March 1969.
Children: Russell and Colette.
Education and qualifications: Abbey Road Primary School; Saltley Grammar School.
Occupation outside cricket: Coaching.
Family links with cricket: None.
County debut: 1964. *County Cap:* 1966.
Benefit: 1979.
Outside interests: Horse-racing.
Nickname: Grabbers.
Other sporting activities: Soccer, golf, squash.
General: Toured Pakistan with M.C.C. 1966–67 but had to return early because of injury.
Address and telephone number: 17 Lugtrout Lane, Solihull, Birmingham.
Telephone: 021–705–1746.
Personal best: Batting f/class 117* Warwicks v Essex, Edgbaston 1966; jpl 76 Warwicks v

Glamorgan, Edgbaston 1974; b & h 113* Warwicks v Hants, Bournemouth 1976; gillette 47 Warwicks v Lincs, Edgbaston 1971. Bowling f/class 2–19 Warwicks v Oxford University, Oxford 1972; jpl 2–26 Warwicks v Gloucs, Cheltenham 1971; b&h 1–23 Warwicks v Leics, Leicester 1973.

ABRAHAMS, John.
County: Lancashire.
Role: Left-hand bat, off-break bowler.
Date and place of birth: 21 July 1952, Capetown, South Africa.
Height: 5′ 7½″. *Weight:* 10 st 4 lbs.
Parents: Cecil John and Cynthia Jean Abrahams.
Wife: Unmarried.
Education and qualifications: Moorhouse County Primary School; Heywood Grammar School (later became Heywood Senior High School).
Occupation outside cricket: Clerk at West Pennine Water Board for five years. Salesman and representative, Hambro Life Assurance Company.
Family links with cricket: Father was professional with Milnrow and Radcliffe in Central Lancashire League. Brothers, Basil and Peter, still play at Milnrow. Basil professional for Heyside in Saddleworth League in 1980.
County debut: 1973.
Outside interests: "Listening to pop music

(Rod Stewart, Fleetwood Mac for example). Reading (fairly light, e.g. Alistair Maclean, cricket books)."
Nickname: Abey.

continued overleaf

Other sporting activities: Badminton, golf.
General: Has lived in UK since 1962.
Address and telephone number: Bolton, Greater Manchester.
Personal best: Batting f/class 126 Lancs v

Cambridge University, Cambridge 1978; jpl 59 Lancs v Hants, Old Trafford 1979; b&h 22 Lancs v Hants, Southampton 1977; gillette 46 Lancs v Northants, Lord's 1976.

ACFIELD, David Laurence.
County: Essex.
Role: Right-hand bat, off-break bowler.
Date and place of birth: 24 July 1947, Chelmsford, Essex.
Height: 5' 9½". *Weight:* 11 st 21 lbs.
Parents: Robert and Ena Acfield.
Wife: Helen.
Married: 27 October 1973.
Children: Clare Louise, 10 December 1977.
Education and qualifications: Brentwood School; Christ's College, Cambridge. M.A. Cantab History.
Occupation outside cricket: Schoolmaster.
Family links with cricket: Late elder brother, Ian, 1944–68, member of MCC, Incogniti, Cambridge University Crusaders, etc.
County debut: 1966. *County cap:* 1970.
Outside interests: Bird-watching; films, especially Westerns.
Nickname: Ackers.
Other sporting activities: Fencing (sabre), British Olympic team 1968 and 1972. Commonwealth Games Gold Medal (team event) 1970, British champion 1969-70-71-72; now retired. Cambridge cricket blue 1967, 1968; also Cambridge blue for fencing.
General: Equipment and clothing supplied by Stuart Surridge Ltd.
Address and telephone number: c/o Essex

County Cricket Club, New Writtle Street, Chelmsford CM2 ORW.
Personal best: Batting f/class 42 Cambridge University v Leics, Leicester 1967; jpl 8 Essex v Kent, Canterbury 1978; b&h 6*14 Essex v Northants, Chelmsford 1977; gillette 2* Essex v Herts, Hitchin 1976. Bowling f/class 7–36 Essex v Sussex, Ilford 1973; jpl 5–14 Essex v Northants, Northampton 1970; b&h 2–14 Essex v Combined Universitys, Chelmsford 1979; gillette 2-51 Essex v Worcs, Worcester 1975.

AGNEW Jonathan Philip.
County: Leicestershire.
Role: Right-hand bat, right arm fast bowler.
Date and place of birth: 4 April 1960, Macclesfield, Cheshire.
Height: 6' 4½". *Weight:* 12 st 7 lbs.
Parents: Philip and Margaret Agnew.
Education and qualifications: Uppingham School, nine O-levels, two A-levels.
Occupation outside cricket: Lorry driver with

S.B.A. (Asbestos), Leicester.
Family links with cricket: First cousin, Mary Duggan, Captain of England's Women's XI in 1960s.
County debut: 1978.
Outside interests: Music (all kinds). Playing piano and tuba. Coaching cricket.
Nickname: Spiro (after U.S. Vice-President Spiro Agnew). Agnes
Other sporting activities: Hockey,

badminton, squash, table tennis.
General: Played for Surrey 2nd XI 1976–77. Won Whitbread Scholarship to Australia 1978–79. Young England tour of Australia, 1978–79.
Back trouble in 1979 season.
Address and telephone number: Flat 6, 15 Parkhill Drive, Aylestone, Leicester LE2 8AD.
Personal best: Batting f/class 9 Leics v Notts, Trent Bridge 1979. Bowling f/class 3–51 Leics v Northants, Leicester 1978.

ALLOTT, Paul John Walter.
County: Lancashire.
Role: right-hand bat, right arm fast medium bowler.
Date and place of birth: 14 September 1956, Altrincham, Cheshire.
Height: 6′ 4″. *Weight:* 14 st
Parents: John Norman and Lillian Patricia Allott
Wife: Helen.
Married: 27 October 1979.
Education and qualifications: Altrincham Grammar School and Bede Colleges Durham.
Occupation outside cricket: Qualified teacher. Cricket coach for Manchester Education Committee.
Family links with cricket: Father was dedicated club cricketer for 20 years with Ashley C.C. and is now active with Bowdon C.C. (Cheshire County League) as selector, administrator and junior organiser.
County debut: 1978.
Outside interests: Playing golf, watching all sports, listening to music ("no preferences but I know what I like!"), eating out.
Nickname: Wally, Walt or Wal.
Other sporting activities: Playing golf, football, squash.
General: Use Crown Sports (Dewsbury) equipment.

Address and telephone number: c/o Lancashire County Cricket Club, Old Trafford, Manchester M16 OPX.
Personal best: Batting f/class 14 Lancs v Warwicks, Old Trafford 1979; jpl 22* Lancs v Middlesex, Old Trafford 1979; gillette 1* Lancs v Kent, Canterbury 1979. Bowling f/class 5–39 Lancs v Worcs, Old Trafford 1979; jpl 3–15 Lancs v Warwicks, Edgbaston 1979; b&h 2–34 Lancs v Hants, Old Trafford 1979; gillette 1 –47 Lancs v Kent, Canterbury 1979

AMISS, Dennis Leslie.
County: Warwickshire.
Role: Right-hand bat, slow left arm chinaman bowler.
Date and place of birth: 7 April 1943, Harborne, Birmingham.
Height: 5' 11" · *Weight:* 13 st.
Wife: Jill.
Children: one son, one daughter.
Family links with cricket: Father, A. V. Amiss, played good club cricket.
County debut: 1960. *County cap:* 1965.
Benefit: £34,947 in 1975.
Outside interests: Bridge, gardening. Smokes a pipe.
Nickname: Sacker.
Other sporting activities: Golf, tennis, squash.
General: One of Wisden's Cricketers of the Year 1974. Toured Pakistan 1966–67; India, Pakistan and Sri Lanka 1972–73; West Indies 1973–74; Australia, New Zealand 1974–75; India, Sri Lanka and Australia 1976–77. Scored two centuries in one match, 155 not out and 112, v Worcestershire at Birmingham 1978. Made highest individual score in 1979 English season of 232 not out. Played for World Series Cricket 1978–79. Played for England v Rest of the World 1970.
Address and telephone number: c/o

Warwickshire County Cricket Club, Edgbaston, Birmingham B5 7QU.
Personal best: Batting 262* England v West Indies, Kingston 1973–74; other f/class 232* Warwicks v Gloucs, Bristol 1979: jpl 110 Warwicks v Surrey, Edgbaston 1974; b&h 73* Warwicks v Minor Counties West, Coventry 1977; gillette 113 Warwicks v Glamorgan, Swansea 1966. Bowling f/class 3–21 Warwicks v Middlesex, Lord's 1970; jpl 1–15 Warwicks v Kent, Canterbury 1972.

ANDERSON, Iain Stuart.
County: Derbyshire.
Role: Right-hand bat, off-break bowler.
Date and place of birth: 24 April 1960, Derby.
Education and qualifications: Dovecliff Grammar School; Wulfric School, Burton-on-Trent.
County debut: 1978.
Address and telephone number: c/o Derbyshire County Cricket Club, Nottingham Road, Derby DE2 6DA.
Personal best: Batting f/class 75 Derby v Worcs, Worcester 1978; jpl 21 Derby v Middlesex, Lord's 1978. Bowling f/class 1—24 Derby v Northants, Derby 1978.

ARNOLD, Geoffrey Graham.
County: Sussex.
Role: Right-hand bat, right arm fast medium bowler.

Date and place of birth: 3 September 1944, Balham, London.
Height: 6' 1". *Weight:* 13 st 12 lbs.
Parents: Arthur Wilfred Arnold and Amelia

12

May Blanche Arnold, deceased.
Wife: Jacqueline, 4 Oct 69.
Children: Matthew Paul, 20 March 72; Joanna Claire, 28 May 75.
Educatiom and qualifications: Elliott Comprehensive, Putney Heath.
Occupation outside cricket: George Wimpey & Co., Hammersmith, as a draughtsman. Cannon Davies Associates, Woking, as a sales executive.
Family links with cricket: Father played club cricket.
County debut: 1978. *County cap:* 1979.
Nickname: Horse.
Other sporting activities: Playing golf, squash, football, training for coming cricket season.
General: Debut for Surrey 1963, cap 1967, benefit £15,000 in 1976. One of Wisden's Cricketers of the Year in 1971. Left Surrey after 1977 season. Toured Pakistan 1966–67; India, Pakistan, Sri Lanka 1972–73; West Indies 1973–74; Australia, New Zealand 1974–75. Took 109 wickets at an average of 18.22 1977. Played for Orange Free State in 1966–67 Currie Cup Competition. Played soccer for Corinthian Casuals.
Address and telephone number: c/o Sussex County Cricket Club, Eaton Road, Hove BN3 3AN. Telephone: Brighton 732161.
Personal best: Batting Tests 59 England v

Pakistan, The Oval 1967; other f/class 73 MCC U-25 v C. Zone, Sahiwal 1966–67; jpl 24* Surrey v Notts, Nottingham 1971; b&h 12* Surrey v Combined Universities, The Oval 1976; gillette 18* Sussex v Northants, Hove 1979. *Personal best:* Bowling Tests 6–45 England v India, New Delhi 1972–1973; other f/class 6–41 Surrey v Gloucs, The Oval 1967; jpl 5–11 Surrey v Glamorgan, The Oval 1969; b&h 3–19 Surrey v Yorkshire, Bradford 1976; gillette 5–9 Surrey v Derby, The Oval 1967.

ARROWSMITH, Robert.

County: Lancashire.
Role: Right-hand bat, slow left arm orthodox bowler.
Date and place of birth: 21 May 1953, Denton.
Height: 5' 11". *Weight:* 13 st 5 lbs.
Parents: Ellis and Lillian Arrowsmith.
Wife: Divorced.
Education and qualifications: Two Trees, Denton, Manchester.
Occupation outside cricket: Representative for club fund-raising company.
Family links with cricket: Cousin is league professional with Northern League club.
County debut: 1976.
Outside interests: Watching amateur football, fishing.
Nickname: Joe Barrow.
Other sporting activities: Golf, snooker, table tennis.
General: Played in one John Player League

match 1975. "I support World Series Cricket in as much as the wages have increased two-

continued overleaf

fold, more sponsorship, better coverage for public.''

Address and telephone number: Smithalls Hall, Smithalls Hall House, Smithalls Dene Road, Bolton, Manchester.

ASIF, Iqbal Razvi.
County: Kent.
Role: Right-hand bat, right arm medium bowler.
Date and place of birth: 6 June 1943, Hyderabad, Deccan, India.
Height: 5' 9½". *Weight*: 10 st 7 lbs.
Wife: Married.
Education and qualifications: Alyia School, Hyderabad; Osmania University, Hyderabad.
Family links with cricket: Nephew of Ghulam Ahmed, former Indian Test cricketer.
County debut: 1968. *County cap*: 1968.
Benefit: 1981.
Off-season 1979-80: Toured India with Pakistan, as captain.
Outside interests: Music, travel, reading.
Other sporting activities: Squash.
General: Debut 1959-60 for Hyderbad in Ranji Trophy. Migrated to Pakistan 1961. Captained Pakistan Under-25s v England Under-25s in 1966-67. County Captain 1977. Toured with Pakistan to Australia and New Zealand 1964-65 and 1972-73, as Vice-Captain; England 1967, and 1971 (Vice-Captain) and 1974 (Vice-Captain); Australia and West Indies 1976-77; Pakistan Eaglets v England 1963, Pakistan A to Sri Lanka 1964; Pakistan International Airways to East Africa 1964. Shared in 9th wicket record partnership of 190 with Intikhab Alam for Pakistan v England at the Oval in 1967, after Pakistan had been 65 for 8: this is the record 9th wicket stand in all Test cricket.

ATHEY, Charles William Jeffrey.
County: Yorkshire.
Role: Right-hand bat, off-break bowler.
Date and place of birth: 27 September 1957, Middlesbrough, Yorkshire.
Role: Height: 5' 11". *Weight:* 12 st.
Parents: Peter and Maree Athey.
Wife: Unmarried.
Education and qualifications: Linthorpe Junior School; Stainsby Secondary School, Acklam Hall Grammar School.

Personal best: Batting f/class 39 Lancs v Derby, Chesterfield 1979. Bowling f/class 6-29 Lancs v Oxford University, Oxford 1977; jpl 1-36 Lancs v Leics, Old Trafford 1975.

Address and telephone number: c/o Kent County Cricket Club, St. Lawrence Ground, Canterbury CT1 3NZ.
Personal best: Batting Tests 175 Pakistan v New Zealand, Dunedin 1972-73; f/class 196 Nation Bank v P.I.A, Lahore 1976-77; jpl 106 Kent v Gloucs, Maidstone 1976; b&h 75 Kent v Middlesex, Canterbury 1973; gillette 89 Kent v Lancs, Lord's 1971. Bowling Tests 5-48 Pakistan v New Zealand, Wellington 1964-65; f/class 6-45 Pakistan Eaglets v Cambridge University, Cambridge 1963; jpl 3-3 Kent v Northants, Tring 1977; b&h 4-43 Kent v Worcs, Lord's 1973; gillette 4-18 Kent v Lancs, Canterbury 1979.

Family links with cricket: Father played league cricket in North Yorkshire and South Durham League for 29 years, 25 of them with Middlesbrough. On Middlesbrough C.C. committee. Assistant-Secretary, then Secretary, and President since 1975.
County debut: 1976.
Off-season 1979-80: Touring Australia with Derrick Robbins Under-23 XI
Outside interests: Modern music, training and keeping fit.

14

Nickname: Bumper.
Other sporting activities: Squash, tennis, swimming.
General: Toured West Indies with England Young Cricketers 1976. Played with Manly-Warringah C.C., Sydney, Australia, 1978–79. Toured South America with Derrick Robbins XI (Vice-Captain) 1978–79. Vice-Captain of Derrick Robbins Under-23 XI on tour to Australasia in February and March 1980. Played for Manly-Warringah C.C. in 1979–80 off-season. Played for Teeside County Schools Under-16s in 1970 at age 12, also 1971–72–73, and approached by Northamptonshire County Cricket Club. Made debut in 1972 North Yorkshire and South Durham League. Played for Yorkshire Colts 1974; played for North of England Young Cricketers XI v West Indies Young Cricketers at Old Trafford in 1974. Played football for Middlesbrough Schools Under-16 XI 1972–73, 1973–74. Played for Middlesbrough Juniors 1974–75, offered but declined apprenticeship terms with Middlesbrough F.C. Captained North Riding Yorkshire Under-19 XI 1975–76.
Address and Telephone number: Holly Garth, 80 Roman Road, Linthorpe, Middlesbrough, Cleveland TS5 5QE. Telephone: 88165.
Personal best: Batting f/class 131* Yorkshire

v Sussex, Leeds 1976; 131 Yorkshire v Somerset, Taunton 1978; jpl 118 Yorkshire v Leics, Leicester 1978; b&h 31 Yorkshire v Minor Counties East, Jesmond 1977; gillette 35 Yorkshire v Middlesex, Lord's 1979. Bowling f/class 3–38 Yorkshire v Surrey, The Oval 1978; jpl 3–10 Yorkshire v Kent, Canterbury 1978; b&h 3–32 Yorkshire v Middlesex, Lord's 1979; gillette 1–18 Yorkshire v Durham, Middlesbrough 1978.

BAILEY, Michael John.
County: Hampshire.
Date and Place of birth: 1 August 1954, Cheltenham, Gloucestershire.
Height: 6' &". *Weight:* 12 st.
Parents: Arthur Maurice and Josephine Mary.
Wife: Unmarried
Education and qualifications: Cheltenham Grammar School.
Occupation outside cricket: Insurance broker with Willis Faber Champness Ltd.
Family links with cricket: Brother, Graham, played Under-19 Schools cricket for Gloucestershire. Father on Gloucestershire

C.C.C. regional committee.
County debut: 1979.
Outside interests: Record-collecting, listening to music.
Other sporting activities: Football, squash.
General: Played for Cheltenham Cricket Club's winning side in 1978 John Haig Trophy at Lords.
Address and telephone number: 46 Willersey Road, Benhall, Cheltenham, Gloucestershire. Telephone: Cheltenham 25118.
Personal best: Batting f/class 24 Hants v Surrey, Portsmouth 1979. Bowling f/class 2–65 Hants v Surrey, Portsmouth 1979.

BAINBRIDGE, Philip.
County: Gloucestershire.
Role: Right-hand bat, right arm medium bowler.
Date and place of birth: 16 April 1958, Stoke-on-Trent.

Height: 5' 10". *Weight:* 11 st 3 lbs.
Parents: Leonard George and Lilian Rose.
Wife: Barbara, 22 Sept. 1979.
Education and qualifications: Hanley High School; Stoke-on-Trent Sixth Form College;

continued overleaf

Borough Road College of Education. B.Ed. MCC coaching certificate.
Occupation outside cricket: Supply teaching.
Family links with cricket: Cousin, Stephen Wilkinson, played for Somerset 1969–72.
Outside interests: Wine-making, beer-brewing.
Nickname: Bains.
Other sporting activities: "All sports—football, rugby, squash in particular."
General: Enjoys coaching. While at college did a lot of coaching at the Lord's Indoor School. Hopes to get coaching and playing job abroad in future off-seasons. Played for four 2nd XIs in 1976: Gloucestershire, Derbyshire, Northamptonshire and Warwickshire. Toured Holland with N.C.A. North of England Youth team. Toured West Indies with British Colleges 1978. Played for Young England v Young Australians 1977.
Address and telephone number: c/o Gloucestershire County Cricket Club, Neville Road, Bristol BS7 9EJ.
Personal best: Batting f/class 81* Gloucs v India, Bristol 1979; jpl 20 Gloucs v

Warwicks, Edgbaston 1978; b&h 3 Gloucs v Worcs, Worcester 1979; Bowling f/class 2–30 Gloucs v Somerset, Taunton 1979; jpl 3–15 Gloucs v Yorkshire, Cheltenham 1979; b&h 2–22 Gloucs v Minor Counties (South) Bristol 1979.

BAIRSTOW, David Leslie.
County: Yorkshire.
Role: Right-hand bat, wicket-keeper.
Date and place of birth: 1 September 1951, Bradford.
Education and qualifications: Hanson Grammar School, Bradford.
Occupation outside cricket: Sales representative.
County debut: 1970, while still at school. *County cap:* 1973.
Off-season 1979–80: Touring Australia with England.
Nickname: Bluey.
Other sporting activities: Played football for Bradford City F.C.
General: Played for M.C.C. Schools at Lord's in 1970. Played for Griqualand West in 1966–67 and 1977–78 as Captain. Toured Australia 1979–80. Holds record of 133 consecutive John Player League matches.
Address and telephone number: c/o Yorkshire County Cricket Club, Headingley Cricket Ground, Leeds LS6 3BU.
Personal best: Batting Tests 59 England v India, The Oval 1979; f/class 106 Yorkshire v Glamorgan, Middlesbrough 1976; 106

Griqualand W v Natal B, Pietermaritzburg 1976–77; jpl 76 Yorkshire v Sussex, Scarborough 1976; b&h 35* Yorkshire v Essex, Middlesbrough 1976; gillette 31* Yorkshire v Durham, Middlesbrough 1978. Bowling f/class 3–82 Griqualand E v Transvaal B, Johannesburg 1976–77.

BALDERSTONE, John Christopher.
County: Leicestershire.
Role: Right-hand bat, slow left arm orthodox bowler.
Date and place of birth: 16 November 1940, Huddersfield, Yorkshire.
Height: 6' 0½".   *Weight:* 12 st 7 lbs.
Parents: Frank and Jenny Balderstone.
Wife: Madeline.
Married: April 1962.
Children: Sally Victoria, 15 September 1970; Michael James, 1 March 73.
Education and qualifications: Paddock County School, Huddersfield. Advanced cricket coach.
Occupation outside cricket: Professional footballer with Huddersfield Town, Carlisle United, Doncaster Rovers, Queen of the South, Enderby Town. Representative for a sports shop.
Family links with cricket: None.
County debut: 1971.   *County cap:* 1973.
Outside interests: Do-it-yourself.
Nickname: Baldy.
Other sporting activities: Golf, professional football.
General: Played for Yorkshire 1961–70. Once played first-class cricket match and a League football match on the same day, 15 September, 1975 (Leicestershire v Derbyshire at Chesterfield 11.30 am to 6.30 pm and Doncaster Rovers v Brentford at Doncaster 7.30 pm to 9.10 pm).

Address and telephone number: 26 Copse Close, Oadby, Leicester.
Personal best: Batting Tests 35 England v West Indies, Leeds 1976; other f/class 178* Leics v Notts, Trent Bridge 1977; jpl 96 Leics v Northants, Leicester 1976; b&h 101* Leics v Hants, Leicester 1975; gillette 119* Leics v Somerset, Taunton 1973. Bowling Tests 1–80 England v West Indies, The Oval 1976; other f/class 6–25 Leics v Hants, Southampton 1978; jpl 3–29 Leics v Worcs, Leicester 1971; b&h 2–13 Leics v Warwicks, Leicester 1972; gillette 4–33 Leics v Herts, Leicester 1977.

BARCLAY, John Robert Troutbeck.
County: Sussex.
Role: Right-hand bat, off-break bowler.
Date and place of birth: 22 January 1954, Bonn, West Germany.
Education and qualifications: Eton College.
County debut: 1970, aged 16 yrs 6 mths while still at school.   *County cap:* 1976.
Outside interests: Fishing, music, golf.
Nickname: Trouters.
General: Was in Eton College 1st XI from age of 14. Played in M.C.C. Schools matches at Lord's since 1971. Toured India 1970–71 with England Schools Cricket Association (Vice-Captain); England Young Cricketers to West Indies 1972 as Captain. Played for Orange Free State 1978–79. Scored 1,000 runs in a season four times. Lord's Taverners/Schweppes Award 1979 for Best Young All-Rounder.
Address and telephone number: 2 Myrtle

continued overleaf

17

Cottages, Weavers Lane, Henfield, Sussex. Telephone: Henfield 3426.

Personal best: Batting f/class 112 Sussex v Warwicks, Hove 1977; jpl 48 Sussex v Derby, Derby 1974; b&h 93* Sussex v Surrey, The Oval 1976; gillette 44 Sussex v Derby, Hove 1977; 44 Sussex v Somerset, Lord's 1978. Bowling f/class 6–61 Sussex v Sri Lanka, Horsham 1979; jpl 3–11 Sussex v Worcs, Eastbourne 1978; b&h 5–43 Sussex v Combined Universities, Oxford 1979; gillette 3–27 Sussex v Lancs, Hove 1978.

BARLOW, Graham Derek.
County: Middlesex.
Role: Left-hand bat, right arm medium bowler.
Date and place of birth: 26 March 1950, Folkestone, Kent.
Height: 5' 10½". *Weight:* 12 st 12 lbs.
Parents: Derek Albert and Millicent Louise (Betty) Barlow.
Wife: Elise.
Married: 22 January 1979.
Education and qualifications: Woolverstone Hall, Ealing Grammar School, Loughborough College of Education. Certificate of Education for Physical Education and English.
Occupation outside cricket: P.E. teacher, Brentside School, Greenford 1973–74. NCA qualified coach to Wynberg Boys' School, Capetown 1975–76. Printing representative for Hildesley Ltd. 1974–75, Captain and coach Greenpoint C.C., Capetown 1977–78. Coach and professional to St Kilda C.C. Melbourne, Australia, 1978–79.
Family links with cricket: "Negligible. Distant great-uncle played good club cricket, but that's it."
County debut: 1969. *County cap:* 1976.
Outside interests: "Music—cross-section of taste from Beethoven and particularly Sibelius to 'Yes' on the 'heavier' side. Reading when time permits; likewise cinema and, to a lesser extent, theatre."
Nickname: "Take your pick! Eddy, Gladys, Duncan."
Other sporting activities: General fitness and particularly squash and running, especially when away in the winter.
General: Played rugby union for Loughborough Colleges, Leicestershire,

England Under-23 and briefly, Rosslyn Park. Endorses Duncan Fearnley bats and sporting goods. Played in MCC Schools matches at Lords in 1968. Spent 1979–80 off-season coaching and playing in Cape Town. Known for talking a lot in the dressing-room.
Address and telephone number: c/o Middlesex County Cricket Club, Lord's Cricket Ground, St John's Wood Road, London NW8 8QN.
Personal best: Batting Tests 7* England v India, Calcutta 1976–77; other f/class 160* Middlesex v Derby, Lord's 1976; jpl 114 Middlesex v Warwicks, Lord's 1979; b&h 129 Middlesex v Northants, Northampton 1977; gillette 76* Middlesex v Warwicks, Edgbaston 1975; Bowling f/class 1–6 Middlesex v Surrey, Lord's 1976; jpl 2–13 Middlesex v Surrey, Lord's 1976; b&h 1–18 Middlesex v Minor Counties East, Lord's 1976.

BARNETT, Kim John
County: Derbyshire.
Role: Right-hand bat, leg-break bowler.
Date and place of birth: 17 July 1960, Stoke-on-Trent.
Height: 6' 0".
Education and qualifications: Leek High School, Leek, Staffs.
Occupation outside cricket: Has worked as bank clerk.

County debut: 1979.
Off-season 1979-80: Playing cricket in Adelaide, Australia, on Whitbread Scholarship.
General: Played for Young England XI in Australia, 1978-79.
Address and telephone number: c/o Derbyshire County Cricket Club, Nottingham Road, Derby DE2 6DA.
Personal best: Batting f/class 96 Derby v Lancs, Chesterfield 1979; jpl 43* Derby v Northants, Long Eaton 1979; b&h 16 Derby v Hants, Derby 1979; gillette 22 Derby v Somerset, Taunton 1979. Bowling f/class 1-14 Derby v Hants, Basingstoke 1979; jpl 3-39 Derby v Yorks, Chesterfield 1979; gillette 1-30 Derby v Somerset, Taunton 1979.

BIRCH, John Dennis.
County: Nottingham.
Role: Right-hand bat, right arm medium bowler.
Date and place of birth: 18 June 1955, Nottingham.
County debut: 1973.
Address and telephone number: c/o Nottingham County Cricket Club, Trent Bridge, Nottingham NG2 6AG.
Personal best: Batting f/class 94* Notts v Yorkshire, Trent Bridge 1979; jpl 71 Notts v Yorkshire, Scarborough 1978; b&h 85 Notts v Minor Counties North, Trent Bridge 1979; gillette 32 Notts v Yorkshire, Bradford 1978. Bowling f/class 6-64 Notts v Hants, Bournemouth 1975; jpl 3-29 Notts v Glamorgan, Swansea 1976; b&h 2-14 Notts v Minor Counties North, Newark 1975; gillette 1-58 Notts v Yorkshire, Bradford 1978.

BIRKENSHAW, Jack
County: Leicestershire.
Role: Left-hand bat, off-break bowler.
Date and place of birth: 13 November 1940, Rothwell, Leeds, Yorkshire.
Height: 5′ 9″. *Weight:* 11st.
Parents: John and Edith Birkenshaw.
Wife: Gloria. *Children:* Mark, 9 December 1962.
Education and qualifications: Rothwell Grammar School.
Occupation outside cricket: "Everything from the bakehouse to promotional work, plus coaching for Leicestershire County Cricket Club."

County debut: 1961. *County cap:* 1965.
Benefit: £13,100 in 1974.
Outside interests: Coaching young people. Music, gardening, wine-making.
Nickname: Birky.
Other sporting activities: Squash and table tennis.
General: Played for Yorkshire in 1958-60. Toured India, Pakistan and Sri Lanka 1972-73; West Indies 1973-74. Took 111 wickets at an average of 21.41 in 1967. Shared in seventh wicket partnership record for county, 206 with B. Dudleston v Kent at Canterbury, 1969.

continued overleaf

Address and telephone number: c/o Leicestershire County Cricket Club, Grace Road, Leicester. Telephone: 832128.

Personal best: Batting Tests 64 England v India, Kanpur 1972–73; other f/class 131 Leics. v Surrey, Guildford 1969; jpl 79 Leics v Yorkshire, Leicester 1978; b&h 35* Leics v Worcs, Worcester 1972; gillette 101* Leics v Hants, Leicester 1976. Bowling Tests 5–57 England v Pakistan, Karachi, 1972–73; other f/class 8–94 Leics v Somerset, Taunton 1972; jpl 5–20 Leics v Essex, Leicester 1975; b&h 2–5 Leics v Minor Counties East, Leicester 1976; gillette 3–19 Leics v Somerset, Leicester 1968.

BOOTH, Peter

County: Leicestershire.
Role: Right-hand bat, right arm fast medium bowler.
Date and place of birth: 2 November 1952, Shipley, Yorkshire.
Height: 6' 0". *Weight:* 11st. 5lbs.
Parents: Both deceased.
Wife: Julia.
Married: 31 Dec. 1977.
Education and qualifications: Whitcliffe Mount Grammar School, Cleckheaton. Loughborough Colleges, Leicestershire. Qualified P.E. teacher.
Occupation outside cricket: Teacher at Stonygate Prep School, Leicester.
County debut: 1972. *County cap*: 1976.
Outside interests: Coaching and watching rugby union, reading.
Nickname: Shaker.
Other sporting activities: "Haven't time for any!"
General: Played for MCC Schools at Lords in 1970–71. Toured West Indies with England Youth team 1972.
Address and telephone number: c/o Leicestershire County Cricket Club, Grace Road, Leicester LE2 8AD.

Personal best: Batting f/class 58* Leics v Lancs, Leicester 1976; jpl 22* Leics v Derby, Leicester 1976; b&h 29* Leics v Derby, Leicester 1979; gillette 40* Leics v Glamorgan, Swansea 1977. Bowling f/class 6–93 Leics v Glamorgan, Swansea 1978; jpl 4–20 Leics v Warwicks, Leicester 1977; b&h 3–27 Leics v Hants, Leicester 1975; gillette 5–33 Leics v Northants, Northampton 1977.

BORE, Michael Kenneth.

County: Nottinghamshire.
Role: Right-hand bat, left arm medium bowler.
Date and place of birth: 2 June 1947, Hull.

Height: 5' 11½". *Weight:* 13 st.
Parents: Kenneth Gordon and Cicely May Bore.
Wife: Ann.
Married: 30 September 1972.

Children: Christopher Mark, 17 July 1977, Suzanne, 23 July 1979.
Education and qualifications: Maybury High School, Hull.
Occupation outside cricket: Various clerical jobs, spanning ten years, in off-seasons, five of which were spent in the Civil Service, at the Department of Health and Social Security.
Family links with cricket: Father played in local amateur league in Hull as left arm spinner.
County debut: 1979.
Outside interests: Cricket coaching at all levels and also arranging cricket forums, etc., gardening, decorating "when I find the time.'
Nickname: Noddy.
Other sporting activities: Competitive badminton, snooker, table tennis, squash.
General: Advanced MCC cricket coach, made debut for Yorkshire County Cricket Club in 1969. Started bowling seamers in one-day cricket in 1979.
Address and telephone number: 18 Waddington Drive, West Bridgford, Nottingham NG2 7GX. Telephone: Nottingham 231424.
Personal best: Batting f/class 37* Yorkshire v Notts, Bradford 1973; jpl 28* Notts v

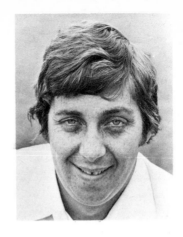

Northants, Northampton 1979; b&h 7* Yorkshire v Lancs, Bradford 1974; gillette 1 Notts v Sussex, Hove 1979; Bowling f/class 8-89 Notts v Kent, Folkestone 1979; jpl 4-21 Yorkshire v Sussex, Middlesbrough 1970; Yorkshire v Worcs, Worcester 1970; b&h 3-29 Yorkshire v Minor Counties North, Leeds 1974; gillette 3-35 Yorkshire v Kent, Canterbury 1971.

BORRINGTON, Anthony John.
County: Derbyshire.
Role: Right-hand bat, leg-break bowler.
Date and place of birth: 8 December 1948, Derby.
Education and qualifications: Spondon Park Grammar School; Loughborough College of Education.
Occupation outside cricket: Teacher.
County debut: 1971.   *County cap:* 1977.
Nickname: Tony. Borrers.
General: Played for MCC Schools at Lord's in 1967. Played in one John Player League match in 1970.
Address and telephone number: c/o Derbyshire County Cricket Club, Nottingham Road, Derby DE2 6DA.
Personal best: Batting f/class 137 Derby v Yorkshire, Dore, Sheffield 1978; jpl 101 Derby v Somerset, Taunton 1977; b&h 81

Derby v Notts, Trent Bridge 1974; gillette 29 Derby v Somerset, Taunton 1979.

21

BOTHAM, Ian Terrance.
County: Somerset.
Role: Right-hand bat, right arm fast medium bowler.
Date and place of birth: 24 November 1955, Hesall, Cheshire.
Height: 6'1". *Weight:* 14 st 7 lbs.
Wife: Kathryn.
Children: Sarah, Liam.
Education and qualifications: Milford School; Buckler's Mead.
Family links with cricket: Father, a regular in the Fleet Air Arm for 20 years, played most sports, including cricket. Mother played cricket for V.A.D. Nursing Service.
County debut: 1974. *County cap:* 1976.
Outside interests: Shooting. Golf. "Even mastered water-skiing after falling over 58 times".
Nickname: Both, Guy (the Gorilla).
Other sporting activities: Has played soccer in Somerset Senior League.
General: Played for 2nd XI 1971. On M.C.C. staff 1972-73. Played for county in last two John Player League matches 1973. Elected Best Young Cricketer of the Year in 1977 by the Cricket Writers' Club. One of Wisden's Cricketers of the Year 1978. Toured Pakistan, New Zealand 1977-78; Australia 1978-79 and 1979-80. Took five Australian wickets in his first day of Test Match cricket aged 21. Holds record for having scored 1,000 runs and taken 100 wickets in fewest Test matches. Has scored 1,000 runs in a season once. Took 100 wickets at an average of 16.40 in 1978. Became first ever player to score a century and take eight wickets in an innings in a Test Match, v Pakistan at Lord's in 1978. Trains with Scunthorpe United F.C.

known as practical joker: carries a water pistol. Awarded Lord's Taverners Schweppes Award for Most Outstanding Match Performance in 1979—his Leeds Test century.
Address and telephone number: c/o Somerset County Cricket Club, St James's Street, Taunton TA1 1JT.
Personal best: Batting Tests 137 England v India, Leeds 1979; other f/class 167* Somerset v Notts, Trent Bridge 1976; jpl 69 Somerset v Hants, Street 1977; b&h 54 Somerset v Sussex, Hove 1978; gillette 91* Somerset v Northumberland, Taunton 1977; Bowling Tests 8-34 England v Pakistan, Lord's 1978; other f/class 7-61 Somerset v Glamorgan, Cardiff 1978; jpl 4-10 Somerset v Yorkshire, Scarborough 1979; b&h 4-16 Somerset v Combined Universities, Taunton 1978; gillette 3-15 Somerset v Kent, Taunton 1979.

BOYCOTT, Geoffrey.
County: Yorkshire.
Role: Right-hand bat, right arm medium bowler.
Date and place of birth: 21 October 1940, Fitzwilliam, Yorkshire.
Height: 5'10". *Weight:* 11 st 7 lbs.
Wife: Unmarried.
Education and qualifications: Hemsworth Grammar School.
County debut: 1962. *County cap:* 1963.
Benefit: £20,639 in 1974.
Off-season 1979-80: Playing in Australia.

Outside interests: Reading, television, theatre, cinema.
Nickname: Fiery or Boycs or Thatch.
Other sporting activities: Golf, tennis.
General: Elected Best Young Cricketer of the Year 1963 by the Cricket Writers' Club. One of the Cricketers of the Year in Wisden 1965. Plays in contact lenses. Wears cap when bowling. County Captain 1971-78. Played for Northern Transvaal 1971-72. Played in two matches for England v. Rest of World 1970. Toured S. Africa 1964-65; Australia, New Zealand 1965-66 and 70-71, returning

home early with broken arm injury; West Indies 1967-68 and 1973-74; Pakistan and New Zealand 1977-78 as Vice-Captain; Australia 1978-79 and 1979-80. Has scored 1,000 runs in a season 17 times. Best season 1971 with 2,503 runs. Finished top of the batting averages 1979 with an average of 102.53, the only English batsman ever to have an average of over 100 for a season. Scored two centuries in a match (103 and 105) v Notts at Sheffield in 1966, and 160 not out and 116 for England v the Rest at Worcester in 1974. Published *Put to the Test*, an account of England's Australian Tour 1978-79.

Address and telephone number: c/o Yorkshire County Cricket Club, Headingley Cricket Ground, Leeds LS6 3BU.

Personal best: Batting Tests 246 England v India, Leeds 1967; other f/class 261* MCC v President's XI, Bridgetown 1973-74; jpl 108* Yorkshire v Northants, Huddersfield 1974; b&h 102 Yorkshire v Northants, Middlesbrough 1977; gillette 146 Yorkshire v Surrey, Lord's, 1965; Bowling Tests 3-47 England v

S. Africa, Cape Town 1964-65; other f/class 4-14 Yorkshire v Lancs, Bradford 1979; jpl 2-5 Yorkshire v Glamorgan, Bradford 1979; gillette 1-33 Yorkshire v Leics, Leicester 1965.

BOYNS, Cedric Nigel.

County: Worcestershire.

Role: Right-hand bat, right arm medium bowler.

Date and place of birth: 14 August 1954, Harrogate, Yorkshire.

Height: 6' 0". *Weight: 12 st. 8 lbs.*

Parents: Blendal Mellor Boyns, B.Sc. Ph.D. and Marian Boyns.

Wife: Unmarried.

Education and qualifications: Adam's Grammar School, Newport, Shropshire. Queen Elizabeth College, London University. Hughes Hall, Cambridge University. B.Sc. 2nd Class Hons in Biology, London University, Post-Graduate Certificate in Education, Cambridge University.

Occupation outside cricket: Secondary school teacher in Biology, General Science and Games.

Family links with cricket: Grandfather and father played club cricket in Westmoreland and Yorkshire. Brother plays for Walton-on-Thames.

County debut: 1976.

Outside interests: Photography—"I develop and print all my own photographs." Wood-

working, engraving, ornithology and natural history in general.

Other sporting activities: "I help with the running of junior rugby at school. This involves refereeing. I play club badminton."

General: Holds N.C.A. cricket coaching

continued overleaf

award. Played for county 2nd XI since 1972 also for Shropshire.
Address and telephone number: 33 Laxton Avenue, Henwick Park, Worcester.
Personal best: Batting f/class 95 Worcs v Yorks., Scarborough 1976; jpl 41* Worcs v Yorkshire, Huddersfield 1976; b&h 15 Worcs v Kent, Lord's 1976; gillette 5 Worcs v Glamorgan, Worcs 1977; Bowling f/class 3–24 Worcs v Oxford University, Oxford 1977; jpl 4–34 Worcs v Leics, Worcester 1978; b&h 2–30 Worcs v Glamorgan, Cardiff 1979; gillette 3–36 Worcs v Glamorgan, Worcester 1977.

BRAIN, Brian Maurice.
County: Gloucestershire.
Role: Right-hand bat, right arm fast medium bowler.
Date and place of birth: 13 September 1940, Worcester.
Height: 6′ 2″.   *Weight:* 11 st 8 lbs.
Parents: Herbert Frank and Eva Brain.
Wife: Eva May.
Married: 24 April 1961.
Children: Sarah Louise, 1 November 62; Helen Mary, 17 June 1964; Susan Claire, 17 June 1964.
Education and qualifications: King's School, Worcester.
Occupation outside cricket: Insurance representative.
Family links with cricket: Two brothers have played some local club cricket.
County debut: 1976.   *County cap:* 1977.
Outside interests: Very keen darts player. Writing articles for *Cricketer International* magazine. Listening to popular music.
Nickname: Brainy.
Other sporting activities: Armchair football supporter of West Bromwich Albion.
General: Made debut for Worcestershire in 1959. Left staff in 1960, rejoined in 1963, cap 1966, left staff again 1971, but rejoined 1973. Not re-engaged after 1975 season and joined Gloucestershire in 1976. Drives 136 miles a day from his home in Worcester when playing at Bristol, having clocked up 14,500 miles during last season. Has been involved in

running several coaching courses for young cricketers.
Address and telephone number: 89 Bromwich Road, St John's, Worcester. Telephone: 0905-424163.
Personal best: Batting f/class 57 Gloucs v Essex, Cheltenham 1976; jpl 33 Gloucs v Kent, Canterbury 1978; b&h 16 Gloucs v Warwicks, Bristol 1978; gillette 21* Worcs v Sussex, Worcester 1967. Bowling f/class 8–55 Worcs v Essex, Worcester 1975; jpl 4–27 Worcs v Somerset, Taunton 1970; b&h 4–30 Gloucs v Somerset, Bristol 1977; gillette 4–13 Worcs v Durham, Chester-le-Street 1968.

BRASSINGTON, Andrew James.
County: Gloucestershire.
Role: Right-hand bat, wicket-keeper.
Date and place of birth: 9 August 1954, Bagnall, Staffordshire.
Height: 6′ 0″.   *Weight:* 10 st 10 lbs.
Parents: John and Joan Brassington.
Wife: Rosalyn.
Married: 26 February 1976.
Children: Emma Louisa, 20 August 1977.
Education and qualifications: Enden Secondary Modern, Enden, Stoke-on-Trent.
Occupation outside cricket: Salesman.
County debut: 1974.   *County cap:* 1978.

Nickname: Imma.
Other sporting activities: Football, squash, golf.
General: Uses Slazenger cricket equipment. Plays soccer as a goalkeeper. Was elected Young Wicket-keeper of the Year.
Address and telephone number: 74 Ashley Down Road, Horfield, Bristol BS7 9JP. Telephone: Bristol 43995.
Personal best: Batting f/class 28 Gloucs v Glamorgan, Cardiff 1975; jpl 8 Gloucs v Kent, Canterbury 1978; b&h 9* Gloucs v Somerset, Bristol 1979; gillette 20 Gloucs v Hants, Bristol 1979.

BREAKWELL, Dennis.

County: Somerset.
Role: Left-hand bat, slow left arm orthodox bowler.
Date and place of birth: 2 July 1948, Brierley Hill, Staffordshire.
Height: 5′ 9″.   *Weight:* 12 st.
Parents: John Morgan and Florence Emily Breakwell.
Wife: Susan.
Married: 11 November 1977.
Children: James Stuart, Donna Louise.
Education and qualifications: Cunsdale Comprehensive School, Wombourne.
Occupation outside cricket: Painter and decorator.
Family links with cricket: Father and his two brothers, Ted and Alan, all played in Birmingham League. Father captained Dudley. Two brothers, Dave and Mike, good cricketers, brother Dave playing for Victoria Tramways, Australia.
County debut: 1973.   *County cap:* 1976.
Outside interests: "Making home-made wine and beer, and drinking it." Making things out of wood.
Nickname: Breakleg.
Other sporting activities: Football, skittles, fishing, shooting, golf.
General: Played for Northants for seven years.
Address and telephone number: 39

Ladymead Road, Taunton, Somerset, Telephone: Taunton 77981.
Personal best: Batting f/class 100* Somerset v New Zealand, Taunton 1978; jpl 44* Somerset v Notts, Trent Bridge 1976; b&h 36* Somerset v Glamorgan, Taunton 1979; gillette 19* Somerset v Essex, Westcliff 1974. Bowling f/class 8-39 Northants v Kent, Dover 1970; jpl 4-10 Northants v Derby, Northampton 1970; b&h 2-16 Somerset v Gloucs, Bristol 1979; gillette 2-29 Somerset v Northumberland, Taunton 1977.

BREARLEY, John Michael.
County: Middlesex.
Role: Right-hand bat, occasional wicket-keeper.
Date and place of birth: 28 April 1942, Harrow, Middlesex.
Height: 5' 11". *Weight:* 11 st 9 lbs.
Parents: Horace and Midge Brearley.
Education and qualifications: City of London School; St. John's College, Cambridge, 1st Class Hons. in Classics. and 2:1 in Moral Sciences. Also came joint top in Civil Service Examination. Has taught at adult education classes and helped at a clinic for disturbed adolescents.
Occupation outside cricket: "Teaching, counselling, writing." Taught philosophy at University of California and Newcastle University.
Family links with cricket: Father played for both Yorkshire (once) and Middlesex (twice).
County debut: 1961. *County cap:* 1964.
Benefit: £31,000 in 1978: a Middlesex record.
Outside interests: Classical music; Indian culture.
Nickname: Scagg.
General: Has served on Cricketers' Association committee. Scored 1,222 runs in first season (1961). Cambridge blue 1961-62-63-64, and captain 1964. Elected Best Young Cricketer of the Year in 1964 by Cricket Writers' Club. Turned out for Cambridgeshire in 1966 and kept wicket to Johnny Wardle. Did not play for Middlesex in 1966 or 1967, but re-appeared in second half of each season between 1968 and 1970. Appointed Captain of Middlesex in 1971. One of Wisden's Cricketers of the Year 1977. Awarded O.B.E. in 1978. Toured South Africa 1964-65; Pakistan 1966-67; India, Sri Lanka, Australia 1976-77; Pakistan and New

Zealand 1977-78 (Captain); Australia 1978-79 and 79-80 both as Captain. Scored 2,178 runs at an average of 44.44 in 1964. Holds record for most runs scored for Cambridge University, 4,310 at 38.48. Published *The Ashes Retained* jointly with Dudley Doust about 1978-79 Australia Tour.
Address and telephone number: c/o Middlesex County Cricket Club, Lord's Cricket Ground, St John's Wood Road, London NW8 8QN.
Personal best: Batting Tests 91 England v India, Bombay 1976-77; other f/class 312* MCC U-25 v N. Zone, Peshawar, 1966-67; jpl 75* Middlesex v Glamorgan, Lord's 1974; b&h 88 Middlesex v Notts, Newark 1976; gillette 124* Middlesex v Bucks, Lord's 1975. Bowling f/class 1-21 Camb U v Sussex, Cambridge 1963; jpl 1-15 Middlesex v Warwicks, Lord's 1979; b&h 2-3 Middlesex v Northants, Northampton 1977.

BRIERS, Nigel Edwin.
County: Leicestershire.
Role: Right-hand bat.
Date and place of birth: 15 January 1955, Leicester.
Height: 6' 0". *Weight:* 12 st 5 lbs.
Parents: Leonard Arthur Roger and Eveline Briers.
Wife: Suzanne Mary Tudor.
Married: 3 September 1977.
Education and qualifications: Lutterworth Grammar School, Borough Road College of

Physical Education. Qualified teacher (Certificate of Education), B.Ed Hons.
Occupation outside cricket: Teacher of P.E., presently lecturing in P.E. at Leicester Polytechnic.
Family links with cricket: Father was captain and wicket-keeper of Narborough and Littlethorpe Cricket Club, first division of Leicestershire League, for 15 years. Mother was scorer for the team. Father was captain of South Leicestershire representative XI and played for the Royal Marines in the same

team as Trevor Bailey. Cousin, Norman Briers played for Leicestershire once in 1967.
County debut: 1971, at age of 16 years, 104 days, being youngest player to appear for county.
Outside interests: Glazed tiling, eating good food ("favourite food, steak"), cinema. Keeping fit.
Other sporting activities: Rugby, basketball, badminton.
General: Uses Duncan Fearnley cricket equipment. Toured South America with Derrick Robins XI in 1978–79.
Address and telephone number: c/o Leicestershire County Cricket Club, Grace Road, Leicester LE2 8AD.
Personal best: Batting f/class 119 Leics v Warwicks, Edgbaston 1979; jpl 81 Leics v Worcs, Worcester 1978; b&h 71* Leics v Hants, Southampton 1979; gillette 20 Leics v Worcs, Leicester 1979. Bowling f/class 1–22 Leics v Glamorgan, Leicester 1978; jpl 1–12

Leics v Surrey, Leicester 1979; gillette 2–6 Leics v Worcs, Leicester 1979.

BROAD, Brian Christopher.
County: Gloucestershire.
Role: Left-hand bat. Right-arm medium.
Date and place of birth: 29 September 1957.
Height: 6' 4". *Weight:* 13 st.
Parents: Kenneth and Nancy Broad.
Wife: Carole.
Married: 14 July 1979.
Education and qualifications: XIV Prep School, Bristol; Colston's School, Bristol; St Paul's College, Cheltenham.
Occupation outside cricket: Floor laying.
Family links with cricket: Father and grandfather both played local cricket. Father a member of Gloucestershire committee for 10 years until retired four years ago. Father on T.C.C.B. development sub-committee.
County debut: 1979.
Outside interests: Woodwork.
Nickname: Chris or Broadie.
Other sporting activities Played rugby for English Colleges, Bristol United, St. Paul's College and now plays for Clifton. Golf, swimming, squash, tennis.
General: Tour of Malawi with Gloucestershire County Cricket Club, 1978–79; tour of West Indies with British Colleges 1978–79.

Address and telephone number: 23 Camelford Road, Greenbank, Bristol BS5 6HW.
Personal best: Batting f/class 129 Gloucs v Northants, Bristol 1979; jpl 22 Gloucs v Derby, Bristol 1979; b&h 39 Gloucs v Glamorgan, Swansea 1979.

BROWN, Alan.

County: Worcestershire.
Role: Wicket-keeper.
Date and place of birth: 23 December 1957, Darwen, Lancs.
Height: 5' 5½". *Weight:* 10 st.
Parents: William and Mary Brown.
Wife: Unmarried.
Education and qualifications: Darwen Grammar School (now Darwen Vale High); St John's College, York. Nine O-levels, three A-levels, B.Ed. Hons.
Occupation outside cricket: Student.

Family links with cricket: None.
County debut: 1979.
Outside interests: Music.
Other sporting activities: Sport in general, college football 1st XI, hockey goalkeeper.
General: Toured West Indies with British Colleges 1979. Released by Worcestershire at the end of the 1979 season.
Address and telephone number: 233 Blackburn Road, Darwen, Lancs. Telephone: Darwen 771407.
Personal best: Batting f/class did not bat.

BROWN, David John.

County: Warwickshire.
Role: Right-hand bat, right arm fast medium bowler.
Date and place of birth: 30 January 1942, Walsall, Staffordshire.
Height: 6' 4". *Weight:* 14 st.
Parents: Henry George and Rose Brown.
Wife: Catherine Patricia.
Married: 21 September 1968.
Children: One son, one daughter.
Educations and qualifications: Queen Mary Grammar School, Walsall.
Occupation outside cricket: Horse-breeding.
Family links with cricket: Father played cricket for B.I.P. Works XI.
County debut: 1961. *County cap:* 1964.
Benefit: £21,109 in 1973.
Outside interests: All sports.
Nickname: Barnsley.
General: County Captain from 1975–77. Played two matches for England v Rest of the World 1970. Toured South Africa 1964–65; Australia, New Zealand 1965–66; Pakistan 1966–67 (Vice-Captain); West Indies 1967–68; Sri Lanka, Pakistan 1968–69. Has his own stud. Steward at Wolverhampton Races. Chairman of Cricketers' Association. Appointed manager of Warwickshire C.C.C. in 1980. Suffered from ankle injury in 1979. Took his 1,000th first-class wicket, after playing 323 matches for Warwickshire.
Address and telephone number: Furnace Mill Farm, Wyre Forest, Kidderminster,

Worcestershire. Telephone: Rock 266160.
Personal best: Batting Tests 44 England v New Zealand, Christchurch 1965–66; 44* England v Pakistan, Lahore 1968–69; other f/class 79 Warwicks v Derby, Edgbaston 1972; jpl 38* Warwicks v Worcs, Edgbaston 1972; b&h 20* Warwicks v Northants, Coventry 1973; gillette 41 Warwicks v Middlesex, Lord's 1977. Bowling Tests 5–42 England v Australia, Lord's 1968; other f/class 8–60 Warwicks v Middlesex, Lord's 1975; jpl 5–13 Warwicks v Worcs, Edgbaston 1970; b&h 3–17 Warwicks v Lancs, Coventry 1978; gillette 5–18 Warwicks v Glamorgan, Swansea 1966.

Full name: BURGESS, Graham Iefvion.

County: Somerset.
Role: Right-arm bat, right arm medium bowler.

Date and place of birth: 5 May 1943, Glastonbury.
Education: Millfield School.
County debut: 1966. *County cap:* 1968.

Testimonial: £24,800 in 1977.
Other sporting activities: Plays football.
General: Retired from County cricket at end of 1979 season. Is to become cricket professional & sports officer at Monmouth School.
Address and telephone number: c/o Somerset County Cricket Club, St James's Street, Taunton TA1 1JT.
Personal best Batting f/class 129 Somerset v Gloucs Taunton 1973; jpl 66* Somerset v Gloucs, Bristol 1971; b&h 58 Somerset v Hants, Yeovil 1972; gillette 73 Somerset v Leics, Taunton 1967. Bowling f/class 7–43 Somerset v Oxford University, Oxford 1975; jpl 6–25 Somerset v Glamorgan, Glastonbury 1972; b&h 4–12 Somerset v Glamorgan, Pontypridd 1972; gillette 3–25 Somerset v Middlesex, Lord's 1979.

BUTCHER, Alan Raymond.
County: Surrey.
Role: Left-hand bat, left arm medium bowler.
Date and place of birth: 7 January 1954, Croydon, Surrey.
Height: 5′ 8″   *Weight 11 st 7 lbs.*
Parents: Raymond and Jacky Butcher.
Wife: Elaine.
Married: 27 September 1972.
Children: Mark, Gary, Lisa.
Education and qualifications: Heath Clark Grammar School, five O-levels, one A-level.
Occupation outside cricket: Football coach, physical education master, Cumnor House School, South Croydon, Surrey.
Family links with cricket: Brother, Martin, M.C.C. Young Pros. Brother, Ian, joined Leicestershire, 1979, debut v Surrey in John Player League.
County debut: 1972   *County cap:* 1975
Outside interests: Most sport, rock music, reading.
Nickname: Butch, Budgie.
Other sporting activities: Football.
Address and telephone number: c/o Surrey County Cricket Club, Kennington Oval, London SE11 5SS.
Personal best: Batting Tests 20 England v

India, The Oval 1979; other f/class 188 Surrey v Sussex, Hove 1978; jpl 113* Surrey v Warwicks, Edgbaston 1978; b&h 61 Surrey v Kent, Canterbury 1976; gillette 51 Surrey v Derby, Ilkeston 1976. Bowling f/class 6–48 Surrey v Hants, Guildford 1972; jpl 5–19 Surrey v Gloucs, Bristol 1975; b&h 3–11 Surrey v Lancs, Old Trafford 1974; gillette 1–43 Surrey v Somerset, The Oval 1974.

BUTCHER, Roland Orlando.
County: Middlesex.
Role: Right-hand bat, right arm medium bowler.

Date and place of birth: 14 October 1953, East Point, St Philip, Barbados.
Height: 5′ 8″.   *Weight:* 12 st.

continued overleaf

29

Parents: Robert & Doreen Butcher.
Wife: Cheryl Denise.
Children: One son, Paul Nicholas Roland.
Education and qualifications: Secondary Advanced Cricket Coaching Certificate. Football Association Preliminary Coaching Certificate.
Occupation outside cricket: Coaching.
Family links with cricket: Cousin is Basil Butcher of Guyana and West Indies.
County debut: 1974.
Outside interests: Television, horse-racing, cinema.
Nickname: Butch.
Other sporting activities Football. Has played semi-professionally.
General: Played for Barbados 1974–75 Shell Shield Competition. Spent 1979–80 off-season playing cricket in Barbados.
Address and telephone number: c/o Middlesex County Cricket Club, Lord's Cricket Ground, St. John's Wood Road, London NW6 8QN. Telephone: 01–289–1300.
Personal best: f/class 142 Middlesex v

Gloucs, Bristol 1978; jpl 94 Middlesex v Surrey, The Oval 1979; b&h 4 Middlesex v Yorkshire, Lord's 1975; gillette 6 Middlesex v Yorkshire, Lord's 1979. Bowling gillette 1–18 Middlesex v Derby, Derby 1978.

CARRICK, Phillip.
County: Yorkshire.
Role: Right-hand bat, slow left arm orthodox bowler.
Date and place of birth: 16 July 1972, Leeds.
Height: 6′ 0″. *Weight:* 12 st 10 lbs.
Parents: Arthur and Ivy Carrick.
Wife: Elspeth.
Married: 2 April 1977.
Occupation outside cricket: Director, Worthington Sports.
Family links with cricket: Father was good league player—Leeds/Bradford.
County debut: 1970. *County cap:* 1976.
Outside interests: Vegetable garden, walking dog.
Nickname: Fergus.
Other sporting activities Golf.
General: Played for Eastern Province in 1976–77 Currie Cup Competition.
Address and telephone number: c/o Yorkshire County Cricket Club, Headingley Cricket Ground, Leeds LS6 3BU.
Personal best: Batting f/class 128* Yorkshire v Gloucs, Cheltenham 1979; jpl 21 Yorkshire v Hants, Leeds 1979; b&h 19* Yorkshire v Notts, Bradford 1979; gillette 18 Yorkshire v Durham, Harrogate 1973; 18 Yorkshire v

Notts, Bradford 1978. Bowling f/class 8–33 Yorkshire v Cambridge University, Cambridge 1973; jpl 3–32 Yorkshire v Notts, Trent Bridge 1979; jpl 3–32 Yorkshire v Hants, Bournemouth 1976; b&h 2–17 Yorkshire v Minor Counties North, Jesmond 1979; gillette 2 –32 Yorkshire v Durham, Harrogate 1973.

CARTER, Robert Michael.
County: Northamptonshire.
Role: Right-hand bat, right arm medium bowler.
Date and place of birth: 25 May 1960, King's Lynn, Norfolk.
Height: 5' 10¾". *Weight:* 12 st.
Parents: Reg and Judy Carter.
Education and qualifications: St. James Primary School; Gaywood Park Secondary Modern School, Kings Lynn; Norfolk College of Arts and Technology, King's Lynn.
Occupation outside cricket: Professional footballer with Norwich City F.C.
Family links with cricket: Grandfather played for Barham village team. Father played for Marham and King's Lynn, which he captained for several years.
County debut: 1978.
Outside interests: "Listening to Earth, Wind and Fire. Reading about anything to do with football and cricket."
Nickname: Bob.
Other sporting activities Football. Golf and squash occasionally—"most when it's raining during a cricket match."
Address and telephone number: 5 Sandholme Close, Borrowdale Drive, Norwich, Norfolk

NR1 4LX. Telephone: Norwich 33327.
Personal best: Batting 26* Northants, v Gloucs, Northampton 1979; jpl 21* Northants, v Surrey, The Oval 1979; b&h 5* Northants, v Surrey, Northampton 1979. Bowling f/class 2–12 Northants, v Warwicks, Edgbaston 1979; jpl 3–35 Northants, v Worcs, Milton Keynes 1978; b&h 1–42 Northants, v Surrey, Northampton 1979.

CARTWRIGHT, Harold.
County: Derbyshire.
Role: Right-hand bat.
Date and place of birth: 12 May 1951, Halfway, Derbyshire.
Occupation outside cricket: Teacher.
County debut: 1973. *County cap:* 1978.
Nickname: Harry.
General: Played in John Player and Gillette Cup matches 1971–72. Not re-engaged.
Address and telephone number: c/o Derbyshire County Cricket Club, Nottingham Road, Derby DE2 6DA.
Personal best: f/class 141* Derby v Warwicks, Chesterfield 1977; jpl 76* Derby v Middlesex, Chesterfield 1973; b&h 56* Derby v Minor Counties (West) 1978; gillette 36 Derby v Somerset, Ilkeston 1977.

CHEATLE, Robert Giles Lenthell.
County: Surrey.
Role: Left-hand bat, slow left arm orthodox bowler.

Date and place of birth: 31 July 1953, London.
Height: 6' 0". *Weight:* 11 st 7lbs.

continued overleaf

Parents: Tony and Peggy Cheatle.
Wife: Amanda,
Married: 18 December 1976.
Education and qualifications: Stowe School (various O- and A-levels).
Occupation outside cricket: Taught for four years. Currently broking in the City.
Family links with cricket: "None with cricket, but both my parents were way above average ability at a number of sports."
County debut: 1974.
Nickname: Cheat, "nickname has nothing to do with my cricket or reputation!", or Giles.
Other sporting activities: Squash (Surrey cap), hockey (Truman League, South).
General: Was Sussex representative on Cricketers' Association. Endorses Grays' cricket, hockey and squash equipment. "Thought to be not the worst mimic in the dressing room!" Toured South America 1979 with Derrick Robins XI. Joined Surrey for 1980 season.
Address and telephone number: 1 Ashley Cottages, Ardingleigh, Sussex. Telephone: Haywards Heath 892559. Also, Norton Warburg Ltd., 68 Cannon Street, London EC4. Telephone: 01–236–5244.

Personal best: Batting f/class 34 Sussex v Kent, Hove 1977; jpl 18* Sussex v Warwicks, Hove 1979; b&h 16 Sussex v Somerset, Hove 1978; gillette 6 Sussex v Yorkshire, Leeds 1978. Bowling f/class 6–32 Sussex v Yorkshire, Hove 1979; jpl 4–33 Sussex v Glamorgan, Eastbourne 1977; b&h 2–31 Sussex v Surrey, Hove 1979; gillette 2–50 Sussex v Somerset, Lord's 1979.

CHILDS, John Henry.

County: Gloucestershire.
Role: Left-hand bat, slow left arm orthodox bowler.
Date and place of birth: 15 August 1951, Plymouth.
Height: 6' 0". *Weight:* 11 st 7 lbs.
Parents: Sydney and Barbara Childs.
Wife: Jane Anne,
Married: 11 November 1978.
Education and qualifications: Audley Park Secondary Modern, Torquay. Advanced cricket coach.
Occupation outside cricket: Signwriter.
County debut: 1975. *County cap:* 1977.
Outside interests: Watching rugby, decorating at home, "walking moors and beaches."
Other sporting activities: Golf.
General: Played for Devon 1973–74.
Address and telephone number: 17 Birch Close, Patchway, Bristol. Telephone: 694949.
Personal best: Batting f/class 12 Gloucs v Derby, Ilkeston 1977; jpl 11* Gloucs v Essex, Cheltenham 1975; b&h 10 Gloucs v Somerset,

Bristol 1979; gillette 0* Gloucs v Hants, Bristol 1979. Bowling f/class 8–34 Gloucs v Hants, Basingstoke 1978; jpl 4–15 Gloucs v Northants, Northampton 1976; b&h 2–26 Gloucs v Minor Counties (West), Chippenham 1978; gillette 1–45 Gloucs v Hants, Bristol 1979.

CLARKE, Sylvester Theophilus.
County: Surrey.
Role: Right-hand bat, right arm fast bowler.
Date and place of birth: 11 December 1955, Lead Vale, Christchurch, Barbados.
Height: 6' 1". *Weight:* 15 st.
Parents: Ashton and Marjorie Smith.
Education and qualifications: St Bartholomew Boys' School.
Occupation outside cricket: Carpenter.
County debut: 1979.
Outside interests: Listening to music and party-movies.
Other sporting activities: Football.
General: Toured with West Indies to India and Sri Lanka, 1978–79. Plays for local club in Barbados Cricket League.
Address and telephone number: Lead Vale, Christchurch, Barbados.

Personal best: Batting Tests 15 West Indies v India, New Delhi 1978–79; other f/class 25 Surrey v Hants, The Oval 1979; jpl 30 Surrey v Lancs, The Oval 1979; b&h 2* Surrey v Essex, The Oval 1979. Bowling Tests 5–126 West Indies v India, Bangalore 1978–79; other f/class 6–39 Barbados v Trinidad, Bridgetown 1977–78; jpl 3–26 Surrey v Lancs, The Oval 1979; b&h 4–23 Surrey v Essex, The Oval 1979.

CLAUGHTON, John Alan.
County: Warwickshire.
Role: Right-hand bat, slow left arm orthodox bowler.
Date and place of birth: 17 September 1956, Leeds, Yorkshire.
Height: 5' 8½". *Weight:* 11 st 3 lbs.
Parents: Ronald and Patricia Claughton.
Education and qualifications: King Edward's School, Birmingham; Merton College, Oxford. BA, 1st Class Hons. Classics.
Family links with cricket: Great-uncle, Hugh Marsden Claughton, played as all-rounder for Yorkshire occasionally in 1914 and 1919. At 89 years old is oldest living Yorkshire professional. Father and three uncles all ex-professionals in Bradford League.
County debut: 1979.
Off-season 1979–80: Touring Australia with Combined Oxford and Cambridge XI.
Outside interests: Reading, music, ("having knee operations").
Nickname: Trapper.
Other sporting activities: Golf, rugby football, squash.
General: Throws with his right hand, bowls with his left. Scored 56 and 112 on first-class

debut for Oxford v Gloucestershire in 1976.
Address and telephone number: 22 Greville Drive, Edgbaston, Birmingham. Telephone: 021–440–4503.
Personal best: Batting 112 Oxford University v Gloucs, Oxford 1976; b&h 15 Combined Universities v Hants, Cambridge 1978.

CLIFFORD, Christopher Craven.
County: Warwickshire.
Role: Right-hand bat, off-break bowler.
Date and place of birth: 5 July 1942, Hoveringham, Yorkshire.
Height: 5′ 11″.   *Weight:* 11 st 7 lbs.
Parents: Stanley and Eva May Clifford.
Wife: Susan.
Married: 1 August 1969.
Children: Kathryn, Elizabeth.
Education and qualifications: Malton Grammar School; Leeds College of Education; Carnegie Hall College of Physical Education.
Occupation outside cricket: Teacher, Scarborough Grammar School.
Family links with cricket: None.
County debut: 1978.
Outside interests: Stamp collecting, bridge.
Nickname: Wef (Wild Eyed Fellow).
Other sporting activities: Soccer, basket-ball, cross-country, badminton, formerly hockey, "getting past them all."
General: Played for Yorkshire 2nd XI in 1963 and made debut for county in 1972. Did not play again until making debut for Warwickshire in 1978. Played for Johannesburg Wanderers C.C. 1969–72 in Transvaal Premier League. Recommended to Warwickshire by Geoff Boycott. Only bowler to have

2,000 runs hit off him in 1979.
Address and telephone number: 2 The Grove, Seamer, Scarborough, Yorkshire. Telephone: Scarborough 863839.
Personal best: Batting f/class 26 Warwicks v Surrey, The Oval 1979; jpl 2* Warwicks v Sussex, Hove 1979; Warwicks v Hants, Edgbaston 1979. Bowling f/class 6–89 Warwicks v Somerset, Weston 1978; jpl 2–35 Warwicks v Sussex, Hove 1979.

CLIFT, Patrick Bernard.
County: Leicestershire.
Role: Right-hand bat, right arm medium bowler.
Date and place of birth: 14 July 1953, Salisbury, Rhodesia.
Education and qualifications: St George's College, Salisbury, Rhodesia.
County debut: 1975.   *County cap:* 1976.
Off-season 1979–80: Playing cricket in Rhodesia.
Nickname: Paddy.
General: Debut for Rhodesia 1971–72. Has to do military service in Rhodesia. Took 8 wickets for 17 in opening match in 1976 season v M.C.C.
Address and telephone number: c/o Leicestershire County Cricket Club, Grace Road, Leicester LE2 8AD. Telephone: Leicester 832128.
Personal best: Batting f/class 88* Leics v Oxford University, Oxford 1979; jpl 51*

f/class 8–17 Leics v MCC, Lord's 1976; jpl 4–14 Leics v Lancs, Leicester 1978; b&h 4–13

Leics v Somerset, Leicester 1979; b&h 58
Leics v Worcs, Worcester 1979; gillette 48*
Leics v Worcs, Leicester 1979; Bowling

Leics v Minor Counties East, Amersham
1978; gillette 3-36 Leics v Worcs, Leicester
1979.

CLINTON, Grahame Selvey.
County: Surrey.
Role: Left-hand bat, right medium bowler.
Date and place of birth: 5 May 1953, Sidcup.
Education and qualifications: Chislehurst
and Sidcup Grammar School.
County debut: 1979.
General: Toured West Indies with England
Young Cricketers 1972. Debut for Kent 1974.
Left after 1978 season to join Surrey.
Address and telephone number: Surrey
County Cricket Club, Kennington Oval,
London SE11 5SS.
Personal best: Batting f/class 134 Surrey v
Kent, The Oval 1979; jpl 34 Surrey v Notts,
Trent Bridge 1979; b&h 66 Kent v Surrey,
Canterbury 1976. Bowling f/class 2-8 Kent v
Pakistan, Canterbury 1978.

COCKBAIN, Ian.
County: Lancashire.
Date and place of birth: 19 April 1958,
Bootle, Lancashire.
County debut: 1979.
Off season 1979-80: In Tasmania.

Address and telephone number: c/o
Lancashire County Cricket Club, Old
Trafford, Manchester M16 0PX.
Personal best: Batting f/class 23 Lancs v
Leics, Old Trafford.

COOK, Geoffrey.
County: Northamptonshire.
Role: Right-hand bat, slow left arm bowler,
orthodox.
Date and place of birth: 9 October 1951,
Middlesbrough, Yorkshire.
Height: 6' 0". *Weight:* 12 st 10 lbs.
Parents: Harry and Helen Cook.
Wife: Judith.
Married: 22 November 1975.
Education and qualifications: Middlesbrough
High School, six O-levels, one A-level.
Occupation outside cricket: Has taught at
Spratton Hall Prep School.
Family links with cricket: Father and brother,
David, very keen club cricketers. "Father was
virtually 'Mr Cricket' in Middlesbrough
cricket in the 1960s. (President, Secretary,
Chairman of various leagues)."
County debut: 1971. *County cap:* 1975.
Outside interests: Walking, reading,
crosswords.

Nickname: Geoff.
Other sporting activities: "All sports when
continued overleaf

given opportunity." Football with Wellingborough in the Southern League. "I'm a Roy-of-the-Rovers-style Centre Forward".
General: "Great believer in organized recreation for young people. Would enjoy time and scope to carry my beliefs through." One of very few opening batsmen not to wear a helmet. Does excellent impersonations of bowlers.
Address and telephone number: c/o

Northants County Cricket Club, County Ground, Wantage Road, Northampton NN1 4TJ.
Personal best: Batting f/class 155 Northants v Derby, Northampton 1978; jpl 85 Northants v Leics, Leicester 1976; b&h 96 Northants v Minor Counties East, Northampton 1978; gillette 114* Northants v Surrey, Northampton 1979.

COOK, Nicholas Grant Billson.
County: Leicestershire.
Role: Right-hand bat, slow left arm orthodox bowler.
Date and place of birth: 17 June 1956, Leicester.
Height: 6′ 0″. *Weight:* 11 st 7 lbs.
Parents: Peter and Cynthia Cook.
Wife: Janet Elizabeth,
Married: 3 November 1979.
Education and qualifications: Stokes Croft Junior; Lutterworth High; Lutterworth Upper. Seven O-levels, one A-level. Advanced cricket coach.
Occupation outside cricket: Has worked for Leicestershire C.C.C., on promotions, organizing lotteries, sponsored walks, general fund-raising projects. Also coaching.
Family links with cricket: None.
County debut: 1978.
Off-season 1979–80: Touring Australasia with Derrick Robins Under-23 XI.
Outside interests: Crosswords, watching horse-racing and football, and most sporting events.
Nickname: Nick.
Other sporting activities: Playing squash.
General: Has played for Leicestershire 2nd XI since 1974. Played for E.S.C.A. 1975. Played for Young England v Young West

Indies 1975. Toured Australasia with Derrick Robins XI February–March 1980.
Address and telephone number: c/o Leicestershire County Cricket Club, Grace Road, Leicester LE2 8AD.
Personal best: Batting f/class 31 Leics v Northants, Leicester 1978; jpl 13* Leics v Kent, Leicester ,1979. Bowling f/class 6–57 Leics v Essex, Leicester 1979; jpl 2–32 Leics v Kent, Leicester 1979.

COOPER, Howard Pennett.
County: Yorkshire.
Role: Left-hand bat, right arm medium bowler.
Date and place of birth: 17 April 1949, Bradford.
Education and qualifications: Buttershaw Comprehensive School, Bradford.
County debut: 1971.
General: Played for Northern Transvaal in 1973–74 Currie Cup Competition.
Address and telephone number: c/o

Yorkshire County Cricket Club, Headingley Cricket Ground, Leeds LS6 3BU.
Personal best: Batting f/class 56 Yorkshire v Notts, Worksop 1976; jpl 29* Yorkshire v Hants, Bournemouth 1976; b&h 20* Yorkshire v Minor Counties East, Jesmond 1977; gillette 17 Yorkshire v Hants, Bournemouth 1977. Bowling f/class 8–62 Yorkshire v Glamorgan, Cardiff 1975; jpl 6–14 Yorkshire v Worcs, Worcester 1975; b&h 4–28 Yorkshire v Middlesex, Lord's 1979; gillette 4–18 Yorkshire v Leics, Leeds 1975.

COOPER, Kevin Edwin.
County: Nottinghamshire.
Role: Left-hand bat, right arm fast medium bowler.
Date and place of birth: 27 December 1957, Sutton-in-Ashfield.
Height: 6' 1". *Weight:* 11 st 13 lbs.
Parents: Gerald Edwin and Margaret Cooper.
Education and qualifications: Secondary modern.
Occupation outside cricket: Has been warehouseman and maintenance man.
Family links with cricket: None.
County debut: 1976.
Off-season 1979–80: Touring Australasia with Derrick Robins Under 23 XI.
Outside interests: Darts, dominoes, snooker, pool.
Nickname: Henry.
Other sporting activities: Football, golf.
General: On 23 June 1974 playing for Hucknall Ramblers C.C. took 10 wickets for six runs in one innings against Sutton Coll. in the Mansfield and District League.
Address and telephone number: 22 Broomhill Road, Welbeck Est., Hucknall, Notts. Telephone 634910.

Personal best: Batting f/class 19 Notts v Cambridge University, Cambridge 1978; jpl 12 Notts v Northants, Northampton 1979; b&h 5* Notts v Yorkshire, Trent Bridge 1978; gillette 5* Notts v Northants, Trent Bridge 1976; Bowling f/class 6–32 Notts v Derby, Derby 1978; jpl 4–25 Notts v Hants, Trent Bridge 1976; b&h 4–23 Notts v Kent, Canterbury 1979.

COPE, Geoffrey Alan.
County: Yorkshire.
Role: Right-hand bat, off-break bowler.
Date and place of birth: 23 February 1947, Leeds.
Education and qualifications: Temple Moor School, Leeds.
County debut: 1966. *County cap:* 1970.
Outside interests: Family.
Nickname: Todge.
General: Suspended from playing in second half of 1972 season because of doubtful bowling action. Action cleared in 1973 by T.C.C.B. Suspended again in 1978. Toured India, Sri Lanka, Australia 1976–77; Pakistan, New Zealand 1977–78. Wears spectacles.
Address and telephone number: c/o Yorkshire County Cricket Club, Headingley Cricket Ground, Leeds LS6 3BU.
Personal best: Batting Tests 22 England v Pakistan, Hyberabad 1977–78; other f/class 78 Yorkshire v Essex, Middlesbrough 1977; jpl 16* Yorkshire v Sussex, Bradford 1974; b&h 18* Yorkshire v Surrey, Bradford 1976; gillette 1* Yorkshire v Gloucs, Leeds 1976.

Bowling Tests 3–102 England v Pakistan, Lahore 1977–78; other f/class 8–73 Yorkshire v Gloucs, Bristol 1975; jpl 3–24 Yorkshire v Northants, Bradford 1969; b&h 1–23 Yorkshire v Surrey, Barnsley 1978; gillette 2–22 Yorkshire v Hants, Bradford 1974.

CORDLE, Anthony Elton.
County: Glamorgan.
Role: Right-hand bat, right arm fast medium bowler.
Date and place of birth: 21 September 1940, St Michael, Barbados.
County debut: 1963. *County cap:* 1967.
Benefit: £8,000 in 1977.
Outside interests: Is a church-warden at St. Luke's Parish Church, Cardiff.
Nickname: Tony.
General: Was elected Glamorgan Player of the Year 1979. Took first hat-trick after 16 years with Glamorgan—and did not notice until told at tea, v Hants at Portsmouth.
Address and telephone number: c/o Glamorgan County Cricket Club, 6 High Street, Cardiff. Telephone: Cardiff 29956.
Personal best: Batting f/class 81 Glamorgan v Cambridge University, Swansea 1972; jpl 87 Glamorgan v Notts, Trent Bridge 1971; b&h 27* Glamorgan v Hants, Swansea 1976; gillette 36 Glamorgan v Lincs, Swansea 1974. Bowling f/class 9–49 Glamorgan v Leics,

Colwyn Bay 1969; jpl 5–24 Glamorgan v Hants, Portsmouth 1979; b&h 4–14 Glamorgan v Hants, Swansea 1973; gillette 4–42 Glamorgan v Worcs, Worcester 1977.

COWDREY, Christopher Stuart.
County: Kent.
Role: Right-hand bat, right arm medium bowler.
Date and place of birth: 20 October 1957, Farnborough, Kent.
Height: 6′ 0″. *Weight:* 12 st 2 lbs.
Parents: Michael Colin and Penelope Susan Cowdrey.
Education and qualifications: Wellesley House, Broadstairs, and Tonbridge School.
Occupation outside cricket: Director, PPG Sporting Enterprises, Sandwich, Kent. Working for Leisuresports, running golf pro-ams in winter months.
Family links with cricket: Grandfather, Stuart Chiesman, on Kent Committee for many years, twelve as Chairman. Pavilion on Kent's ground at Canterbury named after him. Father, Colin, played for Kent and England.
County debut: 1977. *County cap:* 1979.
Off-season 1979–80: Touring Australasia with Derrick Robbins Under-23 XI.
Outside interests: Sport.
Nickname: Chris. Cow.
Other sporting activities: Squash, rackets, golf.
General: Captained Young England to West Indies, 1976. Uses Duncan Fearnley cricket

equipment. Played for Kent 2nd XI at age 15.
Address and telephone number: Yew Tree Cottage, Grub Street, Limpsfield, Oxted, Surrey. Telephone: Limpsfield Chart 2377.
Personal best: Batting f/class 101* Kent v Glamorgan, Swansea 1977; jpl 74 Kent v Worcs, Worcester 1978; b&h 114 Kent v Sussex, Canterbury 1977; gillette 23* Kent v Lancs, Canterbury 1979. Bowling f/class 3–40 Kent v Warwicks, Edgbaston 1979; jpl 2–10 Kent v Surrey, The Oval 1978.

COWLEY, Nigel Geoffrey.
County: Hampshire.
Role: Right-hand bat, off-break bowler.
Date and place of birth: 1 March 1953, Shaftesbury, Dorset.
County debut: 1974. *County cap:* 1978.
Address and telephone number: c/o Hampshire County Cricket Club, Northlands Road, Southampton SO9 2TY.
Personal best: Batting f/class 109* Hants v Somerset, Taunton 1977; jpl 47 Hants v Notts, Trent Bridge 1978; b&h 59 Hants v Gloucs, Southampton 1977; gillette 63* Hants v Gloucs, Bristol 1979. Bowling f/class 5–44 Hants v Derby, Basingstoke 1979; jpl 3–19 Hants v Gloucs, Cheltenham 1978; b&h 2–10 Hants v Combined Universities, Cambridge 1978; gillette 4–20 Hants v Middlesex, Lord's 1979.

CUMBES, James.
County: Worcestershire.
Role: Right-hand bat, right fast medium.
Date and place of birth: 4 May 1944, Didsbury, Manchester.
Height: 6′ 2″. *Weight:* 14 st.
Parents: John William and Hannah Cumbes.
Wife: Elizabeth Anne.
Married: 4 April 1977.
Education: Didsbury Technical High Sch.
Occupation outside cricket: Professional footballer with Tranmere Rovers, West Bromwich Albion and Aston Villa. Played soccer in Oregon, U.S.A., 1976, with Portland Timbers. Winter job as salesman for Martyn Price Ltd. (industrial fasteners). Also did local radio show 1972–76.
Family links with cricket: Brother-in-law, Roy Collins, played for Lancs. 1954–62.
County debut: 1972. *County cap:* 1978.
Outside interests: All types of music. A little gardening. Reading (mostly newspapers).
Nickname: "None other than Cumbesie".
Other sporting activities: Squash. Still playing "very much on a part-time basis with Worcester City F.C. as goalkeeper."
General: Debut for Lancashire 1963. Not re-engaged at end of 1967 season and made debut for Surrey 1968. Not re-engaged after 1970 season and rejoined Lancashire in 1971. Special registration for Worcestershire in 1972. "I only played cricket for two months per season until I retired from professional football in 1976. My first full cricket season was 1977." Professional Cricketers' Associa-

tion representative for Worcestershire. Used to do a Sunday morning radio show for Radio Birmingham comprising Saturday sports round-up, record requests, telephone quizzes and interviewing guests. Believes county cricket matches should be played over four days during the week with one-day matches on Saturdays and Sundays. Has ambitions to run a pub. Very good public speaker. First man to appear for 3 counties in John Player League: Lancs, Surrey and Worcs.
Address and telephone number, c/o Worcestershire County Cricket Club, New Road, Worcester WR2 9QQ.

continued overleaf

Personal best: Batting f/class 25* Surrey v West Indies, The Oval 1969; jpl 14* Worcs v Sussex, Eastbourne 1978; b&h 4* Worcs v Hants, Bournemouth 1978; gillette 6 Worcs v Leics, Leicester 1979. Bowling f/class 6–24 Worcs v Yorks, Worcester 1977; jpl 3–13 Worcs v Middlesex, Worcester 1978; b&h 3–34 Worcs v Somerset, Taunton 1978; gillette 4–23 Worcs v Sussex, Hove 1974.

CURTIS, Timothy Stephen.
County: Worcestershire.
Date and place of birth: 15 January 1960, Chislehurst, Kent.
Height: 5' 11". *Weight:* 11 st 8 lbs.
Parents: Bruce and Betty Curtis.
Wife: Unmarried.
Education and qualifications: The Royal Grammar School, Worcester; Durham University.
Occupation outside cricket: Student, studying English.
Family links with cricket: Father played good club cricket in Bristol and Stafford.
County debut: 1979.
Outside interests: Reading, listening to modern music.
Nickname: Tim.
Other sporting activities: Golf, squash, tennis, rugby.
Address and telephone number: 10 Denison Close, Malvern, Worcestershire, WR14 2EU. Telephone: Malvern 5557.
Personal best: Batting f/class 27 Worcs v Sri Lanka, Worcester 1979.

CURZON, Christopher Colin.
County: Nottinghamshire.
Role: Right-hand bat, wicket-keeper.
Date and place of birth: 22 December 1958, Lenton, Nottingham.
Family links with cricket: Brother of John Timothy Curzon, who made debut for Nottinghamshire C.C.C. v Cambridge University at Cambridge in 1978.
County debut: 1978.
Nickname: Pukey.
Other sporting activities: Football, squash.
General: Played for Notts 2nd XI since 1976.
Address and telephone number: 22 Watford Road, Aspley, Nottingham. Telephone: Nottingham 786020.
Personal best: Batting f/class 26 Notts v Gloucs, Cheltenham 1978; jpl 18* Notts v Yorkshire, Scarborough, 1978.

DANIEL, Wayne Wendell.
County: Middlesex.
Role: Right-hand bat, right arm fast bowler.
Date and place of birth: 16 January 1956, St Philip, Barbados.
County debut: 1977. *County cap:* 1977.
Outside interests: Enjoys listening to soul music.
Nickname: Diamond.
General: Toured England with West Indies Schoolboys team 1974. Played for Middlesex 2nd XI 1975. Debut for Barbados 1975–76. Toured with West Indies to England 1976. Holds best bowling record for Benson & Hedges Competition with 7 for 12 v Minor Counties East at Ipswich in 1978. Spent 1979–80 off-season in Barbados playing island cricket.
Address and telephone number: c/o Middlesex County Cricket Club, Lord's Cricket Ground, St John's Wood Road, London NW8 8QN. Telephone: 01–289–1300.
Personal best: Batting Tests 11 West Indies v

India, Kingston 1975-76; other f/class 30 West Indies v Sussex, Hove 1976; 30* Middlesex v Notts, Lord's 1978; jpl 63 Middlesex v Hants, Lord's 1977; b&h 20 Middlesex v Derby, Derby 1978; gillette 14 Middlesex v Lancs, Old Trafford 1978. Bowling Tests 4-53 West Indies v England, Trent Bridge 1976; other f/class 6-21 West Indies v Yorkshire, Sheffield 1976; jpl 4-13 Middlesex v Derby, Chesterfield 1979; b&h 7-12 Middlesex v Minor Counties East, Ipswich 1978; gillette 4-24 Middlesex v Somerset, Lord's 1977.

DAVIS, Terry.
County: Glamorgan.
Role: Wicket-keeper.
Date and place of birth: 25 October 1960, St Albans.
Height: 5' 6". *Weight:* 10 st.
Parents: Harry and Peggy Davies.
Wife: Unmarried.
Education and qualifications: Townsend Secondary School, St Albans.
Occupation outside cricket: Carpet-fitter. Has worked in sports shop.
Family links with cricket: Brother living in Sydney, Australia, plays cricket for Morebank Sports Club.
County debut: 1979.
Outside interests: Music.
Other sporting activities: Playing football, squash, golf and tennis.
General: Played football for Hertfordshire Under-16s, and had trials with West Ham F.C., Tottenham Hotspur and Luton. Also trained with Watford for a season. On Lord's ground staff 1976-77-78. Runner-up two years in succession, 1978, 1979, for Best

Young Wicket-keeper of the Year. Played grade cricket in Sydney, Australia, for Central Cumberland in 1978-79 off-season.
Address and telephone number: c/o Glamorgan County Cricket Club, 6 High Street, Cardiff. Telephone: Cardiff 29956.

DAVISON, Brian Fettes.
County: Leicestershire.
Role: Right-hand bat, right arm medium bowler.
Date and place of birth: 21 December 1946, Bulawayo, Rhodesia.
Education and qualifications: Gifford Technical High School, Rhodesia.
County debut: 1970. *County cap:* 1971.

Off-season 1979-80: Playing cricket in Tasmania, as captain.
Nickname: Davo.
Other sporting activities: Has played hockey for Rhodesia. Golf.
General: Made debut for Rhodesia 1967-68 in Currie Cup Competition. Has scored 1,000

continued overleaf

runs in a season nine times. Has to do military service in Rhodesia.

Address and telephone number: c/o Leicestershire County Cricket Club, Grace Road, Leicester LE2 8AD. Telephone: Leicester 832128.

Personal best: Batting f/class 189 Leics v Australia, Leicester 1975; jpl 85* Leics v Glamorgan, Cardiff 1974; b&h 158* Leics v Warwicks, Coventry 1972; gillette 99 Leics v Essex, Southend 1977; Bowling f/class 5–52 Rhodesia v Griqualand W, Bulawayo 1967–68; jpl 4–25 Leics v Hants, Portsmouth 1971; b&h 1–16 Leics v Oxford University, Oxford 1973; gillette 2–18 Leics v Derby, Leicester 1971.

DENNESS, Michael Henry.

County: Essex.

Role: Right-hand bat, right arm medium and off-break bowler.

Date and place of birth: 1 December 1940, Bellshill, Lanarkshire.

Height: 5′ 11″. *Weight:* 12 st.

Parents: William Gardiner Denness, deceased, and Elizabeth Stewart Denness.

Wife: Molly.

Married: 9 September 1964.

Children: Lizanne, 27 October 1965; Jane, 17 October 1967, Craig, 3 May 1973.

Education and qualifications: Ayr Academy, Ayr, Scotland.

Occupation outside cricket: Life assurance, insurance broking, financial management and sports promotion. Manager, World Series Cricket, World Squad.

Family links with cricket: Father played with I. A. R. Peebles, of Middlesex and England.

County debut: 1977. *County cap:* 1977.

Benefit: (while with Kent) £19,219 in 1974.

Outside interests: Follows most sports.

Nickname: Mike. Haggis.

Other sporting activities: Golf.

General: Debut for Scotland while still at school 1969. Debut for Kent 1962. Cap 1964. Kent County Captain 1972–76. Left Kent after 1976 season. Captained England in 19

tests, between 1973 and 1974–75. Played v Rest of the World 1970. One of Wisden's Cricketers of the Year 1974.

Address and telephone number: 2 Barton Road, Canterbury, Kent CT1 1YG.

Personal best: Batting Tests 188 England v Australia, Melbourne 1974–75; other f/class 195 Essex v Leics, Leicester 1977; jpl 118* Kent v Yorkshire, Scarborough 1976; b&h 112* Kent v Surrey, The Oval 1973. Bowling f/class 1– Kent v Leicester 1976.

DENNING, Peter William.
County: Somerset.
Role: Left-hand bat, off-break bowler.
Date and place of birth: 16 December 1949, Wells, Somerset.
Height: 5′ 8″. *Weight:* 10 st. 7 lbs.
Parents: Thomas Frederick and Maxine Betty Denning.
Wife: Anne.
Married: 7 April 1973.
Children: Claire, 28 September 1975; Samantha, 6 July 1978.
Education and qualifications: Millfield School, St. Luke's College, Exeter, 10 O-levels, 3 A-levels, teacher's certificate.
Occupation outside cricket: Qualified teacher, demolition, civil service, council.
Family links with cricket: Father had trial with Somerset in 1932.
County debut: 1969. *County cap:* 1973.
Outside interests: Riding, soccer, gardening, decorating, reading.
Nickname: Dasher.
Other sporting activities: Riding, soccer.
General: Always uses County Sports equipment. Honorary member Cleeve Cricket Club.
Address and telephone number: c/o Somerset

County Cricket Club, County Cricket Ground, St James's Street, Taunton TA1 1JT.
Personal best: Batting f/class 122 Somerset v Gloucs, Taunton 1977; jpl 100 Somerset v Northants, Brackley 1974; b&h 87 Somerset v Gloucs, Taunton 1974; gillette 145 Somerset v Glamorgan, Cardiff 1978. Bowling f/class 1–4 Somerset v Derbyshire, Derby 1974.

DEXTER, Roy Evatt.
County: Nottinghamshire.
Role: Right-hand bat.
Date and place of birth: 13 April 1955, Nottingham.
Height: 6′ 1″. *Weight:* 15 st. 3 lbs.
Parents: John Evatt and Barbara Ellen Dexter.
Education and qualifications: Nottingham High School, Lanchester Polytechnic. BA (Hons) Modern Languages.
Occupation outside cricket: Clerical assistant, DHSS.
Family links with cricket: Father played local cricket.
County debut: 1975.
Outside interests: Visiting foreign countries, playing cards, crosswords.
Nickname: Lord Ted.
Other sporting activities: Golf, rugby, badminton.
General: Gained NCA coaching certificate April 1979. Spent 1979/80 winter playing club cricket in New Zealand and coaching.

Address and telephone number: 21 Aspley Park Drive, Aspley, Nottingham.
Personal best: Batting f/class 48 Notts v Derby, Ilkeston 1977.

DILLEY, Graham Roy.
County: Kent.
Role: Left-hand bat, right arm fast bowler.
Date and place of birth: 18 May 1959, Dartford.
Height: 6' 4". *Weight:* 14 st 5 lbs.
Parents: Geoff and Jean Dilley.
Wife: Unmarried.
Education and qualifications: Dartford West Secondary School, three O-levels.
Occupation outside cricket: Diamond-setter.
Family links with cricket: Father and grandfather both played local cricket.
County debut: 1977.
Off-season 1979-80: Touring Australia.
Outside interests: Music.
Nickname: Dill or Picca.
Other sporting activities: Golf.
General: Got sacked from his first job with a Hatton Garden diamond firm after taking time off to play for Kent 2nd XI.
Address and telephone number: c/o Kent County Cricket Club, Canterbury CT1 3NZ.
Personal best: Batting f/class 81 Kent v

Northants, Northampton 1979; jpl 8 Kent v Worcs, Canterbury 1979. Bowling f/class 6-66 Kent v Middlesex, Lord's 1979; jpl 3-13 Kent v Surrey, The Oval 1978; b&h 2-39 Kent v Notts, Canterbury 1979; gillette 2-28 Kent v Somerset, Taunton 1979.

D'OLIVEIRA, Basil Lewis.
County: Worcestershire.
Role: Right-hand bat, right arm medium and off-break bowler.
Date and place of birth: 4 October 1931, Capetown, South Africa.
County debut: 1964. *County cap:* 1965.
Benefit: £27,000 in 1975.
Nickname: Dolly.
General: Played for Middleton in Central Lancashire League 1960-63. First class debut on Commonwealth tour 1961-62. playing two matches in Rhodesia. Further Commonwealth tour of Rhodesia 1962-63 and Pakistan 1963-64. Played for Kidderminster while qualifying for Worcester. Awarded O.B.E. 1969. Played four matches for England v Rest of World 1970; toured West Indies 1967-68, Sri Lanka and Pakistan 1968-69; Australia, New Zealand 1970-71. Scored 1,000 runs in season nine times. Oldest man playing first class cricket in 1979. Retired from first class cricket at end of season.
Address and telephone number: c/o Worcestershire County Cricket Club, New Road, Worcester WR2 4QQ.
Personal best: Batting Tests 158 England v Australia, The Oval 1968; other f/class 227

Worcs v Yorkshire, Hull 1974; jpl 100 Worcs v Surrey, Byfleet 1973; b&h 84 Worcs v Middlesex, Lord's 1974; gillette 102 Worcs v Sussex, Hove 1974. Bowling Tests 3-46 England v Pakistan, Leeds 1971; other f/class 6-29 Worcs v Hants, Portsmouth 1968; jpl 5-26 Worcs v Gloucs, Lydney 1972; b&h 4-6 Worcs v Minor Counties South, High Wycombe 1979; gillette 4-18 Worcs v Notts, Worcester 1974.

DOWNTON, Paul Rupert.
County: Kent.
Role: Right-hand bat, wicket-keeper.
Date and place of birth: 4 April 1957,
Farnborough, Kent.
Height: 5' 10". *Weight:* 11 st 5 lbs.
Parents: George Charles and Jill Elizabeth
Downton.
Wife: Unmarried.
Education and qualifications: Sevenoaks
School, Exeter University.
Occupation outside cricket: Student, reading
Law.
Family links with cricket: Father was capped
for Kent 2nd XI and was first team under-
study to Godfrey Evans 1948-49.
County debut: 1977. *County cap:* 1979.
Outside interests: Reading and listening to
music.
Nickname: Nobby.
Other sporting activities: Rugby, England
Under-19 group, final trialist and squad
member. Exeter University 1st XV. "Limited
tennis, golf, swimming."
General: Played for Kent 2nd XI at age 16.
Vice-captain of England Young Cricketers
team to tour West Indies 1976. 2nd XI Kent
cap 1977. Pakistan and New Zealand tour
1977-78. Was unavailable for first half of

1979 season because of university studies.
Address and telephone number: Raglands,
Stone Street, Sevenoaks, Kent. Telephone:
Plaxtol 457.
Personal best: Batting f/class 31* Kent v
Surrey, Maidstone 1977; 31 Kent v Sussex,
Hove 1978; jpl 19* Kent v Worcs, Canterbury
1979; b&h 9 Kent v Somerset, Taunton 1979;
gillette 6 Kent v Somerset, Taunton 1979.

DREDGE, Colin Herbert.
County: Somerset.
Role: Left-hand bat, right arm medium
bowler.
Date and place of birth: 4 August 1954,
Frome, Somerset.
Height: 6' 5".
Parents: Frederick Herbert James and Kath-
leen Beryl Dredge.
Wife: Mandy.
Married: 9 December 1978.
Education and qualifications: Wesley
Methodist School; Milk Street School;
Oakfield School.
Occupation outside cricket: Served
apprenticeship with Rolls-Royce Ltd.,
Hatchway, Bristol, as a toolmaker.
Family links with cricket: One of ten
children, eight boys and two girls; all the
brothers play cricket for Frome.
County debut: 1976. *County cap:* 1978.
Outside interests: Watching television.
Nickname: Herbie. "The Demon of Frome".
Other sporting activities: Football, golf.

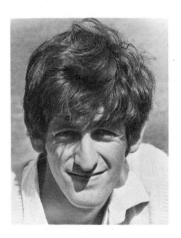

Western League football for Welton Rovers.
Local Sunday side, Jubilee F.C. Played
soccer for Bristol City Reserves, 1974-76.
Address and telephone number: 6 Tankey's
Close, Frome, Somerset.

continued overleaf

Personal best: Batting f/class 56* Somerset v Yorkshire, Harrogate 1977; jpl 14 Somerset v Essex, Taunton 1978; b&h 10* Somerset v Worcs, Taunton 1978; gillette 1* Somerset v Middlesex, Lord's 1977. Bowling f/class

5-53 Somerset v Kent, Taunton 1978; jpl 3-19 Somerset v Middlesex, Taunton 1978; b&h 2-22 Somerset v Sussex, Hove 1978; 2-22 Somerset v Gloucs, Bristol 1979; gillette 4-23 Somerset v Kent, Canterbury 1978.

DUDLESTONE, Barry.
County: Leicestershire.
Role: Right-hand bat, slow left arm orthodox bowler. Occasional wicketkeeper.
Date and place of birth: 16 July 1945, Bebington, Cheshire.
Education and qualifications: Stockport School.
County debut: 1966. *County cap:* 1969.
Benefit: 1980.
Nickname: Danny.
General: Played for Rhodesia from 1966–67 to 1979–80 in Currie Cup Competition. Has scored 1,000 runs in a season eight times. Shared in seventh wicket partnership record for county, 206, with Jack Birkenshaw, v Kent at Canterbury in 1969. Has suffered badly from broken fingers. Broke fingers on same hand 3 times in 1978.
Address and telephone number: c/o Leicestershire County Cricket Club, Grace Road, Leicester LE2 8AD. Telephone: Leicester 832128.
Personal best: Batting f/class 202 Leics v

Derby, Leicester 1979; jpl 152 Leics v Lancs, Old Trafford 1975; b&h 90 Leics v Warwicks, Leicester 1973; gillette 125 Leics v Worcs, Leicester 1979. Bowling f/class 4-6 Leics v Surrey, Leicester 1972.

EALHAM, Alan George Ernest.
County: Kent.
Role: Right-hand bat, off-break bowler.
Date and place of birth: 30 August 1944, Willesborough, Ashford, Kent.
Height: 5′ 8″ *Weight:* 13 st 7 lbs.
Parents: Stuart George Alan and Olive May Ealham.
Wife: Susan Patricia.
Married: 14 September 1968.
Children: Mark Alan, 27 August 1969; Louise Clare, 9 March 1971.
Education and qualifications: Ashford South Secondary School for Boys. Motor vehicle (bodywork), City & Guilds.
Occupation outside cricket: Has worked as sales executive (motor vehicles).
Family links with cricket: Grandfather was Kent County Cricket Club member for over 50 years. Father played for Willesborough C.C., brother for Kingsnorth C.C., two cousins for Willesborough C.C.

County debut: 1966. *County cap:* 1970.
Outside interests: Shooting, walking, cars, family.

46

Nickname: Clogger or Ealy.
Other sporting activities: Table tennis, golf.
General: Writes column for *Kent Gazette* and other papers in the Kent area. County Captain 1978 onwards. Held five catches in an innings v Gloucestershire at Folkestone in 1966, all in the outfield off D. L. Underwood.
Address and telephone number: The Willows, Howfield Lane, Chartham, near Canterbury, Kent.
Personal best: Batting f/class 153 Kent v Worcs, Canterbury 1979; jpl 83 Kent v Leics, Leicester 1977; b&h 94* Kent v Sussex, Canterbury 1977; gillette 46 Kent v Leics, Canterbury 1974. Bowling f/class 1–1 Kent v Middlesex, Lord's 1963.

EAST, Raymond Eric.
County: Essex.
Role: Right-hand bat, slow left arm orthodox bowler.
Date and place of birth: 20 June 1947, Manningtree, Essex.
Height: 6′ 1″. *Weight:* 12 st
Parents: Eric Edward and Paula East.
Wife: Barbara Wilma.
Married: July 1974.
Children: James Peter, 26 November 1976; John Raymond, 24 January 1979.
Education and qualifications: East Bergholt Comprehensive.
Occupation outside cricket: Has been fuel representative.
Family links with cricket: None.
County debut: 1965. *County cap:* 1967.
Benefit: 1978.
Outside interests: Keen Ipswich F.C. fan.
Nickname: Easty. Spindle.
Other sporting activities: Golf, Soccer.
General: One of the best known "characters" in game. Does excellent comic act on and off the field. Holds John Player League record for most expensive spell: 8 overs, 0 maidens, 79 runs, 1 wicket v Glamorgan in 1979. But has taken 5 wickets in a J.P.L. innings 4 times—a record he shares with D. P. Hughes and D. A. Marriott.
Address and telephone number: Walnut Tree

Cottage, Church Street, Great Maplestead, Essex.
Personal best: Batting f/class 113 Essex v Hants, Chelmsford 1976; jpl 25* Essex v Glamorgan, Colchester 1976; b&h 54 Essex v Northants, Chelmsford 1977; gillette 38* Essex v Gloucs, Cheltenham 1973. Bowling f/class 8–30 Essex v Notts, Ilford 1977; jpl 6–18 Essex v Yorkshire, Hull 1969; b& h 5–33 Essex v Kent, Chelmsford 1975; gillette 4–28 Essex v Herts, Hitchin 1976.

EDMONDS, Phillippe Henri.
County: Middlesex.
Role: Right-hand bat, slow left arm orthodox bowler.
Date and place of birth: 8 March 1951, Lusaka, Zambia.
Education and qualifications: Gilbert Rennie High School, Lusaka; Skinner's School, Tunbridge Wells; Cranbrook School; Cambridge University.
County debut: 1971. *County cap:* 1974.
Outside interests: "Reads *Financial Times* avidly at breakfast", crosswords.
Nickname: Goat or Henry.
Other sporting activities: Played rugby for Cambridge but missed blue. Squash.
General: Cambridge cricket blue 1971–72–73, captain 1973. Elected Best Young Cricketer of the Year in 1974 by the Cricket Writers' Club. Played for Eastern Province in 1975–76 Currie Cup Competi-

continued overleaf

tion. Toured Pakistan and New Zealand 1977-78, Australia 1978-79. Constantly listening to news programmes. 7 other counties have made offers. Spent 1979-80 off-season working for sports promoting company.

Address and telephone number: c/o Middlesex County Cricket Club, Lord's Cricket Ground, St John's Wood Road, London NW8 8QN. Telephone: 01-289-1300.

Personal best: Batting Tests 50 England v New Zealand, Christchurch 1977-78; other f/class 141* Middlesex v Glamorgan, Lord's 1979; jpl 43 Middlesex v Leics, Lord's 1977; b&h 44* Middlesex v Notts, Newark 1976; gillette 63* Middlesex v Somerset, Lord's 1979; Bowling Tests 7-66 England v Pakistan, Karachi 1977-78; other f/class 8-132 Middlesex v Gloucs, Lord's 1977; jpl 3-19 Middlesex v Leics, Lord's 1973; b&h

4-11 Middlesex v Kent, Lord's 1975; gillette 3-28 Middlesex v Yorkshire, Lord's 1979.

EMBUREY, John Ernest.

County: Middlesex.
Role: Right-hand bat, off-break bowler.
Date and place of birth: 20 August 1952, Peckham, London.
Height: 6' 2". *Weight:* 13 st 7 lbs.
Parents: John and Rose Emburey.
Wife: unmarried.
Education and qualifications: Peckham Manor Secondary School. Advanced Cricket Coaching Certificate.
Occupation outside cricket: "No other jobs. Has been abroad coaching most years."
Family links with cricket: "An uncle, Charles Roff, was a very good cricketer. His father made him take an apprenticeship which stopped him going any further with cricket." Brother, Stephen, represented London Schools Colts in 1977.
County debut: 1973. *County cap:* 1977.
Off-season 1979-80: Playing for St. Kilda C.C., Victoria, Australia; and then for England, following injury to Geoff Miller.
Outside interests: Fishing, horse-riding, reading, watching television, playing chess, darts, cards.
Nickname: Embers, Ernie.
Other sporting activites: Squash, soccer.
General: Played for Surrey Young Cricketers 1969-70. "I'm happy a settlement has been made with W.S.C. but disappointed that county cricketers have not benefited a great

deal, if any, by W.S.C. which was promised. I believe that any form of advertising should be used by clubs and players and that the T.C.C.B. should be more tolerant towards it."

Address and telephone number: c/o Middlesex County Cricket Club, Lord's Cricket Ground, London NW8 8QN, telephone 01-289-1300.

Personal best: Batting Tests 42 England v Australia, Adelaide 1978-79; other f/class 91* Middlesex v Surrey, The Oval 1979; jpl 30 Middlesex v Lancs, Lord's 1978; b&h 10

Middlesex v Yorkshire, Lord's 1979; gillette 36* Middlesex v Lancs, Old Trafford 1978. Bowling Tests 4–46 England v Australia, Sydney 1978–79; other f/class 7–36 Middlesex v Cambridge Universtiy, Cambridge 1977; jpl 4–43 Middlesex v Worcs, Worcester 1976; b&h 2–18 Middlesex v Minor Counties North, Lord's 1979; gillette 2–22 Middlesex v Derby, Derby 1978.

FEATHERSTONE, Norman George.

County: Glamorgan.
Role: Right-hand bat, off-break bowler.
Date and place of birth: 20 August 1949, Que Que, Rhodesia.
Height: 5' 11". *Weight:* 12 st 2 lbs.
Parents: Jack and Dee Featherstone.
Wife: Dianne.
Married: 19 November 1976.
Education and qualifications: King Edward VII High School, Johannesburg, South Africa.
Occupation outside cricket: Salesman.
County debut: 1968. *County cap:* 1971.
Benefit: 1979.
Nickname: Smokey.
Other sporting activities: Golf. Jogging.
General: Member of South African Schools team to England 1967. Debut for Transvaal B 1967–68 Currie Cup Competition. Asked to be released from contract with Middlesex after 1972 season but subsequently changed his mind. Has scored 1,000 runs in a season twice. Scored two centuries in a match (127 not out and 100 not out) v Kent at Canterbury in 1975. Has been released by Middlesex. Joined Glamorgan.
Address and telephone number: c/o Glamorgan County Cricket Club, 6 High Street, Cardiff. Telephone: Cardiff 29956.

Personal best: Batting f/class 147 Middlesex v Yorkshire, Scarborough 1975; jpl 82* Middlesex v Notts, Lord's 1976; b&h 56* Middlesex v Sussex, Hove 1975; 56 Middlesex v Kent, Lord's 1975; gillette 72* Middlesex v Worcs, Worcester 1975. Bowling f/class 5–32 Middlesex v Notts, Trent Bridge, 1978; jpl 4–10 Middlesex v Worcs, Worcester 1978; b&h 4–35 Middlesex v Minor Counties East, Lord's 1976; gillette 3–17 Middlesex v Glamorgan, Lord's 1977.

FERREIRA, Anthonie Michal.

County: Warwickshire.
Role: Right-hand bat, right arm medium bowler.
Date and place of birth: 13 April 1955, Pretoria, South Africa.
Height: 6' 3". *Weight:* 15 st.
Education and qualifications: Highview High School, Pretoria; Pretoria University; BA.
Occupation outside cricket: Teacher.
County debut: 1979.
Off-season 1979–80: Playing for Northern Transvaal.
Nickname: Yogi, or Anton.
Other sporting activities: Boxing—once fought Gerry Coetzee, who last year fought for W.B.A. World Heavyweight title.
General: Troubled with ankle injury in 1979. Debut for Northern Transvaal 1974–75. Played for Derrick Robins XI v Oxford and Cambridge in 1978. Teetotaller. Non-smoker.
Address and telephone number: c/o
continued overleaf

Warwickshire County Cricket Club, Edgbaston, Birmingham.
Personal best: Batting f/class 84 Northern Transvaal v Griqualand N., Pretoria 1978-79; jpl 36* Warwicks v Middlesex, Lord's 1979; b&h 13* Warwicks v Lancs, Southport 1979; gillette 6 Warwicks v Notts, Edgbaston 1979. Bowling f/class 8-38 Northern Transvaal v Transvaal B, Pretoria 1977-78; jpl 3-32 Warwicks v Kent, Maidstone 1979; b&h 2-37 Warwicks v Hants, Bournemouth 1979; gillette 4-50 Warwicks v Notts, Edgbaston 1979.

FINAN, Nicholas Hugh.
County: Gloucestershire.
Role: Right-hand bat, right arm medium bowler.
Date and place of birth: 3 July 1954, Knowle, Bristol.
Height: 6′ 3″. *Weight:* 15 st.
Parents: Raymond Joseph and Evelyn Mary Finan.
Wife: Monica Frances.
Married: 20 October 1979.
Education and qualifications: St Brendan's College, Bristol.
Occupation outside cricket: Laboratory Technician, Pathology Dept., Bristol University.
Family links with cricket: Brothers played local cricket. Eldest brother, Patrick played in "Possibles v Probables" game to represent Royal Navy. Brother, Bernard, played rugby for Navy.

County debut: 1975.
Outside interests: "Most indoor and outdoor sports, preferably football, rugby, table-tennis, darts and monopoly, and a selection of the usual 'vices'."
Nickname: "Fines, pronounced as in Parking . . .".
General: Has not been re-engaged.
Address and telephone number: c/o Gloucestershire County Cricket Club, Neville Road, Bristol BS7 9EJ.
Personal best: Batting f/class 18 Gloucs v Worcs, Worcester 1977; jpl 11 Gloucs v Essex, Cheltenham 1975; b&h 13 Gloucs v Worcs, Worcester 1979; gillette 4 Gloucs v Hants, Bristol 1979. Bowling f/class 2-57 Gloucs v Sussex, Eastbourne 1975; jpl 2-25 Gloucs v Northants, Northampton 1976; 2-25 Gloucs v Hants, Portsmouth 1977; b&h 2-30 Gloucs v Minor Counties (South) Bristol 1979; gillette 1-23 Gloucs v Worcs, Bristol 1976.

FISHER, Paul Bernard.
County: Middlesex.
Role: Right-hand bat, wicket-keeper.
Date and place of birth: 19 December 1954, Edmonton, Middlesex.
Height: 5′ 10″. *Weight:* 11 st 7 lbs.

Parents: Peter and Sylvia Shipley Fisher.
Wife: Unmarried.
Education and qualifications: St Ignatius College, Enfield, Middlesex; Christchurch College, Oxford; 2nd Class Hons in Classics.
Occupation outside cricket: Schoolmaster at Marlborough College.
County debut: 1979.
Off-season 1979-80: Touring Australia with Combined Oxford and Cambridge XI.
Outside interests: Music.
Nickname: Fish.
Other sporting activities: Rugby, golf.

FLETCHER, Christopher David Bryan.
County: Sussex.
Role: Right-hand bat, right arm fast medium bowler.
Date and place of birth: 10 December 1957, Harrogate, Yorkshire.
Height: 6' 1". *Weight:* 13 st 7 lbs.
Parents: David and Patricia Fletcher.
Wife: Unmarried.
Education and qualifications: Grosvenor House Prep School, Harrogate, Yorkshire. Torquay Boys' Grammar School, Torquay. Exeter College, Exeter, Devon. A-level Art, 5 O-levels, physical education first year certificate, coaching awards (N.C.A.).
Occupation outside cricket: Has worked in the Foreign and Commonwealth Office for nine months.
Family links with cricket: Father had many successful seasons in the Yorkshire League with Harrogate, playing in the same side as his uncle, John Howard, for a few years

FLETCHER, Keith William Robert.
County: Essex.
Role: Right-hand bat, leg-break bowler.
Date and place of birth: 20 May 1944, Worcester.
Height: 5' 11" *Weight:* 10 st 7 lbs.
Parents: Joseph and Doris Fletcher.
Wife: Susan Elizabeth.
Married: 22 March 1969.
Children: Tamara Jane, 2 August 1970; Sara Jane, 19 December 1972.
Occupation outside cricket: Has worked as oil representative.
County debut: 1962. *County cap:* 1963.
Benefit: £13,000 in 1973.
Outside interests: Gardening.
Nickname: Gnome.

General: Debut for Oxford University, 1974. Blue 1975-76-77-78. Played for Middlesex in one Fenner Trophy match and in the last John Player League match 1978.
Address and telephone number: 50A High Street, Marlborough, Wiltshire SN8 1HQ. Telephone: 0672-52643.
Personal best: Batting f/class 42 Oxford University v Warwicks, Oxford 1975; jpl 3 Middlesex v Hants, Bournemouth 1976; b&h 14* Combined Universities v Hants, Cambridge 1978.

during the 1950s and early 1960s.
County debut: 1977.
Outside interests: Photography. Music, ranging from jazz to new wave. Reading.
Nickname: Fletch, Godber.
Other sporting activities: Squash, football, running, golf, swimming.
General: "First came to Sussex's notice after successful season for Torquay Cricket Club and Devon, when asked to attend Tony Greig's 'Find a Fast Bowler' Competition in 1976. Subsequently offered a contract for 1977, played two games and broke down with injury to right shoulder; had major surgery January 1978 to remove part of my collarbone. Despite a loss in pace the operation was 100% successful".
Address and telephone number: Flat 3, 12 Cromwell Road, Hove BN3 3EA, East Sussex. Telephone: Brighton 72053.
Personal best: Bowling f/class 1-35 Sussex v Oxford University, Pagham 1979.

continued overleaf

Other sporting activities: Shooting and golf. *General:* Essex Vice-Captain in 1971, County Captain 1974. Led Essex to first-ever county championship in 1979. Was one of Wisden's Cricketers of the Year in 1973. Scored two centuries in Match, 111 and 102 not out, v Notts., at Nottingham in 1976. *Address and telephone number:* c/o Essex County Cricket Club, New Writtle Street, Chelmsford CM2 0RW. *Personal best:* Batting Tests 216 England v New Zealand, Auckland 1974–75; other f/class 228* Essex v Sussex, Hasting 1968; jpl 99* Essex v Notts, Ilford 1974; b&h 90 Essex v Surrey, The Oval 1974; gillette 74 Essex v Notts, Trent Bridge 1969. Bowling Tests 1–48 England v Australia, Brisbane 1970–71; other f/class 5–51 Essex v Middlesex, Colchester 1979; jpl 1–4 Essex v Leics, Leicester 1979; b&h 1–25 Essex v Minor Counties East, Norwich 1976; gillette 1–16 Essex v Staffs., Stone 1976.

FOAT, James Clive.
County: Gloucestershire.
Role: Right-hand bat, right arm medium bowler.
Date and place of birth: 21 November 1952, Salford Priors, Warwickshire.
Height: 5' 10½". *Weight:* 11 st 3 lbs.
Parents: John and Georgina Foat.
Wife: Olwyn.
Children: Daniel James Foat.
Education and qualifications: Millfield School, Street, Somerset.
Occupation outside cricket: Driving jobs.
County debut: 1972. *County cap:* 1979.
Outside interests: Football programme collecting, watching football, television, listening to records, eating.
Nickname: Jim. Foaty.
Other sporting activities: Football, squash, tennis, golf.
General: Uses Slazenger cricket equipment. Having been awarded county cap in June was told two months later that he was not being re-engaged by county. Good mimic.
Address and telephone number: c/o Gloucestershire County Cricket Club, Neville

Road, Bristol BS7 9EJ.
Personal best: Batting f/class 126 Gloucs v Hants, Gloucester 1979; jpl 60 Gloucs v Glamorgan, Bristol 1973; b&h 73* Gloucs v Somerset, Street 1975; gillette 40* Gloucs v Northants, Bristol 1977.

FOWLER, Graeme.
County: Lancashire.
Role: Right-hand bat, right arm medium bowler.
Date and place of birth: 20 April 1957, Accrington.
Education and qualifications: Accrington Grammar School; Durham University.
County debut: 1979.
General: Has played for 2nd XI since 1973. Played in one John Player League match v Derbyshire at Chesterfield in 1978.
Address and telephone number: c/o Lancashire County Cricket Club, Old Trafford, Manchester M16 0PX.
Personal best: Batting f/class 20 Lancs v Cambridge University, Cambridge 1979; jpl 1 Lancs v Surrey, The Oval 1979.

FRANCIS, David Arthur.
County: Glamorgan.
Role: Right-hand bat, off-break bowler.
Date and place of birth: 29 November 1953, Clydach, Glamorgan.
Education and qualifications: Cwmtawe Comprehensive School, Pontardawe.
County debut: 1973.
Nickname: Arthur.
General: Played for Glamorgan 2nd XI in 1971 and 1972. Played for Gowerton in 1979 in South Wales League.
Address and telephone number: c/o Glamorgan County Cricket Club, 6 High Street, Cardiff. Telephone: Cardiff 29956.
Personal best: Batting f/class 110 Glamorgan v Warwicks, Nuneaton 1977; jpl 50 Glamorgan v Surrey, Byfleet 1976; b&h 59 Glamorgan v Warwicks, Edgbaston 1977; gillette 62* Glamorgan v Worcs, Worcester 1977.

FRENCH, Bruce Nicholas.
County: Nottinghamshire.
Role: Right-hand bat, wicket-keeper.
Date and place of birth: 13 August 1959, Warsop, Nottinghamshire.
Height: 5′ 8″. *Weight:* 10 st.
Parents: Maurice and Betty French.
Wife: Ellen Rose.
Children: Charles Daniel, 31 August 1978.
Education and qualifications: Meden Comprehensive School, Warsop.

Occupation outside cricket: Bricklayer's labourer.
Family links with cricket: Father was Secretary of Welbeck Colliery C.C. Brother, Charles, captain of Welbeck Colliery C.C. Brothers, Joseph, Neil, David, also played for Welbeck Colliery C.C.
County debut: 1976 (age 16 years 10 months).
Outside interests: Furniture-making, joinery, back packing, rock-climbing.
Nickname: Kermit. *continued overleaf*

General: Youngest ever player for Notts. C.C.C. at 16 years, 287 days v Cambridge, 1976.

Address and telephone number: c/o Nottinghamshire County Cricket Club, County Cricket Ground, Trent Bridge, Nottingham NG2 6AG.

Personal best: Batting f/class 66 Notts v Cambridge University, Cambridge 1978; jpl 25 Notts v Northants, Trent Bridge 1978; b&h 5 Notts v Kent, Canterbury 1979; gillette 4* Notts v Yorkshire, Bradford 1978.

GARD, Trevor.

County: Somerset.

Role: Right-hand bat, wicket-keeper.

Date and place of birth: 2 June 1957, West Lambrook, Somerset.

Height: 5' 7". *Weight:* 10 st 7 lbs.

Parents: David and Brenda Gard.

Wife: Amanda Kay

Married: 29 September 1979.

Education and qualifications: Huish Episcopi School, Langport. Four years apprenticeship with Westland Helicopters Ltd.

Occupation outside cricket: Engineer.

Family links with cricket: Father and brother play for local side, South Petherton, as wicket-keeper, and left-hand opening bat.

County debut: 1976.

Outside interests: Rough shooting. Motoring.

Nickname: Gardy.

Other sporting activities: Soccer, golf, badminton.

General: Played for Somerset 2nd XI since 1972.

Address and telephone number: 4 Lambrook Gate, West Lambrook, South Petherton, Somerset. Telephone: South Petherton 40351.

Personal best: Batting f/class 51* Somerset v India, Taunton 1979.

GARNER, Joel.

County: Somerset.

Role: Right-hand bat, right arm fast bowler.

Date and place of birth: 16 December 1952, Barbados.

Height: 6' 8". *Weight:* 17 st.

Education and qualifications: Boys' Foundation School, Christchurch, Barbados.

County debut: 1977. *County cap:* 1979.

Off-season 1979–80: Touring Australia with West Indies.

Outside interests: Sea-bathing, bird-watching.

Nickname: Big Bird.

General: Debut for Barbados in Shell Shield Competition 1975–76. Has played as professional for Littleborough in Central Lancashire League. Toured with West Indies in Australia 1979–80.

Address and telephone number: c/o Somerset County Cricket Club, St James's Street, Taunton, TA1 1JT.

Personal best: Batting Tests 43 West Indies v Pakistan, Bridgetown 1976–77; other f/class 53 Somerset v Yorkshire, Harrogate 1979; jpl 32 Somerset v Kent, Taunton 1979; b&h 17 Somerset v Sussex, Hove 1978; gillette 38* Somerset v Glamorgan, Cardiff 1978; Bowling Tests 4–48 West Indies v Pakistan, Georgetown 1976–77; other f/class 8–31 Somerset v Glamorgan, Cardiff 1977; jpl 3–16 Somerset v Notts, Trent Bridge 1979; b&h 3–23 Somerset v Glamorgan, Taunton 1979; gillette 6–29 Somerset v Northants, Lord's 1979.

GARNHAM, Michael Anthony.

County: Gloucestershire.

Role: Right-hand bat, wicket-keeper.

Date and place of birth: 20 August 1960, Johannesburg, South Africa.

Education and qualifications: Camberwell Grammar School, Melbourne; Scotch College, Perth, Australia. Park School, Barnstaple, Devon. University of East Anglia.

County debut: 1979.

General: Played for Devon and for Gloucestershire 2nd XI since 1976. Played in one John Player League match 1978 v Warwickshire at Birmingham. Toured India with English Schools Cricket Association 1977. Has joined Leicestershire for 1980. Elected Young Wicket-keeper of the Year, 1979.

Address and telephone number: c/o Leicestershire County Cricket Club, Grace Road, Leicester LE2 8AD. Telephone: Leicester 832128.

Personal best: Batting f/class 21 Gloucs v Northants, Bristol 1979; jpl 18 Gloucs v Warwicks, Moreton-in-Marsh 1979.

GATTING, Michael William.

County: Middlesex.

Role: Right-hand bat, right arm medium bowler.

Date and place of birth: 6 June 1957, Kingsbury, Middlesex.

Height: 5′ 10″. *Weight:* 13 st 8 lbs.

Wife: Unmarried.

Education and qualifications: Wykeham Primary School, John Kelly Boys' High School.

Family links with cricket: Father used to play club cricket. Brother, Steve, plays football for Arsenal.

County debut: 1975. *County cap:* 1977.

Outside interests: Reading, "I enjoy mainly sci-fi books or a good thriller." Any sport.

Nickname: Gat.

continued overleaf

Other sporting activities: Football, table-tennis, tennis, swimming. Offered soccer trials but turned them down in favour of cricket.
General: England Young Cricketers 1974. Toured West Indies with England Young Cricketers 1976. Off-season 1979–80: club cricket in Sydney.
Address and telephone number: c/o Middlesex County Cricket Club, Lord's Cricket Ground, St John's Wood Road, London NW8 8QN.
Personal best: Batting Tests 6 England v Pakistan, Karachi 1977–78; other f/class 128 Middlesex v Derby, Lord's 1978; jpl 85 Middlesex v Notts, Lord's 1976; b&h 67 Middlesex v Kent, Canterbury 1979; gillette 62 Middlesex v Kent, Canterbury 1977; Middlesex v Lancs, Old Trafford 1978; Bowling f/class 5–59 Middlesex v Leics, Lord's 1978; jpl 4–32 Middlesex v Kent, Lord's 1978; b&h 3–35 Middlesex v Minor

Counties East, Lord's 1976; gillette 2–53 Middlesex v Derby, Derby 1978.

GIFFORD, Norman.

County: Worcestershire.
Role: Left-hand bat, slow left arm orthodox bowler.
Date and place of birth: 30 March 1940, Alverston, Cumbria.
Height: 5′ 10″. *Weight:* 13 st 7 lbs.
Parents: John Richard and Freda Gifford.
Wife: Janice.
Married: 23 May 1963.
Children: David Ronald, 1 January 1964; Caroline Margaret, 27 March 74.
Occupation outside cricket: Estimator, industrial decorating, City & Guilds.
Family links with cricket: Father played amateur cricket and football, and was also cricket umpire. Uncle Harry Gifford played rugby union for England.
County debut: 1960. *County cap:* 1961.
Benefit: £11,047, 1974.
Outside interests: Horse-racing.
Nickname: 'Oss.
Other sporting activities: Football, golf.
General: County captain from 1971. Was one of Wisden's Cricketers of the Year 1974. Played in one match for Rest of World v Australia 1972. Was awarded MBE in 1979. Suffers badly from the sun on overseas tours.

Toured with Rest of World to Australia 1971–72; India, Pakistan and Sri Lanka 1972–73. Took 100 wickets in a season 3 times.
Address and telephone number: 11 Fernleigh Gardens, Wordsley, Stourbridge, Worcs. Telephone: Kingswinford 278755.
Personal best: Batting Tests 25* England v

New Zealand, Trent Bridge 1973; other f/class 89 Worcs v Oxford University, Oxford 1963; jpl 29 Worcs v Essex, Worcester 1974; b&h 33 Worcs v Kent, Lord's 1973; gillette 38 Worcs v Warwicks, Lord's 1966. Bowling Tests 5–55 England v Pakistan, Karachi 1972–73; other f/class 8–28 Worcs v Yorkshire, Sheffield 1968; jpl 5–28 Worcs v Northants, Worcester 1979; b&h 5–32 Worcs v Northants, Worcester 1973; gillette 4–7 Worcs v Surrey, Worcester 1972.

GOOCH, Graham Alan.

County: Essex.
Role: Right-hand bat, right arm medium bowler.
Date and place of birth: 23 July 1953, Leytonstone.
Height: 6' 0". *Weight:* 13 st.
Parents: Alfred and Rose Gooch.
Wife: Brenda.
Married: 23 October 1976.
Education and qualifications: Norlington Junior High School, Leytonstone.
Occupation outside cricket: Toolmaker (four-year apprenticeship).
Family links with cricket: Father played local cricket for East Ham Corinthians. Second cousin, Graham Saville, played for Essex C.C.C. and is now Assistant-Secretary and N.C.A. coach.
County debut: 1973. *County cap:* 1975.
Off-season 1979–80: Touring Australia with England. Playing for Perth C.C., W. Australia.
Outside interests: "Relaxing at home."
Nickname: Zap.
Other sporting activities: Squash, golf, soccer.
General: Toured West Indies with England Young Cricketers 1972. Shared in second wicket record partnership for county, 321 with K. S. McEwan v Northants. at Ilford in 1978. Toured Australia 1978–79 and 1979–80. Good mimic—"particularly of Geoffrey Boycott". Impersonates bowlers on the field and voices off it.

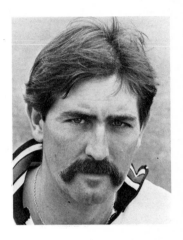

Address and telephone number: c/o Essex County Cricket Club, New Writtle Street, Chelmsford CM2 0RW.
Personal best: Batting Tests 91* England v New Zealand, The Oval 1978; other f/class 136 Essex v Worcs, Westcliff 1976; jpl 90* Essex v Middlesex, Lord's 1978; b&h 138 Essex v Warwicks, Chelmsford 1979; gillette 61 Essex v Somerset, Taunton 1978. Bowling Tests 1–16 England v India, Lord's 1979; other f/class 5–40 Essex v West Indies, Chelmsford 1976; jpl 3–14 Essex v Derby, Derby 1978; b&h 2–36 Essex v Minor Counties East, Norwich 1976; gillette 1–39 Essex v Leics, Southend 1977.

GOULD, Ian James.

County: Middlesex.
Role: Left-hand bat, wicket-keeper.
Date and place of birth: 19 August 1957, Slough, Bucks.
County debut: 1975. *County cap:* 1977.

Nickname: Gouldy.
Other sporting activities: Amateur footballer. Golf.
General: Joined staff in 1972. Toured West Indies with England Young Cricketers 1976.

continued overleaf

Spent 1979–80 off-season in Auckland, New Zealand.

Address and telephone number: c/o Middlesex County Cricket Club, Lord's Cricket Ground, St John's Wood Road, London NW8 8QN. Telephone: 01–289–1300.

Personal best: Batting f/class 128 Middlesex v Worcs, Worcester 1978; jpl 36* Middlesex v Yorkshire, Lord's 1975; b&h 32 Middlesex v Notts, Trent Bridge 1979; gillette 58 Middlesex v Derby, Derby 1978.

GOWER, David Ivon.

County: Leicestershire.

Role: Left-hand bat, off-break bowler.

Date and place of birth: 1 April 1957, Tunbridge Wells, Kent.

Height: 5′ 11¾″ and a bit. *Weight:* 11 st 11 lbs.

Parents: Richard Hallam and Sylvia Mary Gower.

Wife: Unmarried.

Education and qualifications: Marlborough House School, King's School, Canterbury, University College, London. Did not complete Law course. 8 O-levels, 3 A-levels.

Occupation outside cricket: Worked for Bostik Ltd.

Family links with cricket: Father was club cricketer.

County debut: 1975. *County cap:* 1977.

Off-season 1979–80: Touring Australia.

Outside interests: "Photography, sleeping, music, in any order." Does crossword puzzles.

Nickname: Lulu.

Other sporting activities: Squash, golf, tennis, water skiing ("warm water only").

General: Played for King's, Canterbury 1st XI for 3 years. Toured South Africa with English Schools XI 1974–75 and West Indies with England Young Cricketers 1976. One of Wisden's Cricketers of the Year 1978. Elected Best Young Cricketer of the Year in 1978 by Cricket Writers' Club. Has written *Anyone for Cricket* jointly with Bob Taylor about the

1978–79 Australian Tour. Turned down for place at Oxford University. Unkind allegation attributed to Ray Illingworth, that Gower "Bats for England, and fields for Leicestershire".

Address and telephone number: c/o Leicestershire County Cricket Club, Grace Road, Leicester LE2 8AD.

Personal best: Batting Tests 200* England v India, Edgbaston 1979; other f/class 144* Leics v Hants, Leicester 1977; jpl 135* Leics v Warwicks, Leicester 1977; b&h 49 Leics v Middlesex, Lord's 1978; gillette 117* Leics v Herts, Leicester 1977. Bowling f/class 3–47 Leics v Essex, Leicester 1977.

GRAVENEY, David Anthony.
County: Gloucestershire.
Role: Right-hand bat, slow left arm orthodox bowler.
Date and place of birth: 2 January 1953, Bristol.
Height: 6' 4". *Weight:* 14 st.
Parents: Ken Graveney and Jeanne (deceased).
Wife: Julie.
Married: 23 September 1978.
Education and qualifications: Millfield School, Somerset.
Occupation outside cricket: Company Director, Training to be chartered accountant.
Family links with cricket: Son of J. K. Graveney, captain of Gloucestershire, who took 10 wickets for 66 runs v Derbyshire at Chesterfield in 1949, and nephew of Tom Graveney of Gloucestershire, Worcestershire and England. Brother John selected for English Public Schools v English Schools at Lord's.
County debut: 1972. *County cap:* 1976.
Outside interests: "Playing sport, Tv and cinema, and taking the wife out for a good meal and visit to the local pub".
Nickname: Gravity.
Other sporting activities: Golf, soccer, squash.
General: Member of the Executive of the County Cricketers Player Association.

Contracted to Slazengers Ltd.
Address and telephone number: 6 Southover Close, Westbury-on-Trym, Bristol. Telephone: Bristol 500296.
Personal best: Batting f/class 92 Gloucs v Warwicks, Edgbaston 1978; jpl 44 Gloucs v Essex, Cheltenham 1975; b&h 21 Gloucs v Somerset, Street 1975; gillette 44 Gloucs v Surrey, Bristol 1973. Bowling f/class 8–85 Gloucs v Notts, Cheltenham 1974; jpl 4–22 Gloucs v Hants, Lydney 1974; b&h 3–32 Gloucs v Middlesex, Bristol 1977; gillette 3–67 Gloucs v Leics, Leicester 1975.

GRAVES, Peter John.
County: Sussex.
Role: Left-hand bat, slow left arm orthodox bowler.
Date and place of birth: 9 May 1946, Hove.
Height: 5' 10½". *Weight* 11 st 6 lbs.
Parents: Albert and Winifred Graves.
Wife: Susan.
Married: 9 June 1978.
Education and qualifications: Hove Manor School.
Occupation outside cricket: Retail manager, Sussex, Powell Duffryn Group.
County debut: 1965. *County cap:* 1969.
Benefit: 1978.
Outside interests: Gardening, National Trust activities, antiques.
Nickname: "Various, but none specific." Graves—"as in wine".
Other sporting activities: Squash, golf and soccer.

General: Vice-Captain of Sussex County Cricket Club. Played for Orange Free State in
continued overleaf

1969-70, 1970-71 as Captain, 1973-74 to 1976-77, in Currie Cup Competitions. Contracted to Gray Nicholls Ltd. Scored two centuries in match, 119 and 136 not out, for Orange Free State v Border at Bloomfontein in 1966-67.
Address and telephone number: c/o Sussex County Cricket Club, Eaton Road, Hove

GREENIDGE, Cuthbert Gordon.
County: Hampshire.
Role: Right-hand bat, right arm medium bowler.
Date and place of birth: 1 May 1951, St. Peter, Barbados.
Education and qualifications: Black Bess School; St. Peter's Boys School; Sutton Secondary School, Reading, Berkshire.
County debut: 1970. *County cap:* 1972.
Off-season 1979-80: Touring Australia with West Indies.
General: Arrived in England at age of 14. One of Wisden's Cricketers of the Year 1977. Toured with West Indies to India, Sri Lanka and Pakistan 1974-75; Australia 1975-76; England 1976; Australia 1979-80. Scored two centuries in one match (134 and 101)for West Indies v England at Manchester 1976, and v Kent at Bournemouth (136 and 120) in 1978. Holds record for highest score for all one-day competitions with 177 v Glamorgan at Southampton in 1975. Shared in partnership of 285 for second wicket with D. R. Turner v Minor Counties South at Amersham in 1973, being the record partnership for all one-day competitions. Suffered badly from knee injury, but continued to play in 1979. Could have played for either England or West Indies. Persuaded to join Hampshire by John Arlott.
Address and telephone number: c/o

GRIFFITHS, Brian James.
County: Northamptonshire.
Role: Right-hand bat, right arm medium bowler.
Date and place of birth: 13 June 1949, Wellingborough.
Height: 6' 1". *Weight:* 14 st 6 lbs.
Parents: James and Muriel Griffiths.
Wife: Paula.
Married: 30 September 1972.
Children: Rachel, 26 June 1973; Leighton, 6 November 1975.

BN3 3AN.
Personal best: Batting f/class 145* Sussex v Gloucs, Gloucester 1974; jpl 101* Sussex v Middlesex, Eastbourne 1972; b&h 114* Sussex v Cambridge University, Hove 1974; gillette 84* Sussex v Derby, Chesterfield 1973. Bowling f/class 3-69 Orange Free State v Australia, Bloomfontein 1969-70.

Hampshire County Cricket Club, Northlands Road, Southampton SO9 2TY.
Personal best: Batting Tests 134 West Indies v England, Old Trafford 1976; other f/class 273* D. H. Robins' XI v Pakistan, Eastbourne 1974; jpl 163* Hants v Warwicks, Edgbaston 1979; b&h 173* Hants v Minor Counties South, Amersham 1973; gillette 177 Hants v Glamorgan, Southampton 1975; Bowling f/class 5-49 Hants v Surrey, Southampton 1971; jpl 1-36 Hants v Gloucs, Bristol 1972.

Education and qualifications: Irthlingborough Secondary School.
Occupation outside cricket: Has worked for a haulage firm and as a bank porter.
Family links with cricket: Uncle played occasionally for Northamptonshire.
County debut: 1974. *County cap:* 1978.
Outside interests: Reading, quizzes and crosswords.
Nickname: Jim.
Other sporting activities: Football, darts.
General: "As for World Series Cricket, I

don't exactly agree with the type of cricket, but it certainly has helped other ordinary cricketers with money situations."

Address and telephone number: 28 Noble Avenue, Irthlingborough, Northamptonshire. Telephone: Wellingborough 651434.

Personal best: Batting f/class 11 Northants v Middlesex, Lord's 1978; jpl 9 Northants v Warwicks, Northampton 1979; b&h 0*; gillette 0*. Bowling f/class 5–66 Northants v Surrey, Northampton 1978; jpl 4–22 Northants v Somerset, Weston 1977; b&h 5–43 Northants v Sussex, Eastbourne 1979; gillette 3–39 Northants v Leics, Northampton 1979.

GURR, David Robert.

County: Somerset.

Role: Right-hand bat, right arm fast medium bowler.

Date and place of birth: 27 March 1956, Whitchurch, Buckinghamshire.

Height: 6′ 3½″. *Weight:* 12 st 7 lbs.

Parents: Percy William and Mary Elizabeth Blair Gurr.

Wife: Jane Maria.

Married: 15 September 1979.

Education and qualifications: Aylesbury Grammar School, Regent's Park College, Oxford. Theology first year, geography second year.

Occupation outside cricket: Lifeguard, hospital porter, driver. Now employed by Sun Life Assurance Co. of Canada.

Family links with cricket: Father opened the bowling for Whitchurch village team. Brother also played.

County debut: 1976.

Outside interests: Driving, gardening.

Other sporting activities: Football, hockey, squash.

General: Played for Middlesex 2nd XI 1974, Oxford Blue 1976–77, "I will probably spend the 1980 season playing part-time, acting as stand-by. I hope to develop my career in the life assurance market, whilst trying to keep in touch with the first-class game. If all goes well, I hope to try and spend more time in cricket in two or three seasons' time." Suffered from extraordinary spate of wides in 1977.

Address and telephone number: 25 Blackbrook Road, Taunton, Somerset. Telephone: 0823-79269.

Personal best: Batting f/class 46* Oxford University v Cambridge University, Lord's 1977; jpl 4 Somerset v Sussex, Hove 1977; b&h 29* Combined Universities v Sussex, Oxford 1977; gillette 0*. Bowling f/class 6–62 Oxford University v. Warwicks, Edgbaston 1976; jpl 2–21 Somerset v Surrey, Byfleet 1977; b&h 3–42 Combined Universities v Kent, Oxford 1976; gillette 1–15 Somerset v Northumberland, Taunton 1977.

HACKER, Peter John.
County: Nottinghamshire.
Role: Right-hand bat, right arm fast medium bowler.
Date and place of birth: 16 July 1952, Lenton Abbey, Nottingham.
County debut: 1974.
Address and telephone number: c/o Nottinghamshire County Cricket Club, Trent Bridge, Nottingham NG2 6AG.
Personal best: Batting f/class 35 Notts v Kent, Canterbury 1977; jpl 5* Notts v Yorkshire, Trent Bridge 1977; b&h 2* Notts v Lancs, Trent Bridge 1975; gillette 7 Notts v Warwicks, Edgbaston 1979. Bowling f/class 4-46 Notts v Gloucs, Trent Bridge 1979; jpl 3-35 Notts v Sussex, Trent Bridge 1979; gillette 3-27 Notts v Warwicks, Edgbaston 1979.

HADLEE, Richard John.
County: Nottinghamshire.
Role: Left-hand bat, right arm fast bowler.
Date and place of birth: 3 July 1951, Christchurch, New Zealand.
Education and qualifications: Christchurch Boys' High School.
Family links with cricket: Youngest son of W. A. Hadlee and brother of D. R. Hadlee, both New Zealand Test cricketers.
County debut: 1978. *County cap:* 1978.
Off-season 1979-80: Playing for Tasmania.
General: Toured with New Zealand to England in 1973 and 1978; Australia 1973-74; Pakistan and India 1976-77. Made debut for Canterbury in 1971-72 in Plunket Shield Competition.
Address and telephone number: c/o Nottinghamshire County Cricket Club, Trent Bridge, Nottingham NG2 6AG.
Personal best: Batting Tests 87 New Zealand v Pakistan, Karachi 1976-77; other f/class 101* Notts v Derby, Trent Bridge 1978; jpl 25* Notts v Leics, Leicester 1979; b&h 41 Notts v Kent, Canterbury, 1978; gillette 12* Notts v Warwicks, Edgbaston 1979. Bowling

Tests 7-23 New Zealand v India, Wellington 1975-76; other f/class 7-23 Notts v Sussex, Trent Bridge 1979; jpl 5-21 Notts v Leics, Leicester 1979; b&h 3-30 Notts v Minor Counties North, Trent Bridge 1979; gillette 2-27 Notts v Warwicks, Edgbaston 1979.

HAMPSHIRE, John Harry.
County: Yorkshire.
Role: Right-hand bat, leg-break bowler, county captain 1979-.
Date and place of birth: 10 February 1941, Thurnscoe, near Rotherham, Yorks.
Height: 6' 0". *Weight:* 13 st.

Wife: Judith.
Married: 5 September 1964.
Children: Ian, 6 January 1969; Paul, 12 July 1972.
Education and qualifications: Oakwood Technical High School, Rotherham.
Family links with cricket: Father played pre-

62

war for Yorkshire C.C.C. (six games), also brother.
County debut: 1961. *County cap:* 1963.
Benefit: £28,425, 1976.
Outside interests: Gardening, golf, reading.
Nickname: Hamps.
Other sporting activities: Golf.
General: Scored 107 in his first test v West Indies at Lords. Yorkshire Captain 1979.
Address and telephone number: 21 Rayls Road, Todwick, Sheffield S31 0HZ.
Personal best: Batting Tests 107 England v West Indies, Lord's 1969; other f/class 183* Yorkshire v Sussex, Hove 1971; jpl 119 Yorkshire v Leics, Hull 1971; b&h 73 Yorkshire v Kent, Leeds, 1979; gillette 110 Yorkshire v Durham, Middlesbrough 1978. Bowling f/class 7–52 Yorkshire v Glamorgan, Cardiff 1963; jpl 1–22 Yorkshire v Northants, Northampton 1970.

HARDIE, Brian Ross.
County: Essex.
Role: Right-hand bat, right arm medium bowler.
Date and place of birth: 14 January 1950, Stenhousemuir.
Height 5' 10". *Weight:* 12 st 7 lbs.
Parents: James Millar and Elspeth Hardie.
Wife: Fiona.
Married: 28 October 1977.
Education and qualifications: Stenhousemuir Primary School; Larbert High School.
Occupation outside cricket: Bank clerk, computer operator.
Family links with cricket: Father and brother, Keith, played for Scotland.
County debut: 1973. *County cap:* 1974.
Outside interests: Sports.
Nickname: Lager.
Other sporting activities: Football, golf.
General: Played for Stenhousemuir in East of Scotland League. Debut for Scotland 1970. Scored two centuries for Scotland v M.C.C. at Aberdeen in 1971, but not regarded as first-class.
Address and telephone number: c/o Essex County Cricket Club, New Writtle Street,

Chelmsford CM2 0RW.
Personal best: Batting f/class 162 Essex v Warwicks, Edgbaston 1975; jpl 94 Essex v Northants, Northampton 1973; b&h 42* Essex v Cambridge University, Cambridge 1974; gillette 83 Essex v Staffs, Stone 1973. Bowling f/class 2–39 Essex v Glamorgan, Ilford 1979.

HARRIS, Michael John.
County: Nottinghamshire.
Role: Right-hand bat, wicket-keeper, can bowl leg-break and googly.
Date and place of birth: 25 May 1944, St

Just-in-Roseland, Cornwall.
County debut: 1969. *County cap:* 1970.
Benefit: 1977.
General: Debut for Middlesex C.C.C. 1964,

continued overleaf

63

cap 1967. Left staff after 1968 to join Nottinghamshire, 1969. Played for Eastern Province in 1971–72 Currie Cup Competition. Played for Wellington in New Zealand Shell Shield Competition 1975–76. Scored 1,000 in a season eleven times. Scored 2,238 at an average of 50.86 in 1971. Scored nine centuries in 1971 to equal county record. Scored two centuries in match twice in 1971: 118 and 123 v Leicestershire at Leicester, and 107 and 131 not out v Essex at Chelmsford. Shared in first wicket partnership record for Middlesex, 312 with W. E. Russell v Pakistanis at Lord's in 1967.

Address and telephone number: c/o Nottinghamshire County Cricket Club, Trent Bridge, Nottingham NG2 6AG.

Personal best: Batting f/class 201* Notts v Glamorgan, Trent Bridge 1973; jpl 104 Notts v Hants, John Player, Nottingham 1970; b&h 101 Notts v Yorkshire, Hull 1973; gillette 101 Notts v Somerset, Trent Bridge 1970. Bowling f/class 4–16 Notts v Warwicks,

Trent Bridge 1969; jpl 2–24 Notts v Surrey, Trent Bridge 1969; b&h 1–12 Notts v Minor Counties North, Cleethorpes 1972.

HARTLEY, Stuart Neil.

County: Yorkshire.
Role: Right-hand bat, right arm medium bowler.
Date and place of birth: 18 March 1956, Shipley, West Yorkshire.
Height: 5′ 11″. *Weight:* 12 st 7 lbs.
Parents: Horace and Marjorie Hartley.
Wife: Unmarried.
Education and qualifications: Beckfoot Grammar School, Bingley.
Occupation outside cricket: Two years' training as insurance underwriter.
County debut: 1978.
Outside interests: Keeping fit, golf, rugby.
Nickname: Hare.
Other sporting activities: Amateur football with Bradford City 1970–75. Rugby Union with Bingley R.U.F.C.
General: Lived in Perth, Australia, in 1967 and "learnt to play cricket there". Ray Illingworth rates him very highly.
Address and telephone number: 8 Priory Grove, Bingley, West Yorkshire. Telephone:

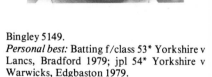

Bingley 5149.
Personal best: Batting f/class 53* Yorkshire v Lancs, Bradford 1979; jpl 54* Yorkshire v Warwicks, Edgbaston 1979.

HASSAN, Basharat.

County: Nottinghamshire.
Role: Right-hand bat, right arm medium bowler, occasional wicket-keeper.

Date and place of birth: 24 March 1944, Nairobi, Kenya.
Education and qualifications: City High School, Nairobi.

County debut: 1966. *County cap*: 1970.
Benefit: 1978.
General: Has scored 1,000 runs in a season
five times. Debut for East Africa Invitation
XI v M.C.C. 1963-64. Played for Kenya
against touring sides. scored a century with
aid of a runner v Kent at Canterbury in 1977.
Address and telephone number: c/o
Nottinghamshire County Cricket Club, Trent
Bridge, Nottingham NG2 6AG.
Personal best: Batting f/class 182* Notts v
Gloucs, Trent Bridge 1977; jpl 111 Notts v
Surrey, The Oval 1977; b&h 98* Notts v
Minor Counties North, Trent Bridge 1973;
gillette 79 Notts v Hants, Southampton 1977.
Bowling f/class 3-33 Notts v Lancs, Old
Trafford 1976; jpl 1-42 Notts v Somerset,
Trent Bridge 1976; gillette 3-20 Notts v
Durham, Chester-le-Street 1976.

HAYES, Frank Charles.
County: Lancashire.
Role: Right-hand bat, right arm medium
bowler.
Date and place of birth: 6 December 1946,
Preston, Lancs.
Education and qualifications: De la Salle
College, Salford; Sheffield University.
County debut: 1970. *County cap:* 1972.
General: Appointed County Captain 1978.
Toured West Indies 1973-74. Has scored
1,000 runs in a season five times. Hit 34 in
one over (six, four, six, six, six, six) off
Malcolm Nash v Glamorgan at Swansea in
1977. Scored 94 on Lancs debut. Scored 106
not out in Test debut v West Indies at Oval in
1973.
Address and telephone number: c/o
Lancashire County Cricket Club, Old
Trafford, Manchester M16 OPX.
Personal best: Batting, Tests 106* England v
West Indies, The Oval 1973; other f/class 187
Lancs v India, Old Trafford 1974; jpl 70

Lancs v Worcs, Worcester 1978; b&h 102
Lancs v Minor Counties North, Old Trafford
1973; gillette 93 Lancs v Warwicks,
Edgbaston 1976.

HEAD, Timothy John.
County: Sussex.
Role: Right-hand bat, wicket-keeper.
Date and place of birth: 22 September 1957,
Hammersmith, London.
Height: 5' 7". *Weight:* 10 st 3 lbs.
Parents: Christopher Edwin and Sheila
Head.
Wife: Unmarried.

Education and qualifications: Lancing
College.
Occupation outside cricket: Teacher at the
Prebendal School, Chichester.
Family links with cricket: None.
County debut: 1976.
Outside interests: Reading, classical music,
horse-racing, wine.

continued overleaf

Nickname: 'Eddy.
Other sporting activities: Hockey, soccer.
General: Contracted to Gunn and Moore
Ltd. and uses their equipment exclusively.
"Regular church-goer of the Anglican
faith." Supporter of World Series Cricket.
Member of the M.C.C. and the Middleton
Sports Club. Held seven catches in his first
match.
Address and telephone number: 8 Harefield
Gardens, Middleton-on-Sea, Sussex.
Telephone: Middleton-on-Sea 3270; or, the
Prebendal School, West Street, Chichester,
West Sussex.
Personal best: Batting f/class 31 Sussex v
Oxford University, Oxford 1976; jpl 12*
Sussex v Yorkshire, Hove 1979.

HEMMINGS, Edward Ernest.
County: Nottinghamshire.
Role: Right-hand bat, off-break bowler.
Date and place of birth: 20 February 1949,
Leamington Spa, Warwickshire.
Height: 5' 10".   *Weight:* 13 st.
Parents: Edward and Dorothy Phyliss
Hemmings.
Wife: Christine Mary.
Married: 23 October 1971.
Children: Thomas Edward, 26 July 1977;
James Oliver, 9 September 1979.
Education and qualifications: Campion
School, Leamington Spa.
Family links with cricket: Father and father's
father both played Minor Counties and
League cricket.
County debut: 1979.
Outside interests: "Watching football at any
level—especially junior. Dining out with my
wife."
Nickname: Eddie. The Whale. Ernie.
Other sporting activities: Played amateur
football, squash.
General: Debut for Warwickshire 1966; cap
1974. Holds John Player League record for
having most runs hit off him in one season:
610 for Warwickshire in 1975.
Address and telephone number: 2 Colwick
Park Close, Old Colwick, Nottingham.
Personal best: Batting f/class 85 Warwicks v

Essex, Edgbaston 1977; 85* Notts v Hants,
Bournemouth 1979; jpl 44* Warwicks v Kent,
Edgbaston 1971; b&h 61* Warwicks v Leics,
Edgbaston 1974; gillette 20 Warwicks v
Worcs, Edgbaston 1973. Bowling f/class
7-33 Warwicks v Cambridge University,
Cambridge 1975; jpl 5-22 Warwicks v
Northants, Edgbaston 1974; b&h 3-18
Warwicks v Combined Universities,
Coventry 1975; gillette 2-27 Warwicks v
Hants, Edgbaston 1971.

HEMSLEY, Edward John Orton.
County: Worcestershire.
Role: Right-hand bat, right arm medium
bowler.

Date and place of birth: 1 September 1943,
Stoke-on-Trent.
Height: 5' 9".   *Weight:* 11 st 8 lbs.
Parents: Ronald and Joan Hemsley.

Wife: Barbara.
Married: 13 October 1968.
Children: Steven, 8 April 1970; Jacqueline, 30 March 1972.
Education and qualifications: Bridgnorth Grammar School.
Occupation outside cricket: Soccer. Shrewsbury Town for six years, two as captain. Sheffield United for nine years, five in First Division, Doncaster Rovers for two years.
Family links with cricket: Younger brother, Colin, was on the staff at Worcester for a year, also plays for Shropshire in Minor Counties competition.
County debut: 1963. *County cap:* 1969.
Outside interests: Reading, horse-racing.
Nickname: Ted.
Other sporting activities: Professional football, golf, swimming.
General: Created novel situation while playing for Worcester v Yorkshire at Bramall Lane (Sheffield United's football ground) by being a cricket visitor playing on football home ground. Shared in sixth wicket partnership record for county, 277 with D. N. Patel v Oxford University at Oxford, 1976.
Address and telephone number: 38 Summerfield Road, Dronfield, Sheffield S18 6GZ, Yorkshire. Telephone: Donfield 415917.

Personal best: Batting 176*Worcs v Lancs, Worcester 1977; jpl 75* Worcs v Glamorgan, Cardiff 1979; b&h 73 Worcs v Warwicks, Edgbaston 1973; gillette 73 Worcs v Sussex, Hove 1972. Bowling f/class 3–5 Worcs v Warwicks, Worcester 1971; jpl 4–42 Worcs v Essex, Worcester 1971; b&h 2–21 Worcs v Notts, Worcester 1973; gillette 2–17 Worcs v Oxfordshire, Cowley 1970.

HENDRICK, Michael.
County: Derbyshire.
Role: Right-hand bat, right arm fast medium bowler.
Date and place of birth: 22 October 1948, Darley Dale, Derbyshire.
Wife: Kathy.
Children: Three.
Occupation outside cricket: Has worked for Electricity Board, Leicester, and as labourer.
Family links with cricket: Father was fast bowler.
County debut: 1969. *County cap:* 1972.
Benefit: 1980.
Off-season 1979–80. Went on tour with England, but returned early through injury.
Outside interests: Shooting, fishing, golf.
Nickname: Hendo.
General: Elected Best Young Cricketer of the Year 1973 by the Cricket Writers' Club. One of Wisden's Cricketers of the Year 1978. Toured West Indies 1973–74; Australia, New Zealand 1974–75; Pakistan, New Zealand 1977–78; Australia 1978–79 and 1979–80.

Sometimes bearded.
Address and telephone number: c/o Derbyshire County Cricket Club,

continued overleaf

Nottingham Road, Derby DE2 6DA.
Personal best: Batting Tests 15 England v Australia, The Oval 1977; other f/class 46 Derby v Essex, Chelmsford 1973; jpl 21 Derby v Warwicks, Buxton 1974; b&h 32 Derby v Notts, Chesterfield 1973; gillette 17 Derby v Middlesex, Derby 1978. Bowling

Tests 4–28 England v India, Edgbaston 1974; other f/class 8–45 Derby v Warwicks, Chesterfield 1975; jpl 6–7 Derby v Notts, Trent Bridge 1972; b&h 5–30 Derby v Notts, Chesterfield 1975; 5–30 Derby v Lancs, Southport 1976; gillette 4–16 Derby v Middlesex, Chesterfield 1975.

HERKES, Robert.
County: Middlesex.
Role: Right-hand bat, right-arm medium bowler.
Date and place of birth: 30 June 1957, Lincoln, Lincolnshire.
Height: 6′ 4″. *Weight:* 13 st.
Parents: Violet and Jack Herkes.
Wife: Unmarried.
Education and qualifications: Lincoln Christ's Hospital Grammar School.
Occupation outside cricket: Trainee accountant in local government.
Family links with cricket: "All my family are members of Harts Holme C.C. in Lincoln. My mother was Secretary, my father Chairman, my brother (Dwane) still plays and has represented Lincolnshire County Cricket Club at various levels. My uncle, Albert, played for Harts Holme C.C. for many years after the war."
County debut: 1978.
Outside interests: "My favourite relaxation is going for short walks around the countryside in Kent where I live. I live on top of a hill in the middle of nowhere where I can completely relax, sometimes with a quiet drink in the local pub."
Nickname: Max (Wall).

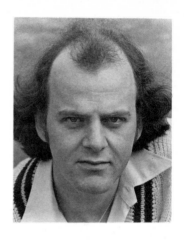

Other sporting activities: Football, squash and most other sports, indoor and outdoor.
General: Played for Lincolnshire in 1977. Took six wickets in bowling debut v Worcs. Not retained.
Personal best: Batting jpl 5 Middlesex v Leics, Leicester 1978. Bowling f/class 6–60 Middlesex v Worcs, Lord's 1979; jpl 2–18 Middlesex v Sussex, Lord's 1979.

HIGGS, Kenneth.
County: Leicestershire.
Role: Left-hand bat, right arm fast medium bowler.
Date and place of birth: 14 January 1937, Sandyford, Stoke-on-Trent.
Height: 6′ 0″.
Parents: James and Elsie Higgs.
Wife: Mary.
Married: 14 December 1957.
Children: Kenneth Paul, 31 August 1960; Terence, 1 October 1963.
Education and qualifications: Secondary modern.
Occupation outside cricket: Professional footballer for Port Vale F.C. Has worked for

a Blackpool grocery firm.
Family links with cricket: None.
County debut: 1972. *County cap:* 1972.
Benefit: £8,390 in 1968 (while at Lancashire).
Outside interests: Gardening, watching all types of sport.
Nickname: Higgy.
Other sporting activities: Squash.
General: Played for Staffordshire in 1957. Debut for Lancashire C.C.C. in 1958, capped 1959. One of Wisden's Cricketers of the Year 1967. Retired after 1969 season. Debut for Leicestershire 1972. Leicestershire Vice-Captain 1973, appointed County Captain 1979. Shared in tenth wicket partnership record for county, 228 with Ray Illingworth

v Northants at Leicester in 1977. Toured Australia and New Zealand 1965–66 and West Indies 1967–68. Took 132 wickets at an average of 19.42 in 1960.

Address and telephone number: c/o Leicestershire County Cricket Club, Grace Road, Leicester LE2 8AD.

Personal best: Batting Tests 63 England v West Indies, The Oval 1966; other f/class 98 Leics v Northants, Leicester 1977; jpl 17* Leics v Notts, Trent Bridge 1975; b&h 8* Leics v Worcs, Worcester 1972; gillette 25 Leics v Somerset, Taunton 1966. Bowling Tests 6–91 England v West Indies, The Oval 1966; other f/class 7–19 Lancs v Leics, Old Trafford 1965; jpl 1–17 Leics v Glamorgan, Leicester 1973; b&h 4–10 Leics v Surrey, Lord's 1974; gillette 6–20 Leics v Staffs, Longton 1975.

HIGNELL, Alastair James.

County: Gloucestershire.

Role: Right-hand bat, leg break bowler.

Date and place of birth: 4 September 1955, Cambridge.

Height: 5′ 7½″. *Weight:* 12 st 7 lbs.

Parents: Antony Francis and Patricia Pearson Hignell.

Wife: Unmarried.

Education and qualifications: Denstone College; Fitzwilliam College, Cambridge. BA Hons (Cantab) and Cambridge Post-Graduate Certificate of Education.

Occupation outside cricket: Schoolteacher at Bristol Cathedral School.

Family links with cricket: Father played for Gloucestershire, Cambridge University Crusaders, Bristol University, RAF, M.E.A.F., Combined Services. Mother and brothers all played at school.

County debut: 1974. *County cap:* 1977.

Outside interests: Bridge, crosswords, reading, theatre, films, sight-seeing, eating, drinking.

Nickname: Higgy.

Other sporting activities: Rugby: England Schools XV Captain; Cambridge University XV four blues and Captain; Bristol; Gloucestershire; England (14 caps); two tours, to Australia and the Far East; Barbarians; non-travelling reserve for Lions' tour of New Zealand 1977.

General: Cambridge cricket blue 1975–76–77–78. Captain in last two years. Played for England Schools v All India Schools at Birmingham in 1973, and for

England Young Cricketers v West Indies Young Cricketers at Arundel 1974. Scored two centuries in a match, 108 and 145 for Cambridge v Surrey at Cambridge in 1978. Bearded. Father was international athlete; threw javelin for England in 1950 Commonwealth Games, New Zealand. Brother, Robert, is junior international canoeist.

Address and telephone number: c/o Gloucestershire County Cricket Club, Neville Road, Bristol BS7 9EJ.

Personal best: Batting f/class 149 Cambridge University v Glamorgan, Cambridge 1977; 149* Gloucs v Northants, Bristol 1979; jpl 51 Gloucs v Northants, Northampton 1976; b&h 63 Combined Universities v Worcs, Worcester 1978; gillette 65* Gloucs v Northants, Bristol 1977.

HILL, Alan.
County: Derbyshire.
Role: Right-hand bat, off-break bowler.
Date and place of birth: 29 June 1950,
Buxworth, Derbyshire.
County debut: 1972. *County cap:* 1976.
Nickname: Bud.
General: Played for Orange Free State in
1976–77 Currie Cup Competition.
Address and telephone number: c/o
Derbyshire County Cricket Club,
Nottingham Road, Derby DE2 6DA.
Personal best: Batting f/class 160* Derby v
Warwicks, Coventry 1976; jpl 120 Derby v
Northants, Buxton 1976; b&h 102* Derby v
Warwicks, Ilkeston 1978; gillette 72 Derby v
Middlesex, Derby 1978. Bowling f/class 3–5
Orange Free State v Northern Transvaal,
Pretoria 1976–77.

HILLS, Richard William.
County: Kent.
Role: Right-hand bat, right arm medium
bowler.
Date and place of birth: 8 January 1951,
Borough Green.
Height: 5′ 10″. *Weight:* 12 st 2 lbs.
Parents: William Arthur Hills.
Wife: Janet Vera.
Married: 11 January 1975.
Children: Christopher Richard Hills, 21
December 1978.
Education and qualifications: Holmdale
Secondary Modern.
Occupation outside cricket: Maintenance
engineer—technical level.
Family links with cricket: None.
County debut: 1973. *County cap:* 1977.
Outside interests: Photography and do-it-
yourself.
Nickname: Vicar. Hill-billy.
Other sporting activities: Golf, squash,
badminton, football, snooker.
Address and telephone number: West
Malling, Kent.
Personal best: Batting f/class 45 Kent v
Hants, Canterbury 1975; jpl 26 Kent v

Somerset, Maidstone 1978; b&h 34 Kent v
Surrey, Canterbury 1977; gillette 9 Kent v
Sussex, Canterbury 1976. Bowling f/class
6–64 Kent v Gloucs, Folkestone 1978; jpl
4–21 Kent v Glamorgan, Cardiff 1979; b&h
5–28 Kent v Combined Universities, Oxford
1976; gillette 1–33 Kent v Middlesex, Canterbury 1977.

HOADLEY, Simon Peter.
County: Sussex.
Role: Right-hand bat, off-break bowler.
Date and place of birth: 16 August 1956,
Eridge, Sussex.
Height: 5′ 11″. *Weight:* 13 st 7 lbs.
Parents: Arthur James and Elizabeth Mary

Hoadley.
Wife: Unmarried.
Education and qualifications: Uckfield
Secondary School. One O-level.
Occupation outside cricket: Salesman. Tree-
felling.
Family links with cricket: Brother, Stephen

John Hoadley, played for Sussex 1974–77.
County debut: 1978.
Outside interests: "Riding a bicycle. Long walks over the Sussex Downs. Drinking in pubs."
Nickname: Hoaders, Bungalow ("nothing up top"), Sid.
Other sporting activities: Football, golf, squash, snooker, table tennis.

HOBBS, Robin Nicholas Stuart.
County: Glamorgan.
Role: Right-hand bat, leg break and googly bowler.
Date and place of birth: 8 May 1942, Chippenham, Wiltshire.
Height: 5′ 10″. *Weight:* 11 st 10 lbs.
Parents: Reg and Betty Hobbs.
Wife: Isabel.
Married: 26 December 1968.
Education and qualifications: Raine's Foundation School, Stepney.
Occupation outside cricket: Employed by Barclays Bank on the credit card side.
Family links with cricket: Father played for Chingford C.C., and uncle played for Finchley and Middlesex 2nd XI.
County debut: 1979.
Outside interests: Bird-watching and travel.
Nickname: Colt.
Other sporting activities: Squash and badminton.
General: Debut for Essex, 1961, cap 1964. Benefit £30,500 in 1974. Retired at end of 1975 season. Played for Suffolk in 1976–78. Joined Glamorgan as County Captain in 1979. Took 102 wickets at an average of 21.40 in 1970. Kept out for much of season through knee injury. Only English leg-spinner in first-class game.
Address and telephone number: c/o Glamorgan County Cricket Club.

HODGSON, Alan.
County: Northamptonshire.
Role: Left-hand bat, right arm fast medium bowler.
Date and place of birth: 27 October 1951, Moorside, County Durham.
Height: 6′ 4½″. *Weight:* 16 st.
Parents: Edward and Olive Hodgson.
Wife: Unmarried.
Education and qualifications: Annfield Plain Grammar Technical School.

General: Started playing cricket for Buxted Park village side. Played for Sussex Schools Under-15s and Sussex Young Cricketers.
Address and telephone number: 43 Vernon Road, Uckfield, Sussex TN22 5 DX. Telephone: Uckfield 5643.
Personal best: Batting f/class 112 Sussex v Glamorgan, Swansea 1978; jpl 17 Sussex v Middlesex, Hove 1978.

Personal best: Batting Tests 15* England v India, Edgbaston 1967; other f/class 100 Essex v Glamorgan, Ilford 1968; 100 Essex v Australia, Chelmsford 1975; jpl 54* Essex v Yorkshire, Colchester 1970; b&h 40 Essex v Middlesex, Lord's 1972; gillette 34 Essex v Lancs, Chelmsford 1971. Bowling Tests 3–25 England v India, Edgbaston 1967; other f/class 8–63 Essex v Glamorgan, Swansea 1966; jpl 6–22 Essex v Hants, Harlow 1973; b&h 3–41 Glamorgan v Derby, Cardiff 1979; gillette 4–55 Essex v Wilts, Chelmsford 1969.

County debut: 1970. *County cap:* 1976.
Benefit: 1980.
Outside interests: Almost all other sports.
Nickname: Hodge.
Other sporting activities: Rugby Union.
General: Spent greater part of 1979 off-season in hospital undergoing a back operation and recovering from it. Has missed much of last 2 seasons through back injuries.

continued overleaf

Address and telephone number: 38 Lutterworth Road, Northampton.
Personal best: Batting f/class 41 Northants v New Zealand, Northampton 1973; 41* Northants v Gloucs, Northampton 1976; jpl 26 Northants v Middlesex, Lord's 1973; b&h 17 Northants v Worcs, Northampton 1975; gillette 20 Northants v Kent, Canterbury 1971. Bowling f/class 5–30 Northants v Oxford University, Oxford 1976; jpl 7–39 Northants v Somerset, Northampton 1976; b&h 3–30 Northants v Minor Counties East, Northampton 1978; gillette 4–32 Northants v Leics, Northampton 1977.

HOGG, William.
County: Lancashire.
Role: Right-hand bat, right arm fast bowler.
Date and place of birth: 12 July 1955, Ulverston, Cumbria.
Height: 6′ 4″. *Weight:* 13 st 12 lbs.
Parents: John Hogg, deceased and Eileen Hogg.
Wife: unmarried.
Education and qualifications: Ulverston Comprehensive School.
Occupation outside cricket: Coppersmith.
Family links with cricket: Brother-in-law plays local amateur cricket.
County debut: 1976.
Nickname: Hoggie.
Other sporting activities: Golf, squash, association football.
General: Played as professional for Preston C.C. in Northern League. Apprentice professional footballer for Barrow-in-Furness F.C.
Address and telephone number: 49 Moorgarth, Swarthmoor, near Ulverston, Cumbria. Telephone: Ulverston 53880.
Personal best: Batting f/class 19 Lancs v Middlesex, Lord's 1978; jpl 5 Lancs v Sussex,

Hastings 1979; gillette 1* Lancs v Kent, Canterbury 1979. Bowling f/class 7–84 Lancs v Warwicks, Old Trafford 1978; jpl 4–23 Lancs v Essex, Ilford 1979; b&h 4–35 Lancs v Hants, Old Trafford 1979; gillette 1–52 Lancs v Kent, Canterbury 1979.

HOLDER, Vanburn Alonza.
County: Worcestershire.
Role: Right-hand bat, right arm fast medium bowler.
Date and place of birth: 8 October 1945, St. Michael, Barbados.
County debut: 1968. *County cap:* 1970.
Benefit: 1979.

General: Debut for Barbados 1966–67 in Shell Shield Competition. Toured with West Indies to England 1969, 1973 and 1976; India, Sri Lanka, Pakistan 1974–75; Australia 1975–76; India and Sri Lanka 1978–79, as Vice-Captain.
Address and telephone number: c/o Worcestershire County Cricket Club, New

72

Road, Worcester WR2 4QQ.

Personal best: Batting Tests 42 West Indies v New Zealand, Port-of-Spain 1971–72, other f/class 122 Barbados v Trinidad, Bridgetown 1973–74; jpl 35* Worcs v Middlesex, Lord's 1970; b&h 17* Worcs v Minor Counties South, High Wycombe 1979; gillette 25* Worcs v Notts, Worcester 1974; Bowling Tests 6–28 West Indies v Australia, Port-of-Spain 1977–78; other f/class 7–40 Worcs v Glamorgan, Cardiff 1974; jpl 6–33 Worcs v Middlesex, Lord's 1972; b&h 5–12 Worcs v Northants, Northampton 1974; gillette 3–14 Worcs v Oxfordshire, Cowley 1970

HOLMES, Geoffrey Clark.

County: Glamorgan.

Role: Right-hand bat, right arm medium bowler.

Date and place of birth: 16 September 1958, Newcastle-on-Tyne.

Height: 5′ 10″. *Weight:* 10 st 10 lbs.

Parents: George and Rita Holmes.

Wife: Unmarried.

Education and qualifications: West Denton High School, A-levels in Maths and Chemistry, 6 O-levels.

Occupation outside cricket: Trainee estimator.

Family links with cricket: Father played in the Northumberland League.

County debut: 1978.

Outside interests: Records and disco music, also "reading—especially a good cricket book".

Other sporting activities: Soccer, squash, badminton.

Address and telephone number: c/o Glamorgan County Cricket Club.

Personal best: Batting f/class 100* Glamorgan v Gloucs, Bristol 1979; jpl 43* Glamorgan v Hants, Portsmouth 1979. Bowling f/class 4–78 Glamorgan v Sri Lanka, Cardiff 1979.

HOPKINS, David Charles.

County: Warwickshire.

Role: Right-hand bat, right arm medium bowler.

Date and place of birth: 11 February 1957, Birmingham.

Height: 6′ 6½″. *Weight:* 14 st.

Wife: Unmarried.

Education and qualifications: Moseley Grammar School.

Occupation outside cricket: Trainee quantity surveyor.

County debut: 1977.

Outside interests: Records, collecting postcards.

continued overleaf

Nickname: Hoppy.
Other sporting activities: Golf, handicap 5; skiing.
General: Has played for 2nd XI since 1975.
Address and telephone number: 48 The Hurst, Kings Heath, Birmingham B13 0D6.
Personal best: Batting f/class 34* Warwicks v Essex, Edgbaston 1979; jpl 13* Warwicks v Sussex, Hove 1979; gillette 2 Warwicks v Notts, Edgbaston 1979. Bowling f/class 6–67 Warwicks v Somerset, Taunton 1979; jpl 3–26 Warwicks v Lancs, Edgbaston 1979; gillette 2–45 Warwicks v Notts, Edgbaston 1979.

HOPKINS, John Anthony.
County: Glamorgan.
Role: Right-hand bat, occasional wicket-keeper.
Date and place of birth: 16 June 1953, Maesteg.
Education and qualifications: Trained as teacher at Trinity College of Education, Carmarthen.
Occupation outside cricket: Teacher.
Family links with cricket: Younger brother of J. D. Hopkins who appeared for Middlesex C.C.C. and formerly on Glamorgan staff.
County debut: 1970. *County cap:* 1977.
General: Dropped down order from opener, then regained form, in 1979.
Address and telephone number: c/o Glamorgan County Cricket Club, 6 High Street, Cardiff. Telephone: Cardiff 29956.
Personal best: Batting f/class 230 Glamorgan v Worcs, Worcester 1977; jpl 62* Glamorgan v Northants, Northampton 1979; b&h 81

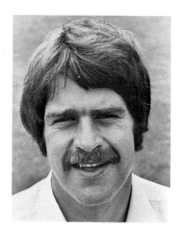

Glamorgan v Worcs, Swansea 1977; gillette 63 Glamorgan v Leics, Swansea 1977.

HOWARTH, Geoffrey Philip.
County: Surrey.
Role: Right-hand bat, off-break bowler.
Date and place of birth: 29 March 1951, Auckland, New Zealand.
Education and qualifications: Auckland Grammar School.
Family links with cricket: Younger brother of H. J. Howarth, New Zealand Test cricketer.

County debut: 1971. *County cap:* 1974.
General: Played for New Zealand Under-23s XI v Auckland at Auckland 1968-69. Joined Surrey staff 1969. Toured with New Zealand to Pakistan and India 1976-77; England 1978. Scored 1,000 runs in a season three times. Scored two centuries in a match (122 and 102) New Zealand v England at Auckland 1977-78.

Address and telephone number: c/o Surrey County Cricket Club, Kennington Oval, London SE11 5SS.
Personal best: Batting Tests 123 New Zealand v England, Lord's 1978; other f/class 183 Surrey v Hants, The Oval 1979; jpl 122 Surrey v Gloucs, The Oval 1976; b&h 80 Surrey v Yorkshire, The Oval 1974; gillette 34 Surrey v Lancs, Old Trafford 1977; 34 Surrey v Northants, Northampton 1979. Bowling Tests 1–13 New Zealand v Pakistan, Lahore 1976–77; other f/class 5–32 Auckland v C. Districts, Auckland 1973–74; jpl 4–16 Surrey v Warwicks, Byfleet 1979; gillette 2–25 Surrey v Lincs, Lincoln 1974.

HUGHES, David Paul.

County: Lancashire.
Role: Right-hand bat, slow left arm orthodox bowler.
Date and place of birth: 13 May 1947, Newton-le-Willows.
Education and qualifications: Newton-le-Willows Grammar School.
County debut: 1967. *County cap:* 1970.
Off-season 1979–80: Playing in Tasmania.
General: Played for Tasmania while coaching there in 1975–76 and 1976–77. Gillette Cup "specialist". Hit 24 runs off John Mortimer v Gloucs in penultimate over in Gillette semifinal in 1972.
Address and telephone number: c/o Lancashire County Cricket Club, Old Trafford, Manchester M16 0PX.
Personal best: Batting f/class 101 Lancs v Cambridge University, Cambridge 1975; jpl 84 Lancs v Essex, Leyton 1973; b&h 42* Lancs v Minor Counties West, Watford 1978; gillette 42* Lancs v Middlesex, Lord's 1974; Bowling f/class 7–24 Lancs v Oxford

University, Oxford 1970; jpl 6–29 Lancs v Somerset, Old Trafford 1977; b&h 5–23 Lancs v Minor Counties West, Watford 1978; gillette 4–61 Lancs v Somerset, Old Trafford 1972.

HUMPAGE, Geoffrey William.

County: Warwickshire.
Role: Right-hand bat, wicket-keeper, can also bowl right arm medium.
Date and place of birth: 24 April 1954, Birmingham.
Height: 5' 9". *Weight:* 12 st 7 lbs.
Parents: Ernest and Mabel Humpage.
Wife: Ingrid Celia.

Married: 5 October 1974.
Children: Philip Andrew Guy, 16 November 1977.
Education and qualifications: Golden Hillock Comprehensive School, Birmingham.
Occupation outside cricket: Former police cadet, then police constable, Birmingham

continued overleaf

75

City Police. Coach, Scarborough C.C., Western Australia, 1978–79.
County debut: 1974. *County cap:* 1976.
Outside interests: Reading, listening to E.L.O.
Nickname: Humpty or Farsley.
Other sporting activities: Soccer, squash, tennis, volleyball, swimming, golf, snooker, table-tennis.
General: Good impressionist, particularly Frankie Howerd. Bowled in John Player League.
Address and telephone number: 387 Shaftmoor Lane, Hall Green, Birmingham B28 8TB. Telephone: 021-778-2825.
Personal best: Batting f/class 125* Warwicks v Sussex, Edgbaston 1976; jpl 58 Warwicks v Yorkshire, Edgbaston 1979; b&h 78 Warwicks v Derby, Derby 1978; gillette 58 Warwicks v Somerset, Taunton 1978;

Bowling jpl 4–53 Warwicks v Gloucs, Moreton-in-Marsh, 1979.

HUMPHRIES, David John.
County: Worcestershire.
Role: Left-hand bat, wicket-keeper.
Date and place of birth: 6 August 1953, Alveley, Shropshire.
Height: 5′ 8″. *Weight:* 13 st.
Parents: Dennis John and Olive Mary Humphries.
Wife: Lorraine Mary.
Married: 7 September 1974.
Children: Rebecca Louise, 10 October 1978.
Education and qualifications: Bridgnorth Secondary Modern, Wulfrun College, Wolverhampton O.N.C. Engineering, Part 1, one A-level, six O-levels, eight C.S.E.
Occupation outside cricket: Has been marketing assistant, Kay & Co. Ltd., Worcester. Lottery manager, Worcs C.C.C.
Family links with cricket: Father club captain of Cannock C.C. and still plays. Brother plays Birmingham League and ex-Staffordshire Schools.
County debut: 1977. *County cap:* 1978.
Outside interests: Skittles, darts.
Nickname: Humpty.
Other sporting activities: Football, golf.
General: Played for Shropshire 1971–73, debut for Leicestershire 1974, left county

after 1976 season.
Address and telephone number: c/o Worcestershire County Cricket Club, County Ground, New Road, Worcester WR2 4QQ.
Personal best: Batting f/class 111* Worcs v Warwicks, Worcester 1978; jpl 62 Worcs v Notts, Dudley 1977; b&h 22* Worcs v Minor Counties West, Worcester 1977; gillette 58 Worcester v Glamorgan, Worcester 1977.

INCHMORE, John Darling.
County: Worcestershire.
Role: Right-hand bat, right arm fast medium bowler.

Date and place of birth: 22 February 1949, Ashington, Northumberland.
Education and qualifications: Ashington Grammar School.

County debut: 1973. *County cap:* 1976.
General: Played for Northumberland 1970. Played for both Worcestershire and Warwickshire 2nd XIs in 1972 and for Stourbridge in the Birmingham League. Played for Northern Transvaal in 1976–77 Currie Cup Competition.
Address and telephone number: c/o Worcestershire County Cricket Club, New Road, Worcester WR2 4QQ.
Personal best: Batting f/class 113 Worcs v Essex, Worcester 1974; jpl 30* Worcs v Essex, Dudley 1976; b&h 49* Worcs v Somerset, Taunton 1976; gillette 19* Worcs v Leics, Leicester 1979. Bowling f/class 8–58 Worcs v Yorkshire, Worcester 1977; jpl 4–9 Worcs v Northants, Dudley 1975; b&h 2–5 Worcs v Minor Counties West, Worcester 1976; gillette 3–11 Worcs v Essex, Worcester 1975.

INGHAM, Peter Geoffrey.
County: Yorkshire.
Role,
Date and place of birth: 28 September 1956, Sheffield.
Height: 5′ 8″. *Weight:* 11 st.
Parents: Geoffrey and Joan Mary Ingham.
Wife: Unmarried.
Education and qualifications: Ashville College, Harrogate; Grosvenor House School, Harrogate.
Occupation outside cricket: Accountancy trainee.
Family links with cricket: Father was a Yorkshire Colt under Arthur Mitchell.

JACKMAN, Robin David.
County: Surrey.
Role: Right-hand bat, right arm fast medium bowler.
Date and place of birth: 13 August 1945, Simla, India.
Height: 5′ 9½″. *Weight:* 12 st 7 lbs.
Parents: Colonel Raymond Clive and Margaret Winifred Joan Jackman.
Wife: Yvonne Lorraine.
Married: 2 November 1970.
Children: Deborah Ann, 3 June 1975; Leigh Ann, 21 November 1978.
Education and qualifications: St. Edmund's School, Canterbury.
Occupation outside cricket: Has run own landscape gardening business, has done broadcasting, worked in advertising and for a production house.

County debut: 1979.
Outside interests: Photography, collecting antiques, music.
Nickname: Ping.
Other sporting activities: Football, hockey, squash.
General: Captain of Birstall C.C. in the Yorkshire League in 1980 when not required for Yorkshire.
Address and telephone number: c/o Yorkshire County Cricket Club, Headingley Cricket Ground, Leeds LS6 3BU.
Personal best: Batting f/class 17 Yorkshire v Warwicks, Sheffield 1979.

continued overleaf

Family links with cricket: Brother, Lt.-Col. B. C. Jackman M.C., played in Malaysian Inter-State competition in the late 1960s, also played for the Army and Hong Kong more recently. Member of I Zingari. "Father played for Fathers v Sons school match with one leg!"
County debut: 1964. *County cap:* 1970.
Outside interests: Other sporting activities.
Nickname: Jackers.
Other sporting activities: Golf, handicap 14; shooting (shotgun) "have never impressed Mickey Stewart (Surrey manager) with my talents as a soccer player!"
General: "Patrick Cargill (actor 'Father, Dear Father', 'Many Wives of Patrick') is my uncle (mother's brother). I appeared on his 'This is Your Life' Show". Played for Western Province 1971-72 and Rhodesia from 1972-73 to 1976-77 in Currie Cup Competition. Spent 1979-80 playing for Rhodesia.
Address and telephone number: c/o Lucas Green Farm, West End, Woking, Surrey. Telephone: Brookwood 3238.
Personal best: Batting f/class 92* Surrey v Kent, The Oval 1974; jpl 43 Surrey v Kent, Maidstone 1977; b&h 36 Surrey v Leics, Lord's 1974; gillette 26* Surrey v Lincs, Lincoln 1974. Bowling f/class 8-40 Rhodesia v Natal, Durban 1972-73; jpl 6-34 Surrey v Derby, Derby 1972; b&h 4-31 Surrey v Kent, Canterbury 1973; gillette 7-33 Surrey v Yorkshire, Harrogate 1970.

JARVIS, Kevin Bartram Sidney.
County: Kent.
Role: Right-hand bat, right arm fast medium bowler.
Date and place of birth: 23 April 1953, Dartford, Kent.
Height: 6' 3". *Weight:* 12 st 7 lbs.
Parents: Herbert John and Margaret Elsie Jarvis.
Wife: Margaret Anne.
Married: 16 September 1978.
Education and qualifications: Springhead School, Northfleet, Kent, and Thames Polytechnic.
Occupation outside cricket: Trainee accountant, now with Hall Aggregates.
Family links with cricket: None.
County debut: 1975. *County cap:* 1977.
Outside interests: Music, reading novels, relaxing.
Nickname: Jarvo, and K.J.
Other sporting activities: Football, squash, badminton, table tennis, tennis.
General: Played and coached for South Melbourne Cricket Club, Australia, in 1978-79 off-season. Suffered injury in 1979 season after falling off a bicycle and damaging knee.
Address and telephone number: 2 Old Castle Walk, Parkwood, Rainham, Kent.

JENNINGS, Keith Francis.
County: Somerset.
Role: Right-hand bat, right arm medium bowler.
Date and place of birth: 5 October 1953, Wellington.

Personal best: Batting f/class 12* Kent v Cambridge University, Canterbury 1977; 12 Kent v Sussex, Hove 1978; jpl 5* Kent v Hants, Canterbury 1976; b&h 4 Kent v Notts, Canterbury 1979; gillette 2* Kent v Notts, Trent Bridge 1975. Bowling f/class 8-97 Kent v Worcs, Worcester 1978; jpl 4-27 Kent v Surrey, Maidstone 1977; b&h 4-34 Kent v Worcs, Lord's 1976; gillette 3-53 Kent v Sussex, Canterbury 1976.

Height: 5' 11".
Parents: Basil and Jean Jennings.
Wife: Unmarried.
Education and qualifications: Kingsmead Secondary School, Wiveliscombe.
Occupation outside cricket: Carpenter and

joiner, City & Guilds.
Family links with cricket: Father plays club cricket.
County debut: 1975. *County cap:* 1978.
Outside interests: Watching motorsports of all kinds, specially rallying.
Nickname: Jenks.
Other sporting activities: Playing rugby.
General: Formerly on M.C.C. staff.
Address and telephone number: c/o Somerset County Cricket Club, County Cricket Ground, St James's Street, Taunton TA1 1JT.
Personal best: Batting f/class 49 Somerset v West Indies, Taunton 1976; jpl 51* Somerset v Notts, Trent Bridge 1976; b&h 2* Somerset v Kent, Taunton 1978; gillette 7 Somerset v Kent, Taunton 1979. Bowling f/class 5-18 Somerset v Sussex, Hove 1978; jpl 4-33 Somerset v Hants, Portsmouth 1976; b&h 4-11 Somerset v Minor Counties South,

Taunton 1979; gillette 3-31 Somerset v Derby, Taunton 1979.

JESTY, Trevor Edward.

County: Hampshire.
Role: Right-hand bat, right arm medium bowler.
Date and place of birth: 2 June 1948, Gosport.
Height: 5' 9". *Weight:* 11 st 10 lbs.
Parents: Aubrey Edward and Sophia Jesty.
Wife: Jacqueline,
Married: 12 September 1970.
Children: Graeme Barry, 27 September 1972; Lorna Samantha, 7 November 1976.
Education and qualifications: Privet County Secondary Modern, Gosport.
Occupation outside cricket: Cricket coach in South Africa and New Zealand. Representative for wine company.
Family links with cricket: Brother, Aubrey Jesty, wicket-keeper and left-hand bat. Could have joined Hampshire staff, but decided to continue with his apprenticeship.
County debut: 1966. *County cap:* 1977.
Outside interests: Watching soccer, and gardening.
Nickname: Jets.
Other sporting activities: Soccer, golf.
General: Played for Border in 1973-74, and Griqualand West in 1974-75 and 1975-76, Currie Cup Competition. Took him 10 years to score first-class century. Models himself on Barry Richards.

Address and telephone number: c/o Hampshire County Cricket Club, Northlands Road, Southampton SO9 2TY.
Personal best: Batting f/class 159* Hants v Somerset, Bournemouth 1976; jpl 107 Hants v Surrey, Southampton 1977; b&h 105 Hants v Glamorgan, Swansea 1977; gillette 69 Hants v Yorkshire, Bournemouth 1977. Bowling f/class 7-75 Hants v Worcs, Southampton 1976; jpl 6-20 Hants v Glamorgan, Cardiff 1975; b&h 4-28 Hants v Somerset, Taunton 1974; gillette 6-46 Hants v Gloucs, Bristol 1979.

JOHNSON, Colin.
County: Yorkshire.
Role: Right-hand bat, off-break bowler.
Date and place of birth: 5 September 1947,
Pocklington, Yorkshire.
Education and qualifications: Pocklington
School.
County debut: 1969.
General: Played in M.C.C. Schools matches
at Lord's in 1966.
Address and telephone number: c/o
Yorkshire County Cricket Club, Headingley
Cricket Ground, Leeds LS6 3BU.
Personal best: Batting f/class 107 Yorkshire v
Somerset, Sheffield 1973; jpl 67* Yorkshire v
Glamorgan, Ebbw Vale 1978; b&h 73*
Yorkshire v Middlesex, Lord's 1977; gillette
44 Yorkshire v Durham, Harrogate 1973.
Bowling f/class 2–22 Yorkshire v Oxford
University, Oxford 1971; jpl 1–0 Yorkshire v
Gloucs, Leeds 1973.

JOHNSON, Graham William.
County: Kent.
Role: Right-hand bat, off-break bowler.
Date and place of birth: 8 November 1946,
Beckenham, Kent.
Education and qualifications: Shooter's Hill
Grammar School: London School of
Economics.
County debut: 1965. *County cap:* 1970.
Address and telephone number: c/o Kent
County Cricket Club, St. Lawrence Ground,
Canterbury CT1 3NZ.
Personal best: Batting f/class 168 Kent v
Surrey, The Oval 1976; jpl 89 Kent v Sussex,
Hove 1976; b&h 85* Kent v Minor Counties
South, Canterbury 1975; gillette 120* Kent v
Bucks, Canterbury 1974. Bowling f/class
6–32 Kent v Surrey, Tunbridge Wells 1978;
jpl 5–26 Kent v Surrey, The Oval 1974; b&h
2–19 Kent v Sussex, Hove 1977; gillette 1–23
Kent v Durham, Canterbury 1974.

JONES, Alan.
County: Glamorgan.
Role: Left-hand bat, off-break bowler.
Date and place of birth: 4 November 1938,
Velindre, Swansea.
Height: 5' 7½". *Weight:* 10 st 8 lbs.
Parents: Beatrice and Evan Jones.
Wife: Megan.
Married: 20 March 1965.
Children: Andrew James, 5 August 1972.

Education and qualifications: Velindre
Primary, Owmtawe Comprehensive.
Occupation outside cricket: Has coached in
South Africa.
Family links with cricket: Brother, Eifion, is
wicket-keeper for Glamorgan County Cricket
Club. Eight brothers all played league cricket
locally. He and his brother, Eifion, were first
brothers to play in John Player League.
County debut: 1957. *County cap:* 1962.

Benefit: £10,000 in 1972. Testimonial in 1980.
Outside interests: Watching rugby and soccer.
Nickname: Sam ("christened by Peter Walker for bowling Sam Trimble in Australia for my first wicket in first-class cricket").
Other sporting activities: Playing golf.
General: Uses Duncan Fearnley equipment. Played for Western Australia in 1963–64, for Northern Transvaal in 1975–76 and for Natal in 1976–77. Glamorgan County Captain from 1976–78. One of Wisden's Criceters of the Year 1977. Played for England v Rest of the World, 1970. Scored two centuries in match, 187 not out, and 105 not out, v Somerset at Glastonbury in 1963; 132 and 156 not out v Yorkshire at Middlesbrough in 1976 and 147 and 100 v Hampshire at Swansea in 1978. Shared in record partnership for any wicket for county, 330 for first wicket with R. C. Fredericks, v Northants at Swansea in 1972. Shared in second wicket partnership record for county, 238 with A. R. Lewis, v Sussex at Hasting in 1962. Scored more runs and centuries for county than any other player. Scored 1,000 runs in season 19 times in succession. Speaks Welsh.

Address and telephone number: c/o

Glamorgan County Cricket Club.
Personal best: Batting f/class 187* Glamorgan v Somerset, Glastonbury 1963; jpl 110* Glamorgan v Gloucs, Cardiff 1978; b&h 89 Glamorgan v Worcs, Cardiff 1979; gillette 124* Glamorgan v Warwickshire, Edgbaston 1976. Bowling f/class 1–24 Western Australia v Queensland, Perth 1963–64; jpl 3–21 Glamorgan v Northants, Wellingborough 1975.

JONES, Allan Arthur.
County: Middlesex.
Role: Right-hand bat, right arm fast medium bowler.
Date and place of birth: 9 December 1947, Horley, Surrey.
Height: 6′ 4″.
Education and qualifications: St. John's College, Horsham.
Occupation outside cricket: Book-maker.
County debut: 1976. *County cap:* 1976.
Outside interests: Racing.
Nickname: Jonah.
General: Made debut for Sussex in 1966. Left staff in 1969 and made debut for Somerset in 1970, cap 1972. Played for Northern Transvaal 1972–73 Currie Cup Competition and for Orange Free State in 1976–77. Left Somerset after 1975 season and made debut for Middlesex 1976. Suffered badly from back injuries throughout career.

Address and telephone number: c/o Middlesex County Cricket Club, Lord's

Cricket Ground, St John's Wood Road, London NW8 8QN. Telephone: 01–289–1300.

continued overleaf

Personal best: Batting f/class 33 Middlesex v Kent, Canterbury 1978; jpl 18* Somerset v Sussex, Hove 1973; b&h 13 Somerset v Gloucs, Bristol 1973; gillette 5* Middlesex v Lancs, Old Trafford 1976. Bowling f/class 9–51 Somerset v Sussex, Hove 1972; jpl 6–34 Somerset v Essex, Westcliffe 1971; b&h 5–16 Middlesex v Minor Counties East, Lakenham 1977; gillette 5–23 Middlesex v Kent, Canterbury 1977.

JONES, Alan Lewis.
County: Glamorgan.
Role: Left-hand bat.
Date and place of birth: 1 June 1957, Alltwen, near Swansea.
Height: 5′ 8½″. *Weight:* 10 st 4 lbs.
Parents: Ieuan and Marion Jones.
Wife: Unmarried.
Education and qualifications: Ystalyfera Grammar School; Cwmtawe Comprehensive School; Cardiff College of Education. Eight O-levels, teacher's training certificate.
Occupation outside cricket: Life assurance salesman for N.M.L.A.
Family links with cricket: Father was very keen club cricketer in South Wales League. Grandfather was also enthusiastic club cricketer.
County debut: 1973, at age of 16 yrs, 99 days. Youngest player for Glamorgan.
Off-season 1979–80: Touring Australasia with Derrick Robins under-23 XI.
Outside interests: Keeps up-to-date with previous biology studies; keep-fit enthusiast.
Nickname: Jonah, occasionally Posh.
Other sporting activities: Squash, rugby, occasional golf.
General: Made debut for Glamorgan 2nd XI in 1972, aged 15. Toured West Indies with England Young Cricketers 1976. Uses Gray

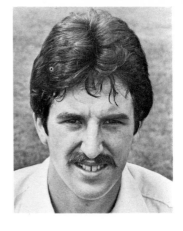

Nicholls cricket equipment. Played for Briton Ferry Town in 1979 in South Wales League.
Address and telephone number: 5 High Street, Alltwen, Pontardawe, Swansea, West Glamorgan. Telephone: Pontardawe 862205.
Personal best: Batting f/class 83 Glamorgan v Worcs, Worcester 1979; jpl 62 Glamorgan v Hants, Cardiff 1975; b&h 36 Glamorgan v Worcs, Cardiff 1979; gillette 11 Glamorgan v Hants, Southampton 1975.

JONES, Barry John Richardson.
County: Worcestershire.
Role: Left-hand bat, right arm medium bowler.
Date and place of birth: 2 November 1955, Shrewsbury.
Height: 5′ 9″. *Weight:* 11 st 7 lbs.
Parents: John Richardson and Helen Joy Jones.
Wife: Unmarried.
Education and qualifications: Mill Mead, Shrewsbury, Kingsland Grange, Shrewsbury, Wrekin College, Wellington.
Occupation outside cricket: Farmer.
Family links with cricket: Two brothers, Peter and Bryan, both played for Wroxeter Cricket Club, Shropshire, and Worcestershire 2nd XI. Father played for Whittington

Cricket Club, Shropshire. "Mum played a bit too!"
County debut: 1976.
Outside interests: "I like playing and watching other sports. My favourite relaxation is sleeping, which I don't get much time for. I enjoy eating, cooking, winemaking and tasting, although quite an amateur at it."
Nickname: Jonah or Ba.
Other sporting activities: Squash, golf, used to play rugby until injured.

JONES, Eifion Wyn.
County: Glamorgan.
Role: Right-hand bat, wicket-keeper.
Date and place of birth: 25 June 1942, Velindre, Glamorgan.
Family links with cricket: Brother of Alan Jones, who plays for Glamorgan C.C.C. He and his brother, Alan, were first brothers to play in John Player League.
County debut: 1961. *County cap:* 1967.
Benefit: £17,000 in 1975.
General: Dismissed 94 batsmen (85 caught, 9 stumped), 1970. Dismissed seven batsmen (6 caught, 1 stumped) against Cambridge University at Cambridge in 1970.
Address and telephone number: c/o Glamorgan County Cricket Club, 6 High Street, Cardiff. Telephone: Cardiff 29956.
Personal best: Batting f/class 146* Glamorgan v Sussex, Hove 1968; jpl 48 Glamorgan v Hants, Cardiff 1971; b&h 39*

KALLICHARRAN, Alvin Isaac.
County: Warwickshire.
Role: Left-hand bat, off-cutter.
Date and place of birth: 21 March 1949, Guyana.
Height: 5' 4".
Married: 1 son Rohan.
Family links with cricket: Brother David Isaac played for Guyana.
County debut: 1971. *County cap:* 1972.
Off-season 1979–80: Touring Australia with West Indies.
Nickname: Kalli.
General: Debut for Guyana 1966–67 in Shell Shield Competition. Played for Queensland in 1977–78 Sheffield Shield Competition. Toured with West Indies to England in 1973 and 1976; India, Sri Lanka and Pakistan 1974–75; Australia 1975–76 and 1979–80; India and Sri Lanka 1978–79 as Captain.

General: "Packer has done good, but what is going on in Australia I find hypocritical." Advocates protective clothing of all kinds, e.g. helmet.
Address and telephone number: Hilley Farm, Nesscliffe, Shropshire. Telephone: Nesscliff 221.
Personal best: Batting f/class 65 Worcs v Warwicks, Edgbaston 1977; jpl 36* Worcs v Warwicks, Worcester 1978.

Glamorgan v Minor Counties West, Amersham 1977; gillette 67* Glamorgan v Herts, Swansea 1969.

continued overleaf

Scored 100 not out and 101 in first two innings in Test Matches, v New Zealand in 1971. Signed for World Series Cricket but resigned before playing.
Address and telephone number: Warwickshire County Cricket Club, Edgbaston, Birmingham.
Personal best: Batting Tests 187 West Indies

KEMP, Nicholas John.
County: Kent.
Role: Right-hand bat, right arm fast medium bowler.
Date and place of birth: 16 December 1956, Bromley, Kent.
Height: 6′ 0″. *Weight:* 15 st.
Parents: Caroline Kemp (father deceased).
Wife: Unmarried.
Education and qualifications: Tonbridge School, Kent.
Occupation outside cricket: Representative for Fell & Briant Ltd., label printers.
Family links with cricket: "My father played at club level for a number of years until killed this summer in a cricket accident."
County debut: 1977.
Outside interests: Road sports cars, music.
Nickname: Jumbo, Nick-Nack.

KENNEDY, Andrew.
County: Lancashire,.
Role: Left-hand bat, right arm medium bowler.
Date and place of birth: 4 November 1949, Blackburn, Lancs.
Education and qualifications: Nelson Grammar School.
County debut: 1970.   *County cap:* 1975.
Off-season 1979-80: Playing cricket and coaching in Tasmania.
General: Elected Best Young Cricketer of the Year in 1975 by the Cricket Writers' Club. Plays in spectacles.
Address and telephone number: c/o Lancashire County Cricket Club, Old Trafford, Manchester M16 0PX.
Personal best: Batting f/class 176* Lancs v Leics, Leicester 1976; jpl 89 Lancs v Yorkshire, Old Trafford 1978; b&h 51 Lancs v Hants, Old Trafford 1979; gillette 131 Lancs v Middlesex, Old Trafford 1978. Bowling

v India, Bombay 1978-79; other f/class 197 Guyana v Jamaica, Kingston 1973-74; jpl 101* Warwicks v Derby, Chesterfield 1972; b&h 109 Warwicks v Gloucs, Bristol 1978; gillette 88 Warwicks v Glamorgan, Edgbaston 1972. Bowling Tests 1-7 West Indies v Australia, Sydney 1975-76; other f/class 4-48 Warwicks v Derby, Edgbaston 1978.

Other sporting activities: Squash, raquets and, particularly, golf.
General: Contracted to Gray Nicholls for all equipment, Toured West Indies with England Young Cricketers, 1976. "As far as World Series Cricket is concerned, it is the best thing that happened to professional cricket in the last 20 years. Whilst not as successful as Mr. Packer planned, it made people sit up and realise that cricket is marketable, and people who play need to earn money to be able to live."
Address and telephone number: Telephone: Westerham 64027.
Personal best: Batting f/class 14 Kent v Lancs, Tunbridge Wells, 1977; jpl 3* Kent v Gloucs, Cheltenham 1977. Bowling f/class 3-83 Kent v Pakistan, Canterbury 1978; jpl 2-38 Kent v Gloucs, Canterbury 1978.

f/class 2-29 Lancs v Cambridge University, Cambridge 1978.

KHAN, Intikhab Alam.

County: Surrey.
Role: Right-hand bat, leg-break and googly bowler.
Date and place of birth: 28 December 1941, Hoshiarpur, India.
Height: 5' 10". *Weight:* 13½ st.
Parents: Late N. D. Khan.
Wife: Mahe Darakshan.
Married: 21 September 1973.
Children: Khuram Alam, 10 October 1974.
Education and qualifications: Church Mission School, Karachi.
Occupation outside cricket: Pakistan International Airlines, Sales.
Family links with cricket: Father and brothers all keen cricketers.
County debut: 1969. *County cap:* 1969.
Benefit: 1978.
Outside interests: Cooking, reading, watching television, classical music.
Nickname: Inti.
Other sporting activities: Swimming, squash.
General: Debut for Karachi 1957–58 aged 16 yrs 9 mths. Professional for West of Scotland Club in Scottish Western Union. Played in five matches for Rest of the World in 1970 and five in 1971. Took a wicket (C. C. McDonald) with the first ball he bowled in Test cricket. Toured with Pakistan to India 1960–61; England 1962, 1967, 1971 and 1974, as Captain on last two tours; Sri Lanka 1964; Australia, New Zealand 1964–65, 1972–73 as Captain; Australia and West Indies 1966–67; toured with Pakistan Eaglets to England in 1962–63. Took 104 wickets at an average of

28.36 in 1971.
Address and telephone number: 34 The Green, Morden, Surrey. Telephone: 01–540–3063.
Personal best: Batting Tests 138 Pakistan v England, Hyderabad 1972–73; other f/class 182 Karachi B v PIA, Karachi 1970–71; jpl 62 Surrey v Northants, Tolworth 1973; jpl 62 Surrey v Middlesex, The Oval 1977; b&h 32 Surrey v Middlesex, Lord's 1973; gillette 50 Surrey v Somerset, The Oval 1975. Bowling Tests 7–52 Pakistan v New Zealand, Dunedin 1972–73; other f/class 8–54 Pakistan v Tasmania, Hobart 1972–73; jpl 6–25 Surrey v Derby, The Oval 1974; b&h 3–42 Surrey v Essex, Chelmsford 1973; gillette 2–28 Surrey v Sussex, The Oval 1970.

NIAZI, Imran Ahmad Khan.

County: Sussex.
Role: Right-hand bat, right arm fast bowler.
Date and place of birth: 25 November 1952, Lahore, Pakistan.
Height: 6' 0". *Weight:* 12 st 21 lb.
Education and qualifications: Aitchison College; Cathedral School, Lahore. Worcester Royal Grammar School; Keble College, Oxford University. BA Hons.
Family links with cricket: Cousin of Pakistan cricketer, Majid Khan.
County debut: 1977. *County cap:* 1978.
Off-season 1979–80: Touring India with Pakistan.
Nickname: Immie.
Other sporting activities: Hockey, squash,

swimming.
General: Debut for Lahore A 1969–70. Debut for Worcestershire 1971, cap 1976. Left Worcestershire in 1977. Oxford cricket blue 1973–74–75, Captain in 1974. Toured with Pakistan to England 1971 and 1974; Australia and West Indies 1976–77. Played for World Series Cricket. Has scored 1,000 runs in a season three times. Scored two centuries in a match, 117 not out and 106, Oxford University v Notts at Oxford in 1974. Had a match double of 111 not out and 13 for 99 v Lancashire at Worcester in 1976.
Address and telephone number: 22 Zaman Park, Lahore, or c/o Sussex County Cricket

continued overleaf

Club, Eaton Road, Hove BN3 3AN.
Telephone: Brighton 732161.
Personal best: Batting Tests 59 Pakistan v
New Zealand, Karachi 1976–77; other f/class
170 Oxford University v Northants, Oxford
1974; jpl 75 Worcs v Warwicks, Worcester
1976; Üx 72 Worcs v Warwicks, Edgbaston
1976; gillette 55* Worcs v Essex, Worcester
1975. Bowling Tests 6–63 Pakistan v
Australia, Sydney 1976–77; other f/class
7–52 Sussex v Gloucs, Bristol 1978; jpl 5–29
Worcs v Leics, Leicester 1973; b&h 5–8
Sussex v Northants, Northampton 1978;
gillette 4–27 Sussex v Staffs, Stone 1978.

KHAN, Javed Miandad.
County: Sussex.
Role: Right-hand bat, leg-break and googly
bowler.
Date and place of birth: 12 June 1957,
Karachi.
Height: 5′ 9″. *Weight:* 11 st 7 lbs.
Education and qualifications: C.M.S.
Secondary School, Karachi.
County debut: 1976. *County cap:* 1977.
Off-season: 1979–80. Toured India with
Pakistan.
Outside interests: Reading sports books,
listening to music.
Nickname: "Noon Ghunna" and "Mummy-
Daddy".
Other sporting activities: Hockey, soccer,
swimming.
General: Toured with Pakistan to Australia
and West Indies 1976–77; England 1978.
Scored 163 for Pakistan v New Zealand on
Test debut, Lahore, 1966–67, and 206 v New
Zealand at Karachi in third Test, becoming
the youngest-ever double century maker in
Test cricket at age of 19 yrs 4 mths. Was Vice-
Captain of Pakistan Under-19 side in
England in 1974 and was Captain of Under-
19 side in Sri Lanka 1974–75. Has joined
Glamorgan for 1980.
Address and telephone number: c/o
Glamorgan County Cricket Club, 6 High

Street, Cardiff. Telephone: Cardiff 29956.
Personal best: Batting Tests 206 Pakistan v
New Zealand, Karachi 1976–77; other f/class
311 Karachi Whites v National Bank,
Karachi 1974–75; jpl 98* Sussex v Lancs,
Hastings 1979; b&h 76 Sussex v Surrey, The
Oval 1977; gillette 75 Sussex v Lancs, Hove
1978. Bowling Tests 3–74 Pakistan v New
Zealand, Hyderabad 1976–77; other f/class
6–93 Sind v Railways, Lahore 1974–75;
gillette 1–12 Sussex v Warwicks, Hove 1977.

KIRSTEN, Peter Noel.
County: Derbyshire.
Role: Right-hand bat, off-break bowler.

Date and place of birth: 14 May 1955,
Pietermaritzburg, Natal, South Africa.
Education and qualifications: South Africa

College School, Capetown.
County debut: 1978.
Off-season 1979–80: Playing in South Africa.
Nickname: Kirsey.
General: Debut for Western Province in Currie Cup Competition 1973–74. Played for Sussex v Australia in 1975 and played for Sussex 2nd XI in 1975. Played for Derbyshire 2nd XI in 1977. Scored four centuries in four consecutive innings, and six in seven innings, including two in one match (173 not out and 103) for Western Province v Eastern Province at Capetown in 1976–77. Captained Derbyshire when G. Miller was absent. Scored highest debut score in John Player League: 88 v Gloucestershire in 1978.
Address and telephone number: c/o Derbyshire County Cricket Club, Nottingham Road, Derby DE2 6DA.
Personal best: Batting f/class 206* Derby v Glamorgan, Chesterfield 1978; jpl 102 Derby v Glamorgan, Swansea 1979; b&h 70 Derby v Surrey, Derby 1979; gillette 6 Derby v Worcs,

Worcester 1978. Bowling f/class 4–44 Derby v Middlesex, Derby 1979; jpl 5–34 Derby v Northants, Long Eaton 1979; b&h 1–6 Derby v Lancs, Chesterfield 1979; gillette 2–15 Derby v Worcs, Worcester 1978.

KITCHEN, Mervyn John.

County: Somerset.
Role: Left-hand bat, right arm medium bowler.
Date and place of birth: 1 August 1940, Nailsea, Somerset.
Height: 5′ 10½″. *Weight:* 13 st 7 lbs.
Parents: Hubert John and Phyllis Elizabeth.
Wife: Anne.
Married: 5 March 1971.
Children: Faye, 30 September 1975; Jody, 6 March 1977.
Education and qualifications: Secondary modern.
Occupation outside cricket: "Many and varied". Company representative, cider maker, etc.
Family links with cricket: Father played club cricket for Nailsea.
County debut: 1960. *County cap:* 1966.
Testimonial: £6,000 in 1973.
Outside interests: Do-it-Yourself. Home-made wine-making. Gardening.
Nickname: M.J.
Other sporting activities: Golf.
General: Joined staff in 1957, left after 1974 season, but rejoined in 1976. Has scored 1,000 runs in a season seven times.
Address and telephone number: c/o Somerset

County Cricket Club, St James's Street, Taunton TA1 1JT.
Personal best: Batting f/class 189 Somerset v Pakistan, Taunton 1967; jpl 82 Somerset v Glamorgan, Yeovil 1977; b&h 70 Somerset v Minor Counties West, Chippenham 1976; gillette 116 Somerset v Lancs, Old Trafford 1972. Bowling f/class 1–4 Somerset v Sussex, Taunton 1969; jpl 2–34 Somerset v Hants, Portsmouth 1976.

KNIGHT, Roger David Verdon.
County: Surrey.
Role: Left-hand bat, right arm medium bowler.
Date and place of birth: 6 September 1946, Streatham.
Height: 6' 3¾". *Weight:* 14 st 2 lbs.
Parents: David Verdon and Thelma Patricia Knight.
Wife: Christine Ann McNab.
Married: 27 March 1971.
Children: Catherine Elizabeth, 29 November 1972; Graeme Edward Verdon, 16 August 1975.
Education and qualifications: Dulwich College; Cambridge University. BA Hons, MA.
Occupation outside cricket: Schoolmaster at Eastbourne College, 1970-78. Schoolmaster at Dulwich College 1978-.
County debut: Originally 1968, rejoined 1978. *County cap:* 1978.
Outside interests: Bridge, music, philosophy, French literature and "reading Ogden Nash".
Nickname: Knighty.
Other sporting activities: Sussex Rugby XV (Captain 1973); played rugby for Cambridge University (no blue); squash, tennis, swimming.
General: Cambridge cricket blue 1967-70. Following debut for Surrey in 1968, left county after 1970 season and made debut for Gloucestershire 1971, gaining cap in 1971. Left Gloucestershire after 1975 season and made debut for Sussex in 1976, gaining Sussex cap in 1976; left Sussex after 1977

season and rejoined Surrey in 1978 as County Captain, gaining cap in 1978. Cricket tours: Derrick Robbins tour of South Africa 1972-73; M.C.C. to East Africa, 1974-75; M.C.C. to West Africa, 1975-76,.
Address and telephone number: c/o Surrey County Cricket Club, Kennington Oval, SE11 5SS.
Personal best: Batting f/class 165* Sussex v Middlesex, Hove 1976; jpl 127 Sussex v Hants, Hove 1976; b&h 117 Sussex v Surrey, The Oval 1977; gillette 75 Gloucs v Glamorgan, Cardiff 1973. Bowling f/class 6-44 Gloucs v Northants, Northampton 1974; jpl 5-42 Sussex v Notts, Trent Bridge 1977; b&h 3-19 Sussex v Surrey, The Oval 1977; gillette 5-39 Gloucs v Surrey, Bristol 1971.

KNOTT, Alan Philip Eric.
County: Kent.
Role: Right-hand bat, wicket-keeper, can bowl off-breaks.
Date and place of birth: 9 April 1946, Belvedere, Kent.
Height: 5' 8". *Weight:* 10 st 10 lbs.
Parents: Eric and Margaret Knott.
Wife: Jan Linda.
Married: 21 March 1969.
Children: James Alan, 14 June 1975.
Education and qualifications: Northumberland Heath Secondary Modern School; Erith, Kent. Advanced cricket coach.
Occupation outside cricket: Proprietor of sports shop.

Family links with cricket: "My father, uncle, brother, cousin and myself have all played for the same club in club cricket, Belvedere C.C. My father was a fine club wicket-keeper who kept me out of the side as keeper. I used to bowl off-spinners while he kept. He taught me cricket from the age of four".
County debut: 1964. *County cap:* 1965.
Benefit: £27,037 in 1976.
Outside interests: Listening to music, "watching movies either on TV or at the cinema." Watching soccer. Family.
Nickname: Knotty.
Other sporting activities: Most sports, especially soccer and table-tennis, badminton, squash.

General: Uses Slazenger cricket equipment. Elected Best Young Cricketer of the Year 1965 by Cricket Writers' Club. One of Wisden's Cricketers of the Year 1969. Holds record for most dismissals in Test cricket. Dismissed seven batsmen, seven caught, in Test debut v Pakistan (Nottingham 1967). Played for World Series Cricket.

Address and telephone number: c/o Alan Knott Sports, 118 High Street, Herne Bay, Kent. Telephone 02273–4862.

Personal best: Batting Tests 135 England v Australia, Trent Bridge 1977; other f/class 156 M.C.C. v South Zone, Bangalore 1972–73; jpl 60 Kent v Hants, Canterbury 1969; b&h 65 Kent v Combined Universities, Oxford 1976; gillette 46 Kent v Notts, Trent Bridge 1975. Bowling f/class 1–40 M.C.C. v Pakistan U-23, Lahore 1966–67.

LAMB, Allan Joseph.

County: Northamptonshire.

Role: Right-hand bat.

Date and place of birth: 20 June 1954, Langebaanweg, Cape Province, South Africa.

Height: 5′ 8″. *Weight:* 12 st 12 lbs.

Parents: Michael and Joan Lamb.

Wife: Lindsay St Leder Lamb.

Married: 8 December 1979.

Education and qualifications: Wynberg Boys' High School; matriculated.

Occupation outside cricket: timber representative and diamond investment broker.

Family links with cricket: father played in the Boland League; brother played for Western Province 'B'.

County debut: 1978. *County cap:* 1978.

Outside interests: skin diving, collecting antiques, reading, "lying on beach".

Nickname: Lambie.

Other sporting activities: squash, tennis, golf, skiing.

General: Debut for Western Province in Currie Cup 1972–73.

Address and telephone number: 14 Wakefield Road, Wynberg, Cape Town, South Africa.

Telephone: 692545 or 776959.

Personal best: Batting f/class 178 Northants v Leics, Leicester 1979; jpl 77 Northants v Warwicks, Northampton 1979; b&h 77 Northants v Essex, Northampton 1979; gillette 101 Northants v Sussex, Hove 1979. Bowling f/class 1–1 Northants v Derby, Derby 1978.

LAMB, Hon. Timothy Michael.
County: Northamptonshire.
Role: Right-hand bat, right arm medium bowler.
Date and place of birth: 24 March 1953, Hartford, Cheshire.
Parents: Lord and Lady Rochester.
Education and qualifications: Shrewsbury School; Oxford University.
County debut: 1978. *County cap:* 1978.
Off-season 1979-80: Playing in Perth, Australia.
Nickname: Tim.
General: Oxford University cricket blue 1973 and 1974. Debut for Middlesex 1974. Left county after 1977 season for Northants.
Address and telephone number: c/o Northamptonshire County Cricket Club, Wantage Road, Northampton MN1 4TJ. Telephone: Northampton 32917.
Personal best: Batting f/class 77 Middlesex v Notts, Lord's 1976; jpl 27 Middlesex v Hants, Basingstoke 1976; b&h 7* Northants v Surrey, Northampton 1979; gillette 11*

Middlesex v Lancs, Lord's 1975. Bowling f/class 6-49 Middlesex v Surrey, Lord's 1975; jpl 5-13 Northants v Notts, Northampton 1979; b&h 5-44 Middlesex v Yorkshire, Lord's 1975; gillette 4-52 Northants v Sussex, Hove 1979.

LARKINS, Wayne.
County: Northamptonshire.
Role: Right-hand bat, right arm medium bowler.
Date and place of birth: 22 November 1953, Roxton, Bedfordshire.
Height: 5' 11". *Weight:* 12 st.
Parents: Mavis Larkins (father deceased).
Wife: Jane Elaine.
Married: 22 March 1975.
Education and qualifications: Bushmead, Eaton Socon, Huntingdon.
Family links with cricket: Father was umpire. Brother, Melvin, "played for Bedford Town for many years."
County debut: 1972. *County cap:* 1976.
Off-season 1979-80: Touring Australia with England.
Nickname: Ned.
Other sporting activities: Golf, Semi-pro footballer for Wellingborough Town (Southern League).
General: Northants considered releasing him in 1974. Lord's Taverners/Schweppes Award 1979 for Best Young Batsman.
Address and telephone number: c/o Northamptonshire County Cricket Club, County Ground, Wantage Road, Northampton NN1 4TJ.

Personal best: Batting f/class 170* Northants v Worcs, Northampton 1978; jpl 111 Northants v Leics, Wellingborough, 1979; b&h 73* Northants v Essex, Chelmsford 1977; gillette 92* Northants v Leics, Northampton 1979. Bowling f/class 3-34 Northants v Somerset, Northampton 1976; jpl 5-32 Northants v Essex, Ilford 1978; b&h 3-13 Northants v Essex, Chelmsford 1977; gillette 1-51 Northants v Kent, Northampton 1978.

LAWSON, Geoffrey Francis.
County: Lancashire.
Role: Right arm fast bowler.
Date and place of birth: 7 December 1957, New South Wales.
General: Playing for New South Wales v England in 1978, bowled 4 successive bouncers to G. Boycott, with England

needing to make 4 in second innings to win.
Address and telephone number: c/o Lancashire County Cricket Club, Old Trafford, Manchester M16 0PX.
Personal best: Batting f/class 39 New South Wales v Western Australia, Perth 1978–79. Bowling f/class 4–71 New South Wales v Southern Australia, Adelaide 1978–79.

LEADBEATER, Barrie.
County: Yorkshire.
Role: Right-hand bat, right arm medium bowler.
Date and place of birth: 14 August 1943, Leeds.
Height: 6′ 0″. *Weight:* 13 st.
Parents: Ronald and Nellie Leadbeater.
Wife: Jacqueline.
Married: 18 September 1971.
Children: Richard Barrie, 23 November 1972; Michael Spencer, 21 March 1975.
Education and qualifications: Brownhill County Primary, Hare Hills County Secondary, Leeds.
Occupation outside cricket: Assistant to the buyer, Metal Box Co. Ltd., Shipley. Clerk/cashier with Leeds & Holbeck Building Society.
Family links with cricket: Father was ex-member of works team, Metal Box Co. Ltd., Shipley. Distant cousin, E. Leadbeater, played for Yorkshire 1949–56.
County debut: 1966. *County cap:* 1969.
Benefit: 1980, jointly with Geoff Cope.
Outside interests: Gardening, astronomy, wild life and "the unknown." "Relaxing with my family."
Nickname: Leady, and Bungalow.
Other sporting activities: Golf, soccer referee, table tennis, squash, snooker, darts, athletics.
General: Would like to be a first-class

umpire. Known as strongly anti-Packer. Scored maiden century in 1976 in 208th innings in first-class cricket.
Address and telephone number: 3 Elmet Road, Barwick-in-Elmet, Leeds LS15 4HD. Telephone: Leeds 812028.
Personal best: Batting f/class 140* Yorkshire v Hants, Portsmouth 1976; jpl 86* Yorkshire v Northants, Bramall Lane, Sheffield 1972; b&h 90 Yorkshire v Lancs, Bradford 1974; gillette 76 Yorkshire v Derby, Lord's 1969. Bowling f/class 1–1 Yorkshire v Middlesex, Leeds 1971; jpl 1–12 Yorkshire v Surrey, The Oval 1976; gillette 3–47 Yorkshire v Hants, Bradford 1974.

LEE, Peter Granville.
County: Lancashire.
Role: Right-hand bat, right arm fast medium bowler.
Date and place of birth: 27 August 1945, Arthingworth, Northamptonshire.
Wife: Sue.
Children: Two daughters, Maxine and Rachel.
Family links with cricket: Brothers all played

for Arthingworth village team.
County debut: 1972. *County cap:* 1972.
Nickname: Leapy.
Other sporting activities: Keeps fit by playing local football.
General: Debut for Northamptonshire C.C.C. 1967. One of Wisden's Cricketers of the Year 1976. Played in only one match in 1978 because of injury. Has twice taken 100

continued overleaf

wickets in a season. Plagued by injuries for last 2 seasons.

Address and telephone number: c/o Lancashire County Cricket Club, Old Trafford, Manchester M16 0PX.

Personal best: Batting f/class 26 Northants v Gloucs, Northampton 1969; jpl 27* Northants v Derby, Chesterfield 1971; b&h 4* Lancs v Warwicks, Edgbaston 1976; gillette 10* Lancs v Middlesex, Lord's 1974. Bowling f/class 8–53 Lancs v Sussex, Hove 1973; jpl 4–17 Lancs v Derby, Chesterfield 1972; b&h 4–32 Lancs v Worcs, Old Trafford 1973; gillette 4–7 Lancs v Cornwall, Truro 1977.

LEVER, John Kenneth.

County: Essex.

Role: Right-hand bat, left arm fast medium bowler.

Date and place of birth: 24 February 1949, Stepney.

Height: 6′ 0½″. *Weight:* 13 st.

Parents: Ken and Doris Lever.

Wife: Unmarried.

Education and qualifications: Highlands Junior; Dane County Secondary School. Three G.C.E.s and "a few R.S.A.s".

Occupation outside cricket: Clerk with Access Social Club; Byron Shipping; Dominion Insurance.

Family links with cricket: "Dad played at school, but this was cut short when he had to go to work. He encouraged me all the way."

County debut: 1967. *County cap:* 1970.

Benefit: 1980.

Outside interests: Driving, music, jogging.

Nickname: Jake or J.K.

Other sporting activities: "All sports." Football, squash, badminton, tennis, snooker.

General: One of Wisden's Cricketers of the Year, 1978. Toured India, Sri Lanka, Australia, 1976–77; Pakistan and New Zealand, 1977–78; Australia 1978–79 and 1979–80. Took 106 wickets at an average of 15.80 in 1978 and 106 wickets at an average of 17.30 in 1979, being top wicket taker jointly with Derek Underwood. President of Blythswood C.C. Member of Ilford C.C. since the age of 14. Contracted with Stuart Surridge equipment. Another of the renowned Essex comedians. Has reputation

of "not breaking down". Was unjustly accused of putting Vaseline on the ball during a Test Match in India, to keep the shine on.

Address and telephone number: c/o Essex County Cricket Club, New Writtle Street, Chelmsford CM2 0RW.

Personal best: Batting Tests 53 England v India, Delhi 1976–77; other f/class 91 Essex v Glamorgan, Cardiff 1970; jpl 23 Essex v Worcs, Worcester 1974; b&h 12* Essex v Warwicks, Edgbaston 1975; gillette 8 Essex v Herts, Hitchin 1976. Bowling Tests 7–46 England v India, Delhi 1976–77; other f/class 8–49 Essex v Warwicks, Edgbaston 1979; jpl 5–13 Essex v Glamorgan, Ebbw Vale 1975; b&h 5–16 Essex v Middlesex, Chelmsford 1976; gillette 5–8 Essex v Middlesex, Westcliff 1972.

LILLEY, Alan William.
County: Essex.
Role: Right-hand bat, wicket-keeper.
Date and place of birth: 8 May 1959, Ilford, Essex.
Height: 5′ 11″. *Weight:* 13 st 4 lbs.
Parents: Min and Ron Lilley.
Wife: Unmarried.
Education and qualifications: Gilbert Colvin and Caterham High School, Ilford.
Occupation outside cricket: Has coached at Ilford Cricket School.
Family links with cricket: Father played for Osborne C.C. as a bowler for 18 years.
County debut: 1978.
Off-season 1979–80: Playing cricket for Perth C.C. in Western Australia.
Nickname: Peanut.
Other sporting activities: Badminton, swimming.
General: Was on M.C.C. Young Pro staff at Lord's one season after leaving school. Scored century in second innings of debut v Notts.
Address and telephone number: Barkingdale,

Ilford, Essex.
Personal best: Batting f/class 100* Essex v Notts, Trent Bridge 1978; jpl 54 Essex v Surrey, Southend 1978; b&h 119 Essex v Combined Universities, Chelmsford 1979.

LISTER, John Wilton.
County: Derbyshire.
Role: Right-hand bat.
Date and place of birth: 1 April 1959, Darlington.
County debut: 1978.
Address and telephone number: c/o Derbyshire County Cricket Club, Nottingham Road, Derby DE2 6DA.
Personal best: Batting f/class 48 Derby v warwicks, Edgbaston 1978; jpl 8 Derby v Kent, Chesterfield 1979; gillette 0 Derby v Somerset, Taunton 1979.

LLEWELLYN, Michael John.
County: Glamorgan.
Role: Left-hand bat, off-break bowler.
Date and place of birth: 27 November 1953, Clydach, Swansea.
Height: 6′ 0″. *Weight:* 13 st 10 lbs.
Parents: David and Marlene Llewellyn.
Wife: Kathleen Pearl.
Married: 15 September 1973.

Children: Michael Dean, 3 October 1977.
Education and qualifications: Comprehensive. Advanced cricket coach.
Family links with cricket: Father played for Royal Navy. Grandfather played for Clydach C.C. and still coaches.
County debut: 1970. *County cap:* 1977.
Outside interests: Carpentry, keep fit, music.

continued overleaf

Nickname: M.J.
Other sporting activities: Football, table tennis, snooker, squash.
General: Toured Malta with Welsh Cavaliers 1978–79. Hit a six into top tier of Lord's Pavilion in Gillette Final v Middlesex, 1977. Played for Skewen in 1979 in South Wales League.
Address and telephone number: 201 Birchgrove Road, Birchgrove, Swansea, Glamorgan. Telephone: Swansea 814337.
Personal best: Batting f/class 129* Glamorgan v Oxford University, Oxford 1977; jpl 79* Glamorgan v Gloucs, Bristol 1977; b&h 63 Glamorgan v Hants, Swansea 1973; gillette 62 Glamorgan v Middlesex, Lord's 1977. Bowling f/class 4–35 Glamorgan v Oxford University, Oxford 1970.

LLOYD, Barry John.
County: Glamorgan.
Role: Right-hand bat, off-break bowler.
Date and place of birth: 6 September 1953, Neath.
Height: 6' 0". *Weight:* 12 st.
Parents: Leslie John and Patricia Mary Lloyd.
Wife: Janice Prydderch.
Married: 11 September 1976.
Children: Hannah Jayne, 25 August 1979.
Education and qualifications: Llangatwg Comprehensive School, Cadoxton, Neath, West Glamorgan; Bangor Normal College, Holyhead Road, Bangor, North Wales. Advanced coaching award.
Occupation outside cricket: P.E. teacher during off-season, cricket coach.
Family links with cricket: Father and grandfather played cricket with Pontneddfechan C.C., a small village in the Neath Valley.
County debut: 1972.
Outside interests: Any sport, including fishing; gardening, family life.
Nickname: Lloydy.
Other sporting activities: Plays rugby for Bryncoch R.F.C., Neath.

General: Formerly on M.C.C. ground staff.
Address and telephone number: c/o Glamorgan County Cricket Club.
Personal best: Batting f/class 45* Glamorgan v Hants, Portsmouth 1973; jpl 13 Glamorgan v Derby, Swansea 1976; Glamorgan v Leics, Leicester 1979. Bowling f/class 4–49 Glamorgan v Hants, Portsmouth 1973; jpl 3–32 Glamorgan v Lancs, Cardiff 1979.

LLOYD, Clive Hubert.
County: Lancashire.
Role: Left-hand bat, right arm medium bowler.
Date and place of birth: 31 August 1944, Queenstown, Georgetown, Guyana, South America.
Height: 6' 4½". *Weight:* 14 st.
Parents: Arthur Christopher and Sylvia Thelma Lloyd.

Wife: Waveney.
Married: 11 September 1971.
Children: Melissa Monica Simone, 22 February 1974; Samantha Louise, 26 January 1976.
Education and qualifications: Fountain A.M.E. School and Chatham High School, Georgetown, Guyana. Cricket coaching certificate.
Occupation outside cricket: Civil servant, Guyana Ministry of Health.
Family links with cricket: Cousin of Lance Gibbs of Warwickshire C.C.C. and West Indies.
County debut: 1968. *County cap:* 1969.
Testimonial: £27,199 in 1977.
Off-season 1979–80: Touring Australia with West Indies, as captain.
Outside interests: Reading, listening to good music.
Nickname: Big C. Hubert.
Other sporting activities: Lawn and table tennis, squash, golf, jogging.
General: Played for Haslingden in Lancashire League in 1967 and also for Rest of the World XI in 1967 and 1968. One of Wisden's Cricketers of the Year in 1970. Currently Captain of the West Indies. Played five matches for Rest of the World XI in 1970 and two in 1971 and 1972. Wears spectacles. Scored 201 not out in 120 minutes for West Indies v Glamorgan, Swansea, 1976, to equal record for fastest double century in first class cricket. Has written articles for *Lancashire Evening Post* and *Bolton Express.* Endorses bats of Gray Nicholls. Played for World Series Cricket and is strong supporter of the idea. Has had knee-injury problems since

1976, causing rumours of retirement. Regarded as strong calming influence in difficult situations for West Indies. Won the first Courage International Batsman of the Year tournament at the Oval in September 1979.
Address and telephone number: c/o Lancashire County Cricket Club, Old Trafford, Manchester M16 0PX.
Personal best: Batting Tests 242* West Indies v India, Bombay 1974–75; other f/class 217* Lancs v Warwicks, Old Trafford 1971; jpl 134* Lancs v Somerset, Old Trafford 1970; b&h 73 Lancs v Notts, Old Trafford 1974; gillette 126 Lancs v Warwicks, Lord's 1974. Bowling Tests 2–13 West Indies v England, Bridgetown 1973–74; other f/class 4–48 Lancs v Leics, Old Trafford 1970; jpl 4–33 Lancs v Middlesex, Lord's 1971; b&h 3–23 Lancs v Derby, Old Trafford 1974; gillette 3–39 Lancs v Somerset, Taunton 1970.

LLOYD, David.
County: Lancashire.
Role: Left-hand bat, slow left arm orthodox bowler.
Date and place of birth: 18 March 1947, Accrington.
Education and qualifications: Accrington Secondary Technical School.
County debut: 1965. *County cap:* 1968.
Testimonial: 1978.
Outside interests: Horse-racing.
Nickname: Bumble.
Other sporting activities: Golf.
General: County Captain from 1973–77. Toured Australia, New Zealand 1974–75.

continued overleaf

Has scored 1,000 runs in a season nine times.
Address and telephone number: c/o
Lancashire County Cricket Club, Old
Trafford, Manchester M16 0PX.
Personal best: Batting Tests 214* England v
India, Edgbaston 1974; other f/class 195
Lancs v Gloucs, Old Trafford 1973; jpl 103*

Lancs v Northants, Peterborough 1971; b&h
113 Lancs v Minor Counties North, Old Traf-
ford 1973; gillette 121* Lancs v Gloucs, Old
Trafford 1978. Bowling f/class 7-36 Lancs v
Gloucs, Lydney 1966; jpl 2-11 Lancs v
Middlesex, Lord's 1976; gillette 1-22 Lancs v
Beds, Luton 1973.

LLOYD, Timothy Andrew.
County: Warwickshire.
Role: Left-hand bat, right arm medium
bowler.
Date and place of birth: 5 November 1956,
Oswestry.
Height: 5' 10". *Weight:* 11 st 3 lbs.
Wife: Unmarried.
Education and qualifications: Oswestry
Boys' High School; Higher National
Diploma, Tourism.
Occupation outside cricket: Coaching and
playing in South Africa.
County debut: 1977.
Off-season 1979-80: Playing in South
Africa, for Orange Free State.
Outside interests: Horse-racing, gardening.
Nickname: Teflon, Jasper.
Other sporting activities: Soccer, golf.
General: Scored 202 not out for Shropshire
Schools v Worcs. Played for Shropshire and
Warwickshire 2nd XI, both in 1975. Played
in one John Player League match in 1976 v
Yorkshire at Leeds.
Address and telephone number: Timber Top,

High Street, Whittington, Shropshire.
Personal best: Batting f/class 104 Warwicks v
Notts, Edgbaston 1979; jpl 54* Warwicks v
Middlesex, Edgbaston 1978; b&h 35*
Warwicks v Glamorgan, Edgbaston 1978.

LLOYDS, Jeremy William.
County: Somerset.
Role: Left-hand bat.
Date and place of birth: 17 November 1954,
Penang, Malaya.
Height: 6' 0". *Weight:* 11 st 7 lbs.
Parents: Edwin William and Grace Cicely
Lloyds.
Wife: Unmarried.
Education and qualifications: Curry Rivel
V.C. Primary School, St Dunstan's Prep

School, Burnham-on-Sea, Somerset. Blun-
dell's School, Tiverton, Devon.
Occupation outside cricket: One and a half
years with Lloyds Bank, Taunton, prior to
joining M.C.C. Young Professionals at
Lord's in 1975 for four years. Cricket
Council, N.C.A., advanced coaching certi-
ficate 1977.
Family links with cricket: Father played for
Blundell's 1st XI, capped in 1935, selected for
Public Schools Rest v Lord's Schools at

Lord's 1935, Inter-State cricket in Malaya and Singapore 1950–55. Brother, Christopher Edwin Lloyds, played for Blundell's 1st XI 1964–66 and Somerset 2nd XI 1966.
County debut: 1979.
Off-season 1979–80: Cricket coach to St. Stithian's College, Johannesburg, South Africa.
Outside interests: Reading, music, bird-watching and wild-life.
Other sporting activities: Captain Taunton Rugby Football Club 1977–78, golf, squash, tennis, swimming.
General: Endorses Stuart Surridge sporting goods. Committee member Taunton R.F.C. 1977–78.
Address and telephone number: c/o Somerset County Cricket Club, St. James's Street, Taunton, TA1 1JT.

Personal best: Batting f/class 43 Somerset v Sussex, Hove 1979.

LONG, Arnold.

County: Sussex.
Role: Left-hand bat, wicket-keeper.
Date and place of birth: 18 December 1940, Cheam, Surrey.
Height: 5′ 8″. *Weight:* 10 st 12 lbs.
Parents: Joseph and Edna Long.
Wife: Barbara.
Married: 26 September 1964.
Children: Martin, 6 March 1969; Matthew, 27 January 1972; Natalie, 31 May 1974.
Education and qualifications: Wallington County Grammar School, seven O-levels, three A-levels.
Occupation outside cricket: Partner in an insurance broker firm, Arnold Long & Partners. Fellow of the Chartered Insurance Institute. Director, East Surrey Building Society.
Family links with cricket: Father played local club cricket.
County debut: 1976. *County cap:* 1976.
Benefit: (while at Surrey) £10,353 in 1971.
Outside interests: Traditional jazz.
Nickname: Oblong, "which I've had since 1959 when I first went into cricket. My recent nickname at Sussex is 'Buzby', because I'm always on the telephone."
Other sporting activities: "I played football for Corinthian Casuals many years ago. I now play the occasional game of football which I still enjoy." Squash, golf, handicap 12.
General: Debut for Surrey 1960 and Surrey

cap in 1962. Appointed Surrey Vice-Captain 1973, and left after 1975 season. Appointed Sussex County Captain in 1978. Dismissed seven batsmen in one innings and eleven in match (all caught) v Sussex at Hove 1964, being world record for most catches in a match and only one short of record for most dismissals in a match.
Address and telephone number: 4 Mellow Close, Banstead, Surrey. Telephone: Borough Heath 55572.
Personal best: Batting f/class 92 Surrey v Leics, Leicester 1970; jpl 71 Surrey v Warwicks, Edgbaston 1971; b&h 46 Surrey v Kent, The Oval 1973; gillette 42 Surrey v Sussex, The Oval 1970.

97

LOVE, James Derek.
County: Yorkshire.
Role: Right-hand bat.
Date and place of birth: 22 April 1955, Leeds.
Height: 6′ 2″. *Weight:* 14 st.
Parents: Derek Oliver and Betty Love.
Wife: Unmarried.
Education and qualifications: Brudenell County Secondary, Leeds.
Occupation outside cricket: Civil servant for three years until left to become professional cricketer.
Family links with cricket: Father played local cricket; brother, Robert, aged 13, plays local cricket and for 1st XI at Tadcaster Grammar School.
County debut: 1975.
Outside interests: Shooting.
Nickname: Jim.
Other sporting activities: Represented Leeds Schoolboys at Under-13 and Under-15 at rugby league.
General: Whitbread Scholarship to Sydney, Australia, 1977–78 off-season.
Address and telephone number: c/o Yorkshire County Cricket Club, Headingley Cricket Ground, Leeds LS6 3BU.

Personal best: Batting f/class 170* Yorkshire v Worcs, Worcester 1979; jpl 90 Yorkshire v Derby, Chesterfield 1979; b&h 18 Yorkshire v Notts, Trent Bridge 1978; gillette 2 Yorkshire v Hants, Bournemouth 1977; 2 Yorkshire v Middlesex, Lord's 1979; Bowling jpl 1–6 Yorkshire v Sussex, Hove 1979.

LUMB, Richard Graham.
County: Yorkshire.
Role: Right-hand bat, right arm medium bowler.
Date and place of birth: 27 February 1950, Doncaster, Yorkshire.
Height: 6′ 4″. *Weight:* 13 st 10 lbs.
Parents: John Edward Lumb, deceased, and Dorothy Lumb.
Wife: Susan Jane.
Married: 4 November 1976, Married in Johannesburg, South Africa.
Education and qualifications: Percy Jackson Grammar School, and Mexborough Grammar School.
Occupation outside cricket: Assistant hotel manager for three years during off-season.
Family links with cricket: Grandfather, Joe Thomas Lumb, member of Yorkshire General Committee for 20 years. Joe Lumb Cricket Competition for young cricketers named after him. Brother, John, played for Yorkshire 2nd XI and now with Smethwick in Birmingham League. Brother-in-law Tony "Titch" Smith, wicket-keeper for Natal in Currie Cup Competition.
County debut: 1970. *County cap:* 1974.

Outside interests: Gardening, reading, theatre.
Nickname: Lummy, and "Too numerous to mention".
Other sporting activities: Golf, tennis.
General: Contracted to use St. Peter sporting products. Agent: Mr Dave Mitchell, Global Entertainments, 77 Great George Street,

Leeds, West Yorkshire. Played in M.C.C. Schools matches at Lord's 1968. Played in one John Player League match in 1969. *Address and telephone number:* c/o Yorkshire County Cricket Club, Headingley Cricket Ground, Leeds LS6 3BU.

LYNCH, Monte Allan.
County: Surrey.
Role: Right-hand bat, right arm medium and off-break bowler.
Date and place of birth: 21 May 1958, Georgetown, Guyana.
Weight: 12 st.
Parents: Lawrence and Doreen Austin Lynch.
Wife: Unmarried.
Education and qualifications: Ryden's School, Walton-on-Thames.
Family links with cricket: "Father and most of family played at some time or another."
County debut: 1977.
Outside interests: Dancing.
Nickname: Mont.
Other sporting activities: Football, table tennis.
Address and telephone number: Erica Thorman Court, Ellesmere Hospital, Queen's Road, Walton-on-Thames, Surrey. Walton on Thames 44601.
Personal best: Batting f/class 101 Surrey v

Pakistan, The Oval 1978; jpl 52 Surrey v Leics, Leicester 1979; b&h 67 Surrey v Worcs, Worcester 1979; gillette 5 Surrey v Northants, Northampton 1979. Bowling f/class 1-14 Surrey v Sussex, Hove 1978.

LYON, John.
County: Sussex.
Role: Right-hand bat, wicket-keeper.
Date and place of birth: 17 May 1951, St Helen's, Merseyside.
Height: 5′ 7½″. *Weight:* 10 st 13 lbs.
Parents: Peter and Margaret Victoria Lyon.
Wife: Cynthia Mary.
Married: 1 December 1972.
Education and qualifications: Central Modern Secondary School, St Helen's.
Occupation outside cricket: Glass-cutter at Pilkington's.
County debut: 1973. *County cap:* 1975.
Outside interests: Reading detective stories, cinema, "quiet meal out with my wife".
Nickname: Lenny.
Other sporting activities: Rugby League before full-time cricket.
General: Not re-engaged by Lancashire after 1979 season. Played once for M.C.C. in 1978 and was regarded as Test possible.

Address and telephone number: 3 Bridgeman Street, St. Helen's, Merseyside, Telephone St Helen's 57260.

continued overleaf

Personal best: Batting f/class 123 Lancs v Warwicks, Old Trafford 1979; jpl 31 Lancs v Gloucs, Gloucester 1975; b&h 19 Lancs v Derby, Old Trafford 1978; gillette 14 Lancs v Kent, Canterbury 1979.

McCURDY, Rodney John.
County: Derbyshire.
Role: Right-hand bat, right arm fast bowler.
Date and place of birth: 30 December 1959, Melbourne, Australia.
County debut: 1979.
General: Played one match v Sri Lanka, 1979. Played for Pudsey St. Lawrence, Bradford League, 1979. Plays for Ringwood C.C. in Melbourne.
Address and telephone number: c/o Derbyshire County Cricket Club, Nottingham Road, Derby DE2 6DA.
Personal best: Bowling f/class 1–50 Derby v India, Derby 1979.

McEVOY, Michael Stephen Anthony.
County: Essex.
Role: Right-hand bat, right arm medium bowler.
Date and place of birth: 25 January 1956, Jorhat, Assam, India.
Height: 5′ 10½″. *Weight:* 11 st.
Parents: Tony and Peggy McEvoy.
Wife: Unmarried.
Education and qualifications: Holmwood House School, Colchester Royal Grammar School, Borough Road College of Education. Certificate of Education, Physical Education teacher.
Occupation outside cricket: P.E. teacher.
County debut: 1976.
Nickname: Mac.
Other sporting activities: Most sports, squash, rugby, hockey.
Address and telephone number: 5 Vane Court, Dorothy Sayers Drive, Witham, Essex.

Personal best: Batting 67* Essex v Yorks, Middlesbrough 1977; jpl 7 Essex v Lancs, Old Trafford 1978.

McEWAN, Kenneth Scott.
County: Essex.
Role: Right-hand bat, off-break bowler.
Date and place of birth: 16 July 1952, Bedford, Cape Province, South Africa.
Education and qualifications: Queen's College, Queenstown, South Africa.
County debut: 1974. *County cap:* 1974.
Off-season 1979–80: Playing in Perth, Australia.
Nickname: Ken.
General: Debut for Eastern Province in 1972–73 Currie Cup Competition. Played for T. N. Pearce's XI v West Indies at Scarborough in 1973. Scored four consecutive centuries in 1977. Shared in second wicket record partnership for county,

321 with Graham Gooch v Northants at Ilford in 1978. Was originally recommended to Sussex C.C.C. by Tony Greig, who coached him at school. "Quietest member of Essex XI." Spent off-season 1979–80 playing for Perth, Western Australia.
Address and telephone number: c/o Essex County Cricket Club, New Writtle Street, Chelmsford CM2 0RW.
Personal best: Batting f/class 218 Essex v Sussex, Chelmsford 1977; jpl 123 Essex v Warwicks, Ilford 1976; b&h 133 Essex v Notts, Chelmsford 1978; gillette 63 Essex v Somerset, Westcliff 1974. Bowling f/class 1–0 Essex v Glamorgan, Swansea 1974.

McFARLANE, Leslie Leopold.
County: Northamptonshire.
Role: Right-arm medium bowler.
Date and place of birth: 19 August 1952, Jamaica.
County debut: 1979.
General: Played in Northampton Town League.
Address and telephone number: c/o Northampton County Cricket Club, Wantage Road, Northampton NN1 4TJ. Telephone: Northampton 32917.
Personal best: Batting jpl 6 Northants v Derby, Long Eaton 1979. Bowling f/class 3–83 Northants v Gloucs, Northampton 1979; jpl 2–27 Northants v Middlesex, Milton Keynes 1979.

MACK, Andrew James.
County: Glamorgan.
Role: Left-hand bat, left arm fast medium bowler.
Date and place of birth: 14 January 1956, Aylsham, Norfolk.
Height: 6′ 5″.
County debut: 1978.
General: Joined Surrey staff in 1973. Played in five John Player League matches 1975 for Surrey. Made debut for Surrey 1st XI 1976. Left Surrey after 1977 season.
Address and telephone number: c/o Glamorgan County Cricket Club, 6 High Street, Cardiff. Telephone: Cardiff 29956.
Personal best: Batting f/class 18 Glamorgan v India, Swansea 1979; jpl 16 Surrey v Hants, Southampton 1977; b&h 3 Surrey v Sussex, The Oval 1977; gillette 1* Glamorgan v Kent, Swansea 1979. Bowling f/class 4–28 Glamorgan v Worcs, Worcester 1978; jpl 3–48 Surrey v Hants, Southampton 1977;

b&h 3–34 Surrey v Combined Universities, The Oval 1976.

MACKINTOSH, Kevin Scott.
County: Nottinghamshire.
Role: Right-hand bat, right arm medium bowler.
Date and place of birth: 30 August 1957, Kingston-on-Thames.
Height: 6' 0". *Weight:* 12 st. 9 lbs.
Parents: Ian Alistair and Hazel Doris Ann Mackintosh.
Wife: Unmarried.
Education and qualifications: Kingston Grammar School, Kingston College of Further Education.
Occupation outside cricket: Representative for plan-a-Year Ltd.
Family links with cricket: Brother, Neil, plays cricket for Lancaster University and has also played for Surrey 2nd XI.
County debut: 1978.

Outside interests: Eating and making curries, pop music, driving, "visiting Young's Pubs."
Nickname: Toffo, Mac.
Other sporting activities: Football, hockey, Old Kingstonians.
General: On Surrey staff from 1975–77.
Address and telephone number: 38 Heathside, Hinchley Wood, Esher, Surrey.

Telephone: 01–398–6299.
Personal best: Batting f/class 23* Notts v Essex, Trent Bridge 1978; jpl 12* Notts v Lancs, Trent Bridge 1978; b&h 3 Notts v Yorkshire, Trent Bridge 1978. Bowling f/class 4–49 Notts v Surrey, The Oval 1978; jpl 4–26 Notts v Gloucs, Trent Bridge 1979; b&h 1–17 Notts v Yorkshire, Trent Bridge 1978.

McLELLAN, Alan James.
County: Derbyshire.
Role: Right-hand bat, wicket-keeper.
Date and place of birth: 2 September 1958, Ashton-under-Lyne, Lancashire.
Education and qualifications: Williamstown High School, Melbourne, Australia; Hartshead Secondary School, Ashton-under-Lyne.
County debut: 1978.
General: Played for both Lancashire and Derbyshire 2nd XIs in 1977.

Address and telephone number: c/o Derbyshire County Cricket Club, Nottingham Road, Derby DE2 6DA.
Personal best: Batting f/class 41 Derby v Hants, Basingstoke 1979; jpl 4* Derby v Worcs, Worcester 1978.

MALONE, Michael Francis.
County: Lancashire.
Date and place of birth: 9 October 1950, Perth, Western Australia.
County debut: 1979.
Nickname: Mick.

General: Took 19 wickets in last two games for Lancashire. Finished top of bowling averages in 1979. Played for World Series Cricket. Signed for Lancashire by special registration near end of season.
Address and telephone number: c/o

Lancashire County Cricket Club, Old Trafford, Manchester M16 0PX.
Personal best: Batting Tests 46 Australia v England, The Oval 1977; other f/class 38 Western Australia v M.C.C., Perth 1976–77.

MARKS, Victor James.
County: Somerset.
Role: Right-hand bat, off-break bowler.
Date and place of birth: 25 June 1955, Middle Chinnock, Somerset.
Education and qualifications: Blundell's School; Oxford University.
County debut: 1975.
General: Half-blue for rugby fives at Oxford University. Debut for Oxford University C.C. 1975, blue 1975–76–77–78. Captain from 1976–77.
Address and telephone number: c/o Somerset County Cricket Club, St. James's Street, Taunton TA1 1JT.
Personal best: f/class 105 Oxford University v Worcs, Oxford 1976; jpl 32* Somerset v Hants, Weston 1975; b&h 59 Combined Universities v Glamorgan, Oxford 1978; gillette 33* Somerset v Essex, Taunton 1978. Bowling f/class 6–33 Somerset v Northants, Taunton 1979; jpl 3–19 Somerset v Derby,

Bowling Tests 5–63 Australia v England, The Oval 1977; other f/class 7–88 Lancs v Notts, Old Trafford 1979; jpl 2–27 Lancs v Somerset, Old Trafford 1979.

Taunton 1979; b&h 2–18 Somerset v Minor Counties South, Taunton 1979.

MARSHALL, Malcolm Denzil.
County: Hampshire.
Role: Right-hand bat, right arm fast medium bowler.
Date and place of birth: 18 April 1958, Barbados.
Height: 5' 11". *Weight:* 11 st 8 lbs.
Parents: Eleanor Marshall.
Wife: Unmarried.
Education and qualifications: Parkinson Comprehensive School.
Occupation outside cricket: Has worked as assistant storekeeper then in advertising department of Banks Products.
Family links with cricket: Cousin plays for Texaco Second XI as a "fast bowler who can also bat."
County debut: 1979.
Off-season 1979–80: Touring Australia with West Indies.
Nickname: Denz, Maco.
Other sporting activities: Road tennis, darts, table tennis.
General: Took 9 wickets in debut match v Glamorgan in May 1979. The fact that it

snowed "almost sent him home to the West Indies".
Address and telephone number: Station Hill, St. Michael, Barbados, West Indies, Telephone: St. Michael 94314.

continued overleaf

Personal best: Batting Tests 5 West Indies v India, Bangalore 1978-79; other f/class 59 West Indies v West Zone, Baroda 1978-79; jpl 20 Hants v Middlesex, Lord's 1979; b&h 15 Hants v Derby, Derby 1979; gillette 21* Hants v Middlesex, Lord's 1979. Bowling Tests 1-44 West Indies v India, Calcutta 1978-79; other f/class 6-42 West Indies v Karnataka, Ahmedabad 1978-79; jpl 5-13 Hants v Glamorgan, Portsmouth 1979; b&h 2-19 Hants v Leics, Southampton 1979.

MAYNARD, Christopher.
County: Warwickshire.
Role: Right-hand bat, wicket-keeper, occasional right arm medium bowler.
Date and place of birth: 8 April 1958, Haslemere, Surrey.
Height: 6' 0". *Weight:* 11 st 7 lbs.
Parents: John and Joan Maynard.
Wife: Unmarried.
Education and qualifications: Bishop Vesey's Grammar School, Sutton Coldfield. Ten O-levels, one A-level.
Occupation outside cricket: Has been salesman and worked for jewellery firm.
Family links with cricket: Father and brother, Steve, play for Sutton Coldfield C.C.
County debut: 1979.
Off-season 1979-80: Touring Australia with Derrick Robins Under-23 XI.
Outside interests: Reading.
Nickname: Fish, Bill.
Other sporting activities: Golf, darts, hockey, football.
General: Played for 2nd XI since 1976.
Address and telephone number: 29 Moor

Meadow Road, Sutton Coldfield, West Midlands. Telephone: 021-378-1031.
Personal best: Batting f/class 85 Warwicks v Kent, Edgbaston 1979; jpl 35 Warwicks v Essex, Edgbaston 1979; b&h 8 Warwicks v Leics, Edgbaston 1979.

MELLOR, Alan John.
County: Derbyshire.
Role: Right-hand bat, slow left arm orthodox bowler.
Date and place of birth: 4 July 1959, Burton-on-Trent.
County debut: 1978.
General: Played for Derbyshire 2nd XI since 1976.
Address and telephone number: c/o Derbyshire County Cricket Club, Nottingham Road, Derby DE2 6DA.
Personal best: Batting f/class 10* Derby v Essex, Southend 1978. Bowling f/class 5-52 Derby v Kent, Maidstone 1978; jpl 1-37 Derby v Worcs, Derby 1979.

MENDIS, Gehan Dixon.
County: Sussex.
Role: Right-hand bat, and wicket-keeper.
Date and place of birth: 24 April 1955, Colombo, Sri Lanka.
Height: 5' 8". *Weight:* 10 st 7 lbs.
Parents: Sam Dixon Charles and Sonia Marcelle Mendis.
Wife: Angela.
Married: 12 June 1976.
Education and qualifications: St. Thomas College, Mount Lavinia, Sri Lanka; Brighton, Hove & Sussex Grammar School; Bede College, Durham University; B.Ed. Mathematics, Durham.
Occupation outside cricket: Teacher at Rosemead School, Littlehampton, Sussex. Has worked in sales division of Caffyn's Ltd., Hove.
County debut: 1974.
Outside interests: Cinema and theatre, "buying and listening to prog. music (especially Bob Dylan)".
Nickname: Mendo, Jack, Sergio.
Other sporting activities: Played table tennis for Sussex at junior level.
General: Played for Sussex 2nd XI since 1971. Played in one John Player League

match 1973.
Address and telephone number: c/o Sussex County Cricket Club, Eaton Road, Hove BN3 3AN. Telephone: Brighton 732161.
Personal best: Batting f/class 128 Sussex v Essex, Hove 1976; jpl 56 Sussex v Gloucs, Bristol 1978; b&h 39 Sussex v Northants, Eastbourne 1979; gillette 69 Sussex v Northants, Hove 1979.

MERRY, William Gerald.
County: Middlesex.
Role: Right-hand bat, right arm fast medium bowler.
Date and place of birth: 8 August 1955, Newbury.
Height: 6' 1". *Weight:* 12 st.
Parents: Gerald and Doreen Merry.
Wife: Sue.
Married: 3 January 1976.
Education and qualifications: Secondary modern.
Occupation outside cricket: Quantity surveyor.
County debut: 1979.
Off-season 1979-80: Touring Australasia with Derrick Robins Under-23 XI.
Nickname: Bill.
Other sporting activities: Most sports—golf, football, etc.
General: M.C.C. tour to Bangladash 1978-79. Derrick Robins Under-23 team tour of Australasia, February and March 1980.
Address and telephone number: c/o Middlesex County Cricket Club, Lord's

Cricket Ground, St. John's Wood Road, London NW8 8QN.
Personal best: Batting f/class 4* Middlesex v Leics, Leicester 1979; jpl 4 Middlesex v Surrey, The Oval 1979; b&h 3 Minor

continued overleaf

Counties West v Lancs, Watford 1973; gillette 1* Herts v Leics, Leicester 1977. Bowling f/class 3-46 Middlesex v Kent, Tunbridge Wells 1979; jpl 3-29 Middlesex v

Lancs, Old Trafford 1979; b&h 3-19 Minor Counties West v Derby, Derby 1978; gillette 2-21 Middlesex v Yorkshire, Lord's 1979.

MILLER, Geoffrey.
County: Derbyshire.
Role: Right-hand bat, off-break bowler.
Date and place of birth: 8 September 1952, Chesterfield.
Education and qualifications: Chesterfield Grammar School.
County debut: 1973. *County cap:* 1976.
Off-season 1979–80: With England in Australia until returned home early with back trouble.
Outside interests: Crosswords, reading.
Nickname: Dusty, Mills.
Other sporting activities: Golf, tennis.

General: Toured India 1970–71 and West Indies 1972 with England Young Cricketers. Won Sir Frank Worrell Trophy as outstanding boy cricketer of 1972. Elected Best Young Cricketer of the Year in 1976 by the Cricket Writers' Club. Toured India, Sri Lanka, Australia 1976–77; Pakistan, New Zealand 1977–78; Australia 1978–79 and 79–80. Had to return in December 1979 through injury. Became Captain of Derbyshire in middle of 1979 season on resignation of D. S. Steele.
Address and telephone number: c/o Derbyshire County Cricket Club, Nottingham Road, Derby DE2 6DA.
Personal best: Batting Tests 98* England v

Pakistan, Lahore 1977–78; other f/class 95 Derby v Lancs, Old Trafford 1978; jpl 44 Derby v Kent, Chesterfield 1973; b&h 75 Derby v Warwicks, Derby 1977; gillette 59* Derby v Worcs, Worcester 1978. Bowling Tests 5-44 England v Australia, Sydney 1978–79; other f/class 7-54 Derby v Sussex, Hove 1977; jpl 4-22 Derby v Yorks, Huddersfield 1978; b&h 3-23 Derby v Surrey, Derby 1979; gillette 2-14 Derby v Lincs, Ilkeston 1976.

MOSELEY, Hallam Reynold.
County: Somerset.
Role: Right-hand bat, right arm fast medium bowler.
Date and place of birth: 28 May 1948, Christchurch, Barbados.
Height: 6' 0". *Weight:* 13 st.
Parents: Eustace and Sheila Moseley.
Wife: Marcia Ophelia.
Married: 25 October 1975.
Children: Charmaine Fiona Michele.
Education and qualifications: Primary: Providence Boys' School; secondary; The Rural Studio.
Family links with cricket: Father played as fast bowler/batsman in village cricket in Barbados. Brother, Collin, played as fast bowler for his school, Princess Margaret High

School, now plays as a medium to fast bowler for Banks Breweries team in the first and intermediate divisions of the Barbados Cricket Association.
County debut: 1971.   *County cap:* 1972.
Testimonial: 1979.
Outside interests: Meeting people, gardening.
Nickname: Moses the Lawgiver, Black Flash and Mojo.
Other sporting activities: Darts, skittles, athletics.
General: Toured England with Barbados team in 1969 and made debut v Notts, at Nottingham. Subsequently played for Barbados in Shell Shield. Bowls in spectacles.
Address and telephone number: 55 Whiteoaks Lane, Cowgate Road, Greenford, Middlesex. Telephone: 01-575-5053.
Personal best: Batting f/class 67 Somerset v Leics, Taunton 1972; jpl 24 Somerset v Notts, Torquay 1972; 24 Somerset v Hants, Weston 1975; b&h 33 Somerset v Hants, Bournemouth 1973; gillette 15 Somerset v Lancs, Old Trafford 1972. Bowling f/class 6-34 Somerset v Derby, Bath 1975; jpl 5-30 Somerset v Middlesex, Lord's 1973; b&h 3-17 Somerset v Leics, Taunton 1977; gillette 4-31 Somerset v Surrey, Taunton 1974.

NASH, Malcolm Andrew.
County: Glamorgan.
Role: Left-hand bat, left arm fast medium bowler.
Date and place of birth: 9 May 1945, Abergavennie, Monmouthshire.
County debut: 1966.   *County cap:* 1969.
Benefit: 1978.
General: All six balls of an over by him were hit for 6 by Gary Sobers at Swansea.
Address and telephone number: c/o Glamorgan County Cricket Club, 6 High Street, Cardiff. Telephone: Cardiff 29956.
Personal best: Batting f/class 130 Glamorgan v Surrey, The Oval 1976; jpl 68 Glamorgan v Essex, Purfleet 1972; b&h 103* Glamorgan v Hants, Swansea 1976; gillette 51 Glamorgan v Lincs, Swansea 1974. Bowling f/class 9-56 Glamorgan v Hants, Basingstoke 1975; jpl 6-29 Glamorgan v Worcs, Worcester 1975;

b&h 4-12 Glamorgan v Surrey, Cardiff 1975; gillette 3-14 Glamorgan v Staffs, Stoke 1971.

NEALE, Phillip Anthony.
County: Worcestershire.
Role: Right-hand bat, right arm medium bowler.
Date and place of birth: 5 June 1954, Scunthorpe.
Height: 5' 11".   *Weight:* 11 st 4 lbs.
Parents: Geoffrey and Elsie Neale.
Wife: Christine,
Married: 26 September 1976.
Education and qualifications: Frederick Gough Grammar School, Scunthorpe, John Leggot Sixth Form College, Scunthorpe, Leeds University, BA Hons. in Russian.
Occupation outside cricket: Professional footballer, Lincoln City F.C.
County debut: 1975.   *County cap:* 1978.
Outside interests: Reading and watching television.

continued overleaf

Nickname: Phil.
Other sporting activities: Professional football, occasional game of snooker or squash; coaches two schoolboy football teams in Lincoln.
General: Played for Lincolnshire 1973-74. Uses Duncan Fearnley cricket equipment. Scored 100 runs before lunch v Warwickshire at Worcester, 1979.
Address and telephone number: c/o

Worcestershire County Cricket Club, New Road, Worcester WR2 4QQ.
Personal best: 163* Worcs v Notts, Worcester 1979; jpl 79* Worcs v Somerset, Worcester 1976; b&h 52* Worcs v Combined Universities, Worcester 1978; gillette 68 Worcs v Gloucs, Bristol 1976. Bowling f/class 1-15 Worcs v Derby, Worcester 1976; jpl 2-46 Worcs v Warwicks, Worcester 1976.

NEEDHAM, Andrew.
County: Surrey.
Role: Right-hand bat. Off-break bowler.
Date and place of birth: 23 March 1957, Calow, near Chesterfield, Derbyshire.
Height: 5' 10". *Weight:* 10 st. 7 lbs.
Parents: Thomas Robin and Peggy Needham.
Wife: Unmarried.
Education and qualifications: Ecclesbourne Grammar School, Derby, Paisley Grammar School, Watford Grammar School, six O-levels.
Family links with cricket: Father played for 20 years in Bassetlaw League.
County debut: 1979.
Outside interests: Keen soccer fan (Chesterfield), horse-racing, reading science fiction and thrillers, music.
General: Debut in Paisley Grammar School 1st XI at age 13, Captain of Watford Grammar School 1st XI 1974.
Address and telephone number: 270 Hempstead Road, Watford, Hertfordshire

WD1 3LY. Telephone: Watford 42660.
Personal best: Batting f/class 21 Surrey v Sussex, Hove 1978; jpl 18 Surrey v Lancs, The Oval 1979. Bowling f/class 3-25 Surrey v Oxford University, Oxford 1977.

NICHOLAS, Mark Charles Jefford.
County: Hampshire.
Role: Right-hand bat, right arm fast medium bowler.
Date and place of birth: 29 September 1957, London.
Education and qualifications: Bradfield College.
County debut: 1978.
Address and telephone number: c/o Hampshire County Cricket Club, Northlands Road, Southampton SO9 2TY.
Personal best: Batting f/class 105* Hants v Oxford University, Oxford 1979; jpl 33* Hants v Somerset, Taunton 1979.

OLD, Christopher Middleton.
County: Yorkshire.
Role: Left-hand bat, right arm fast medium bowler.
Date and place of birth: 22 December 1948, Middlesbrough, Yorks.
Height: 6′ 3″.   *Weight:* 14 st 7 lbs.
Parents: Christopher Middleton Old, deceased, and Phyllis Old.
Wife: Alison.
Children: Juliette Louise, 28 June 1973; Simon Christopher and Paul Edward, 5 November 1975.
Education and qualifications: Acklam Hall Secondary Grammar School, Middlesbrough.
Occupation outside cricket: Started as a bank clerk.
Family links with cricket: Father played local league cricket in Middlesbrough. Brother, Alan, played cricket for Durham, rugby union for England. On 2 February 1974, Chris played cricket in a Test v West Indies, while Alan played rugger for England v Ireland.
County debut: 1966.   *County cap:* 1969.
Benefit: 1979.
Outside interests: Gardening.
Nickname: Chilly.
Other sporting activities: Golf, rugby union, squash.
General: Joined Yorkshire originally as "a batsman who could bowl". Elected Best Young Cricketer of the Year in 1970 by the Cricket Writers' Club. One of Wisden's Cricketers of the Year 1978. Scored century in 37 minutes v Warwickshire at Birmingham in 1977, second fastest century in first class cricket. Took four wickets in five balls

England v Pakistan, Birmingham in 1978. "Hates the sunshine". Plagued by injuries: both knees were operated on in 1970 and 1971.
Address and telephone number: Bramhope; and c/o Yorkshire County Cricket Club, Headingley Cricket Ground, Leeds LS6 3BU.
Personal best: Batting Tests 65 England v Pakistan, The Oval 1974; other f/class 116 Yorkshire v India, Bradford 1974; jpl 82 Yorkshire v Somerset, Bath 1974; 82* Yorkshire v Somerset, Glastonbury 1976; b&h 72 Yorkshire v Surrey, Hove 1976; gillette 29 Yorkshire v Lancs, Leeds 1974. Bowling Tests 7–50 England v Pakistan, Edgbaston 1978; other f/class 7–20 Yorkshire v Gloucs, Middlesbrough 1969; jpl 5–33 Yorkshire v Sussex, Hove 1971; b&h 4–17 Yorkshire v Derby, Bradford 1973; gillette 4–9 Yorkshire v Durham, Middlesbrough 1978.

OLIVER, Philip Robert.
County: Warwickshire.
Role: Right-hand bat, right arm off-spin bowler.
Date and place of birth: 9 May 1956, West Bromwich.
Height: 6′ 1″.   *Weight:* 13 st 7 lbs.
Parents: Jack and Gladys Oliver.
Wife: Sue.
Married: 20 October 1979.
Education and qualifications: Burton Borough, Newport, Shropshire.
Occupation outside cricket: Works for BP

Shell Oil.
Family links with cricket: Father and brother played for Penn C.C.
County debut: 1975.
Nickname: Olly or Dude.
Other sporting activities: Golf, football, squash. Has played soccer for Telford in Southern League.
General: Played for Shropshire, 1972–74.
Address and telephone number: 52 Hordern Crescent, Brierley Hill, West Midlands. Lye 6610.

continued overleaf

Personal best: Batting f/class 83 Warwicks v Yorkshire, Edgbaston 1979; jpl 78* Warwicks v Hants, Southampton 1978; b&h 46 Warwicks v Essex, Chelmsford 1979; gillette 22 Warwicks v Notts, Edgbaston 1979. Bowling f/class 2-28 Warwicks v Sussex, Edgbaston 1978; jpl 3-36 Warwicks v Middlesex, Lord's 1977; b&h 1-12 Warwicks v Minor Counties West, Edgbaston 1978; gillette 1-46 Warwicks v Notts, Edgbaston 1979.

OLDHAM, Stephen.

County: Derby.
Role: Right-hand bat, right arm fast medium bowler.
Date and place of birth: 26 July 1948, High Green, Sheffield.
County debut: 1974.
Nickname: Esso.
Address and telephone number: c/o Yorkshire County Cricket Club, Headingley Cricket Ground, Leeds LS6 3 BU.
Personal best: Batting f/class 50 Yorkshire v Sussex, Hove 1979; jpl 38* Yorkshire v Glamorgan, Cardiff 1977; b&h 4* Yorkshire v Notts, Trent Bridge 1978; gillette 7* Yorkshire v Middlesex, Lord's 1979. Bowling f/class 5-40 Yorkshire v Surrey, The Oval 1978; jpl 4-21 Yorkshire v Notts, Scarborough 1974; b&h 5-32 Yorkshire v Minor Counties North, Scunthorpe 1975; gillette 3-45 Yorkshire v Lancs, Leeds 1974.

OLIVE, Martin.

County: Somerset.
Role: Right-hand bat, right arm medium bowler.
Date and place of birth: 18 April 1958, Watford.

Height: 5′ 10″.   *Weight:* 11 st 7 lbs.
Parents: Dan and Margaret Olive.
Wife: Catherine Anne.
Married: 15 March 1980.
Education and qualifications: Millfield School, three A-levels.

County debut: 1977.
Outside interests: Most forms of music, watching most sports.
Nickname: Palm ("i.e. Palmolive!").
Other sporting activities: Played hockey for West of England Under-21, occasional golf.
Address and telephone number: c/o Somerset County Cricket Club, County Cricket Ground, St James's St., Taunton TA1 1JT.
Personal best: Batting f/class 39 Somerset v Cambridge University, Bath 1979; jpl 2* Somerset v Glamorgan, Yeovil 1977.

ONTONG, Rodney Craig.
County: Glamorgan.
Role: Right-hand bat, right arm fast medium bowler.
Date and place of birth: 9 September 1955, Johannesburg, South Africa.
Education and qualifications: Selbourne College, East London, South Africa.
County debut: 1975.
General: Made debut in 1972-73 for Border in Currie Cup Competition. Transferred to Transvaal for 1976-77 season.
Address and telephone number: c/o Glamorgan County Cricket Club, 6 High Street, Cardiff. Telephone: Cardiff 29956.
Personal best: Batting f/class 135* Glamorgan v Warwicks, Edgbaston 1979; jpl 55 Glamorgan v Lancs, Cardiff 1979; b&h 50* Glamorgan v Gloucs, Swansea 1979; gillette 47* Glamorgan v Somerset, Cardiff 1978; 47 Glamorgan v Kent, Maidstone 1978. Bowling f/class 7-60 Border v Northern Transvaal, Pretoria 1975-76; jpl 4-31

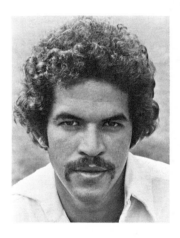

Glamorgan v Middlesex, Lord's 1979; b&h 4-28 Glamorgan v Worcs, Cardiff 1979; gillette 2-47 Glamorgan v Kent, Swansea 1979.

ORMROD, Joseph Alan.
County: Worcestershire.
Role: Right-hand bat, off-break bowler.
Date and place of birth: 22 December 1942, Ramsbottom, Lancashire.

Education and qualifications: Kirkcaldy High School.
County debut: 1962. *County cap:* 1966.
Benefit: £19,000 in 1977.

continued overleaf

General: Toured Pakistan 1966–67. Has scored 1,000 runs in a season eleven times.

Address and telephone number: c/o Worcestershire County Cricket Club, New Road, Worcester WR2 4QQ.

Personal best: Batting f/class 204* Worcs v Kent, Dartford 1973; jpl 110* Worcs v Kent, Canterbury 1975; b&h 124* Worcs v Gloucs, Worcester 1976; gillette 59 Worcs v Essex, Worcester 1975. Bowling f/class 5–27 Worcs v Gloucs, Bristol 1972; jpl 3–51 Worcs v Hants, Worcester 1972; b&h 1–29 Worcs v Warwicks, Worcester 1972.

PARKER, Paul William Giles.

County: Sussex.

Role: Right-hand bat, right arm medium bowler.

Date and place of birth: 15 January 1956, Bulawayo, Rhodesia.

Height: 5′ 10″. *Weight:* 12 st.

Parents: Anthony John and Margaret Parker.

Wife: Teresa.

Married: 26 January 1980.

Education and qualifications: Collyer's Grammar School and St. Catherine's College, Cambridge. B.A. Hons, Cantab.

Family links with cricket: "My father was a very keen cricketer; he played for Essex second team in the 1950s before emigrating to Rhodesia, where he continued to play in their strong club competition in Salisbury. Two of my brothers, Guy and Rupert, are also very keen and active cricketers." Father wrote *The Village Cricket Match*, and was sports editor of I.T.N.

County cap: 1976.

Off-season 1979–80: Playing for Sturt C.C. in Adelaide. First reserve for England in Australia tour. Touring Australia with Combined Oxford and Cambridge XI.

Outside interests: Reading and music.

Nickname: Porky. Polly.

Other sporting activities: Rugby, squash, football, golf, tennis. Played rugger at Cambridge.

General: Uses Gray Nicholls cricket bats. Was selected for Cambridge against Oxford

Rugby match in 1977 but had to withdraw through injury. Tony Greig once said of him, when 17, that he would be "the best cover fielder in the world".

Address and telephone number: c/o Sussex County Cricket Club, County Ground, Eaton Road, Hove, Sussex BN3 3AN. Telephone Brighton 732161.

Personal best: Batting f/class 215 Cambridge University v Essex, Cambridge 1976; jpl 57 Sussex v Gloucs, Hove 1979; b&h 36* Combined Universities v Sussex, Cambridge 1976; gillette 69 Sussex v Lancs, Hove 1978. Bowling f/class 2–23 Cambridge University v Essex, Cambridge 1978; jpl 1–12 Sussex v Northants, Hove 1979.

PARSONS, Gordon James.

County: Leicestershire.
Role: Left-hand bat, right arm medium bowler.
Date and place of birth: 17 October 1959, Slough, Berkshire.
Height: 6' 1". *Weight:* 12 st 8 lbs.
Parents: David and Evelyn Parsons.
Wife: Unmarried.
Education and qualifications: Woodfield County Secondary School, Slough, five O-levels.
Occupation outside cricket: Clerk at J. L. Bennett, Ratby, Leicester.
County debut: 1978.
Off-season 1979–80: Touring Australasia with Derrick Robins Under-23 XI.
Other sporting activities: Football.
General: Played for Leicester 2nd XI since 1976 and also for Buckinghamshire in 1977.
Address and telephone number: Flat 7, 15 Park Hill Drive, Aylestone, Leicester LE2 8AD.

Personal best: Batting f/class 17 Leics v Worcs, Leicester 1979; jpl 1* Leics v Lancs, Old Trafford 1979. Bowling f/class 4–43 Leics v Oxford University, Oxford 1979.

PARTRIDGE, Martin David.

County: Gloucestershire.
Role: Left-hand bat, right arm medium bowler.
Date and place of birth: 25 October 1954, Birdlip.
Weight: 13 st 5 lbs.
Parents: Cyril Martin and Mary Elizabeth Partridge.
Wife: Unmarried.
Education and qualifications: Birdlip Primary, Marling School, Stroud, Bradford University. B. Tech Civil and Structural Engineering, 2nd class, 1st div.
Occupation outside cricket: Trafalgar House Engineering Services (civil engineers).
Family links with cricket: Grandfather, father, six uncles, five cousins, a brother, have all played for Birdlip village team. Brother, John, plays for Gloucestershire Young Cricketers and County Schools Under-19. The Partridge family have twice put out full teams, one in 1948, one in 1975.
County debut: 1976.
Outside interests: Driving and gardening, "I enjoy walking alone in deep countryside."
Nickname: Fez (derivation: Partridge-Pheasant-Pheas-Fez.)
Other sporting activities: Particularly table tennis: football, squash and golf.
General: "I enjoy civil engineering very

much. I also enjoy country life and have set my mind on playing for my own county cricket team ever since I was five years old, so I have now achieved part of my ambition."
Address and telephone number: Cotswold Cottage, Birdlip, near Gloucester. Telephone: Whitcombe 2318.
Personal best: Batting f/class 90 Gloucs v Notts, Trent Bridge 1979; jpl 33 Gloucs v Warwicks, Moreton-in-Marsh 1979; b&h 27

continued overleaf

Gloucs v Warwicks, Bristol 1978; gillette 9 Gloucs v Hants, Bristol 1979. Bowling f/class 5-29 Gloucs v Worcs, Worcester 1979; jpl

5-47 Gloucs v Kent, Cheltenham 1977; b&h 2-27 Gloucs v Middlesex, Bristol 1977; gillette 1-60 Gloucs v Hants, Bristol 1979.

MIR, Parvez Jamil.

County: Glamorgan.
Role: Right-hand bat, right arm fast medium bowler.
Date and place of birth: 24 September 1953, Dacca, Bangladesh.
County debut: 1979.

General: Played for Pakistan in 1975 Prudential Cup. Played one match for Glamorgan in 1979 v India.
Address and telephone number: c/o Glamorgan County Cricket Club, 6 High Street, Cardiff. Telephone: Cardiff 29956.

PATEL, Dipak Narshi.

County: Worcestershire.
Role: Right-hand bat, off-break bowler.
Date and place of birth: 25 October 1958, Nairobi, Kenya.
Height: 5' 11½". *Weight:* 10 st.
Parents: Narshibhai and Laxmiben Patel.
Wife: Unmarried.
Education and qualifications: George Salter Comprehensive School, West Bromwich, West Midlands.
Occupation outside cricket: Sales assistant, Oakfield Tile Co. Ltd., Worcs.
Family links with cricket: Three uncles played for Kenya XI.
County debut: 1976.
Off-season 1979-80: Playing in Australia on Whitbread Scholarship. Touring Australia with Derrick Robins Under-23 XI.
Outside interests: Indian music, football, art.
Nickname: Dipstick or Dip.
Other sporting activities: Golf, badminton.
General: Has lived in UK since 1967. Shared in sixth wicket partnership record for county, 227 with E. J. O. Hemsley, v Oxford University at Oxford, 1976. Discovered by Basil D'Oliveira.
Address and telephone number: c/o Worcestershire County Cricket Club, New

Road, Worcester WR2 4QQ. Telephone: 0905-422694.
Personal best: Batting f/class 118* Worcs v Sri Lanka, Worcester 1979; jpl 40 Worcs v Gloucs, Worcester 1979; b&h 39 Worcs v Glamorgan, Cardiff 1979; gillette 3 Worcs v Derby, Worcester 1979. Bowling f/class 5-22 Worcs V Sussex, Eastbourne 1978; jpl 3-22 Worcs v Gloucs, Moreton-in-Marsh 1978; b&h 1-28 Worcs v Surrey, Worcester 1979.

PAULINE, Duncan Brian.

County: Surrey.
Role: Right-hand opening bat.
Date and place of birth: 15 December 1960. Aberdeen.

Height: 5' 11". *Weight:* 10 st 7 lbs.
Parents: Brian and Vivienne Pauline.
Education and qualifications: Ashley Road School, Aberdeen. Bishop Fox, East Molesey.

114

Family links with cricket: Father and uncle both played in Aberdeen.
County debut: 1979.
Other sporting activities: Football, Golf, Table-tennis.
General: Played for Surrey Schools under-12 and under-15. Played for South-East England under-15. England under-19 v West Indies and v Australia. Young England XI in Australia, 1978. Surrey C.C.C. Far East Tour, 1979. "Opening bat for one of England's oldest clubs, East Molesey, 1730".
Address and telephone number: 28 Merton Way, East Molesey, Surrey. Telephone: 01-979-3149.

PERRY, Neil James.

County: Glamorgan.
Role: Slow left arm bowler.
Date and place of birth: 27 May 1958, Sutton, Surrey.
Height: 6' 0". *Weight:* 11 st 7 lbs.
Parents: Michael and Anne Perry.
Wife: Unmarried.
Education and qualifications: Secondary.
Occupation outside cricket: Lorry driver.
County debut: 1979.
Outside interests: Playing all forms of sport, particularly football, watching Chelsea F.C., motor-cycle racing, hot-rod racing, squash, badminton.
Nickname: Ziggy.
Address and telephone number: c/o Glamorgan County Cricket Club.
Personal best: Batting f/class 5* Glamorgan v India, Swansea 1979. Bowling f/class 3-51 Glamorgan v India, Swansea 1979.

PERRYMAN, Stephen Peter.

County: Warwickshire.
Role: Right-hand bat, right arm medium bowler.
Date and place of birth: 22 October 1955, Yardley, Birmingham.
Height: 5' 10". *Weight:* 12 st.
Parents: James Perryman, deceased, and Mary Winifred Perryman.
Wife: Unmarried.
Education and qualifications: Greet Primary School: Sheldon Heath Comprehensive.

Occupation outside cricket: Cricket coach.
County debut: 1974. *County cap:* 1977.
Off-season 1979-80: Coaching at Warwickshire indoor school.
Outside interests: Horse-racing, football, golf, rugby, squash.
Nickname: Art.
General: Voted Player of the Year by Warwickshire members 1979.
Address and telephone number: 64 Geraldine

continued overleaf

Road, Yardley Birmingham. Telephone: 021-706-8725.

Personal best: Batting f/class 43 Warwicks v Somerset, Edgbaston 1977; jpl 17* Warwicks v Worcs, Edgbaston 1975; b&h 18 Warwicks v Essex, Chelmsford 1979; gillette 4* Warwicks v Middlesex, Edgbaston 1975. Bowling f/class 7-49 Warwicks v Hants, Bournemouth 1978; jpl 4-19 Warwicks v Surrey, The Oval 1975; b&h 4-17 Warwicks v Minor Counties West, Edgbaston 1978; gillette 3-35 Warwicks v Middlesex, Lord's 1977.

PHILLIP, Norbert.

County: Essex.

Role: Right-hand bat, right arm fast medium bowler.

Date and place of birth: 12 June 1948, Bioche, Dominica, West Indies.

Height: 6′ 0″.   *Weight:* 12 st 4 lbs.

Parents: Philbert and Irene Phillip.

Wife: Elizabeth.

Married: 31 October 1975.

Children: Twin boys, Frank and Franklyn.

Education and qualifications: Dominica Grammar School, National Cricketers' Association coaching certificate.

Occupation outside cricket: Sports officer.

County debut: 1978.   *County cap:* 1978.

Outside interests: Reading and listening to music, "specially Reggae, Soul and Calypso".

Nickname: Nobbie in England and Zidi in Dominica.

Other sporting activities: Football.

General: "I acted as Assistant-Secretary of the Dominica Cricket Association, and Chairman of the Youth Sub-Committee of the Dominica Cricket Association. I am involved in cricket coaching as a Sports Officer to the Government of Dominica." Drinks sweet Martini.

Address and telephone number: In Dominica: 4 Bowers Lane, Goodwill, Dominica, West Indies. Telephone: 4341. In England, c/o Essex County Cricket Club,

New Writtle Street, Chelmsford, Essex. Telephone: Chelmsford 354533.

Personal best: Batting Tests 47 West Indies v India, Calcutta 1978-79; other f/class 134 Essex v Gloucs, Gloucester 1978; jpl 17* Essex v Warwicks, Colchester 1978; b&h 14 Essex v Surrey, The Oval 1979; gillette 24* Essex v Leics, Leicester 1978. Bowling Tests 4-48 West Indies v India, Madras 1978-79; other f/class 6-33 Essex v Pakistan, Chelmsford 1978; jpl 4-23 Essex v Kent, Chelmsford 1979; b&h 3-42 Essex v Surrey, Lord's 1979; gillette 2-35 Essex v Leics, Leicester 1978.

PHILLIPSON, Christopher Paul.
County: Sussex.
Role: Right-hand bat, Right-arm medium bowler.
Date and place of birth: 10 February 1952, Urindaban, India.
Height: 6' 2". *Weight:* 13 st 7 lbs.
Parents: Rev. Christopher Quentin & Muriel Regina Phillipson.
Wife: Adell,
Married: 24 March 1979
Education and qualifications: Prebindal School, Chichester. Ardingley College. Loughborough College of Education. Teaching Certificate in P.E. and Geography.
Occupation outside cricket: Coaching. "No other full-time jobs".
Family links with cricket: "My wife's mother's family (Dell) achieved fame in the Eastern Cape in 1908 when they formed a cricket team in Bathurst made up solely of their own family, and played as such for several years."
County debut: 1970.
Nickname: Phillipo.
Other sporting activities: Had a Southern Schools trial at soccer, 1969.
Address and telephone number: Flat 2, 255 Dyke Road, Hove, Sussex. Telephone: Brighton 500426.

Personal best: Batting f/class 70 Sussex v Oxford University, Oxford 1978; jpl 71 Sussex v Lancs, Hastings 1979; b&h 38* Sussex v Essex, Chelmsford 1979; gillette 34 Sussex v Lancs, Hove 1978. Bowling 6–56 Sussex v Notts, Hove 1972; jpl 4–25 Sussex v Middlesex, Eastbourne 1972; b&h 5–32 Sussex v Combined Universities, Oxford 1977; gillette 2–14 Sussex v Lancs, Hove 1978.

PIGOTT, Anthony Charles Shackleton.
County: Sussex.
Role: Right-hand bat, right arm fast medium bowler.
Date and place of birth: 4 June 1958, London.
Height: 6' 1". *Weight:* 12 st 4 lbs.
Parents: Tom and Juliet Pigott.
Wife: Unmarried.
Education and qualifications: Harrow School.
Occupation outside cricket: Groundsman and sportsmaster at Holmewood House Prep School.
Family links with cricket: Father played for Harrow 1st XI in 1948, also keen club cricketer.
County debut: 1978.
Off-season 1979–80: Playing cricket in Sydney, Australia, on Whitbread Scholarship. Touring Australia with Derrick Robins Under-23 XI.
Outside interests: Listening to Capital Radio, playing pop records, reading sports papers,

watching Brighton play football, drinking in pubs—"specially The Greyhound at Langton Green, Tunbridge Wells."
Nickname: Lester.

continued overleaf

117

Other sporting activities: Rugger, hockey, squash, raquets, soccer.
General: Public School Raquets Champion 1975. Played cricket cricket for Waverley Cricket Club, Sydney, Australia, 1976–77 and 1977–78.
Address and telephone number: Old Birchton Farm, Groombridge, Sussex. Telephone: Groombridge 373.

PILLING. Harry.
County: Lancashire.
Role: Right-hand bat, off-break bowler.
Date and place of birth: 23 February 1943, Ashton-under-Lyme.
Height: 5′ 3″.
Education: Ashton Technical School.
County debut: 1962.   *County cap:* 1965.
Testimonial: £9,500 in 1974.
General: Scored two centuries in one match, 119 not out and 104 not out, v Warwickshire at Manchester in 1970. Smallest player in first-class cricket. Coach in Tasmania 1978/79.
Address and telephone number: c/o Lancashire County Cricket Club, Old Trafford, Manchester M16 OPX.
Personal best: Batting f/class 149* Lancs v Glamorgan, Liverpool 1976; jpl 85 Lancs v Sussex, Hove 1970; b&h 109* Lancs v Glamorgan, Old Trafford 1973; gillette 90 Lancs v Middlesex, Lord's 1973. Bowling

Personal best: Batting f/class 55 Sussex v Yorkshire, Hove 1979; jpl 49 Sussex v Warwicks, Hove 1979; b&h 2 Sussex v Middlesex, Hove 1978. gillette 30 Sussex v Northants, Hove 1978. Bowling f/class 4–40 Sussex v Cambridge University, Cambridge 1979; jpl 2–8 Sussex v Middlesex, Hove 1978; b&h 1–19 Sussex v Middlesex, Hove 1978; gillette 3–43 Sussex v Notts, Hove 1979.

f/class 1–42 Lancs v Somerset, Old Trafford 1971; jpl 1–0 Lancs v Leics, Old Trafford 1970.

POCOCK, Nicholas Edward Julian.
County: Hampshire.
Role: Right-hand bat, left-arm medium bowler.
Date and place of birth: 15 December 1951, Maracaibo, Venezuela.
Height: 6′ 1″.   *Weight:* 13 st 3 lbs.
Parents: Carmichael Charles Peter Pocock, deceased, and Nina Alice Hilary Pocock.
Wife: Gina Mary,
Married: 11 September 1976.
Children: Emma Mary, 10 July 1979.
Education and qualifications: Sandroyd School, near Salisbury, Wiltshire; Shrewsbury School. Partly qualified insurance exams.
Occupation outside cricket: Holmwoods & Back & Manson Ltd, insurance brokers, working for Colin Ingleby-Mackenzie.
Family links with cricket: Father and uncle played for Rossall School 1st XI. Uncle,

Duncan Pocock, played for the Army after the war.
County debut: 1976.

Outside interests: Theatre, light music and family.
Nickname: Pokers.
Other sporting activities: Squash, tennis and Eton fives.
General: Believes that "points system should be revised to reward risk-taking by a captain in pursuit of victory, i.e. too many tame draws where equally balanced sides oppose each other. It would help to bring back disenchanted three-day spectators." Ap-

POCOCK, Patrick Ian.
County: Surrey.
Role: Right-hand bat, off-break bowler.
Date and place of birth: 24 September 1946, Bangor, Caernarvonshire.
Height: 6' 1½". *Weight:* 13 st.
Parents: James Reginald and Cecelia Frances Pocock
Wife: Diane,
Married: 8 March 1966.
Children: Samantha, 8 March 1971, Toby, 18 May 1973.
Education and qualifications: Merton C. of E. Secondary Boys, Wimbledon Technical School, M.C.C. Advanced Coach.
Occupation outside cricket: Various posts in sales and marketing. Has own company Pat Pocock Sports Promotions Ltd.
Family links with cricket: Brothers' Nigel and Tim, are very active members of Merton Cricket Club, London S.W. 20 "W. G. Grace's mother was a Pocock & a relative of mine".
County debut: 1964. *County cap:* 1967.
Benefit: £18,500 in 1977.
Outside interests: "Holidays".
Nicknames: Percy.
Other sporting activities: Squash and golf.
General: Played for Northern Transvaal in 1971–72 Currie Cup Competition. Toured Pakistan in 1966–67; West Indies 1967–68 and 1973–74; Sri Lanka and Pakistan 1968–69; India, Pakistan and Sri Lanka 1972–73. Took 112 wickets at an average of 18.22 in 1967. Took four wickets in four balls, five in six, six in nine and seven in eleven v Sussex at Eastbourne in 1972. Organised the Chubb World Double Wicket

PONT, Keith Rupert.
County: Essex.
Role: Right-hand bat, right arm medium bowler.

pointed Hants C.C.C. Captain for 1980.
Address and telephone number: 12 Melrose Gardens, London W6.
Personal best: Batting f/class 143* Hants v Middlesex, Portsmouth 1979; jpl 53* Hants v Northants, Northampton 1978; b&h 3 Hants v Warwicks, Bournemouth 1979; 3 Hants v Lancs, Old Trafford 1979. Bowling gillette 33 Hants v Gloucs, Bristol 1979. Bowling f/class 1–4 Hants v Sussex, Bournemouth 1979.

Championship at Wembley in April 1979, the first time a cricket competition had been televised indoors.
Address and telephone number: c/o Surrey County Cricket Club, Kennington Oval, London SE11 5SS.
Personal best: Batting Tests 33 England v Pakistan, Hyderabad, 1972–73, other f/class 75* Surrey v Notts, The Oval 1968; jpl 22 Surrey v Notts, Nottingham 1971; b&h 19 Surrey v Middlesex, The Oval 1972; gillette 14 Surrey v Essex, Colchester 1978. Bowling Tests 6–79 England v Australia, Old Trafford 1968; other f/class 9–57 Surrey v Glamorgan, Cardiff 1979; jpl 4–27 Surrey v Essex, Chelmsford 1974; b&h 4–11 Surrey v Yorkshire, Barnsley 1978; gillette 3–34 Surrey v Somerset, The Oval 1975.

Date and place of birth: 16 January 1953, Wanstead.
Height: 6' 2". *Weight:* 13 st.

continued overleaf

Wife: Veronica.
Education and qualifications: Secondary school education.
Occupation outside cricket: Has been furniture representative, insurance clerk and in road haulage management.
Family links with cricket: Younger brother, Ian, played for England Under-19.
County debut: 1970. *County cap:* 1976.
Outside interests: Music, opera.
Nickname: Monty, Plod.
Other sporting activities: Hockey golf.
General: Played and coached in Johanesburg in 1979-80 off-season. Strong comic sense, e.g. has been known to field outside ground when Ray East comes on to bowl. Other counties have expressed interest in him.
Address and telephone number: c/o Essex County Cricket Club, County Ground, New Writtle Street, Chelmsford CM2 ORW.
Personal best: Batting f/class 113 Essex v Warwicks, Edgbaston 1973; jpl 52 Essex v Glamorgan, Chelmsford 1979; b&h 60* Essex v Notts, Ilford 1976; gillette 39 Essex v Somerset, Taunton 1978. Bowling f/class

4-100 Essex v Middlesex, Southend 1977; jpl 4-24 Essex v Derby, Chelmsford 1979; b&h 2-20 Essex v Northants, Horton 1976; gillette 2-18 Essex v Durham, Chester-le-Street 1973.

POPPLEWELL, Nigel Francis Mark.
County: Somerset.
Role: Right-hand bat. Right-arm medium bowler.
Date and place of birth: 8 August 1957, Farnborough, Kent.
Height: 5' 10" *Weight:* 13 st.
Parents: Oliver and Margaret Popplewell.
Wife: Unmarried.
Education and qualifications: Radley College, Selwyn College, Cambridge; BA Hons 2:1 in Natural Science.
Occupation outside cricket: Temporary jobs during university vacations.
Family links with cricket: Father played for Cambridge University for three years, 1949-51. Younger brother has played for Cambridge 2nd XI.
County debut: 1979.
Off-season 1979-80: Touring Australia with Combined Oxford & Cambridge XI.
Outside interests: "Very limited since I've spent most of my life working or playing one sport or another, but include reading, especially English social history in the twentieth century, sailing, throwing weights around and running miles before breakfast".
Nickname: "Any mutations of Pops, Poppers, etc."

Other sporting activities: Rugby, squash, boxing, hockey. Played rugby and squash for College. Boxed in a single bout for Cambridge at Middleweight. "Athletics in a very amateur and incompetent manner."
Address and telephone number: Telephone: 024-020356.
Personal best: Batting f/class 92 Cambridge University v Lancs, Cambridge 1979; jpl 8 Somerset v Middlesex, Lord's 1979; b&h 22*

Combined Universities v Sussex, Oxford 1979. Bowling f/class 3-18 Cambridge University v Somerset, Bath 1979; jpl 1-7

Somerset v Middlesex, Lord's 1979; b&h 2-31 Combined Universities v Hants, Cambridge 1978.

PRIDGEON, Alan Paul.
County: Worcestershire.
Role: Right-hand bat, right arm medium bowler.
Date and place of birth: 22 February 1954, Wall Heath, Staffordshire.
Height: 6' 3". *Weight:* 12 st 12 lbs.
Parents: Albert Ernest and Sybil Ruby Pridgeon.
Wife: Jane.
Married: 7 October 1978.
Education and qualifications: Summerhill Secondary Modern, Kingswinford, West Midlands.
Occupation outside cricket: Semi-professional footballer, F.A. coach (not full badge). Salesman. Has also worked for Manpower Commission.
County debut: 1972.
Outside interests: Horse-racing, gardening, taking dog for walks.
Nickname: Pridge.
Other sporting activities: Semi-professional footballer for Ledbury Town F.C., West Midlands League. Golf.
Address and telephone number: c/o Worcestershire County Cricket Club, New Road, Worcester WR2 4QQ.

Personal best: Batting f/class 32 Worcs v Yorkshire, Middlesbrough 1978; jpl 16* Worcs v Essex, Dudley 1976; b&h 10 Worcs v Leics, Leicester 1976; gillette 1 Worcs v Gloucs, Bristol 1976. Bowling f/class 7-35 Worcs v Oxford University, Oxford 1976; jpl 6-26 Worcs v Surrey, Worcester 1978; b&h 3-57 Worcs v Warwicks, Edgbaston 1976.

PROCTER, Michael John.
County: Gloucestershire.
Role: Right-hand bat, right arm fast and off-break bowler.
Date and place of birth: 15 September 1946, Durban, South Africa.
Education and qualifications: Hilton College, Natal.
County debut: 1965. *County cap:* 1968.
Benefit: £15,500 in 1976.
Nickname: Prock.
Family links with cricket: Father and brother played Currie Cup in S. Africa.
Other sporting activities: Played rugger in South Africa.
General: County Captain 1977 onwards. Vice-Captain of South African schools team to England 1963. Having made debut for Gloucestershire in 1965 in one match v South Africans, returned home to make debut for Natal in 1965-66 Currie Cup Competition.

Rejoined Gloucestershire staff in 1968. Was one of Wisden's Cricketers of the Year in
continued overleaf

1969. Played for Western Province in 1969–70 Currie Cup Competition, Rhodesia in 1970–71 and Natal in 1976–77. Played in five matches for Rest of the World v England in 1970. Took 109 wickets at an average of 18.04 in 1977. Scored six centuries in six consecutive innings for Rhodesia, 1970–71, to equal world record. Scored two centuries in match, 114 and 131, for Rhodesia v International Wanderers at Salisbury in 1972–73. Took a hat trick and scored century for Gloucestershire v Essex at Southend in 1977. Had match double of 100 runs and ten wickets (108 and 13 for 73) v. Worcestershire at Cheltenham in 1977. Spent off-season 1979–80 captaining Natal. Bowled first ball in W.S.C. to Rick McCosker, at Melbourne.

Address and telephone number: c/o Gloucestershire County Cricket Club, Neville Road, Bristol BS7 9EJ.
Personal best: Batting Tests 48 South Africa v Australia, Cape Town 1969–70; other f/class 254 Rhodesia v Northern Province, Salisbury 1970–71; jpl 109 Gloucs v Warwicks, Cheltenham 1972; b&h 154* Gloucs v Somerset, Taunton 1972; gillette 107 Gloucs v Sussex, Hove 1971. Bowling Tests 6–73 South Africa v Australia, Port Elizabeth 1969–70; other f/class 9–71 Rhodesia v Transvaal, Bulawayo 1972–73; jpl 5–8 Gloucs v Middlesex, Gloucester 1977; b&h 6–13 Gloucs v Hants, Southampton 1977; gillette 4–21 Gloucs v Yorkshire, Leeds 1976.

RADLEY, Clive Thornton.
County: Middlesex.
Role: Right-hand bat, leg break bowler.
Date and place of birth: 13 May 1944, Hertford.
Height: 5′ 10″. *Weight:* 12 st.
Parents: Laura Radley.
Wife: Linda.
Married: 27 February 1973.
Children: Louise, 18 September 1978.
Education and qualifications: King Edward VI Grammar School, Norwich.
Occupation outside cricket: Has coached in South Africa and Australia.
Family links with cricket: Father played club cricket.
County debut: 1964. *County cap:* 1967.
Benefit: £26,000 in 1977.
Nickname: Grizzly.
Other sporting activities: Squash, golf.
General: Toured Pakistan and New Zealand 1977–78, Australia 1978–79. Shared in sixth wicket partnership record for county, 227 with Fred Titmus v South Africans at Lord's in 1965. Played for Norfolk under W. J. Edrich, who eased his way to Middlesex. First fielder to hold 50 catches in John Player League.
Address and telephone number: c/o Middlesex County Cricket Club, Lord's Cricket Ground, St John's Wood Road,

London NW8 8QN.
Personal best: Batting Tests 158 England v New Zealand, Auckland 1977–78; other f/class 171 Middlesex v Cambridge University, Cambridge 1976; jpl 133* Middlesex v Glamorgan, Lord's 1969; b&h 121* Middlesex v Minor Counties East, Lord's 1976; gillette 105* Middlesex v Worcs, Worcester 1975. Bowling f/class 1–7 Middlesex v Surrey, The Oval 1964; 1–7 Middlesex v Leics, Lord's 1966.

RAMAGE, Alan.
County: Yorkshire.
Role: Left-hand bat; right-arm fast medium

bowler.
Date and place of birth: 29 November 1957, Guisborough, Yorkshire.

Height: 6′ 2″. *Weight:* 13 st 8 lbs.
Parents: James and Anne Ramage.
Wife: Alison.
Married 1 February 1978.
Education and qualifications: Warsett Comprehensive, Brotton.
Occupation outside cricket: Professional footballer.
Family links with cricket: Father played local league cricket. "My father coached me to become what I am now."
County debut: 1979.
Outside interests: Driving, music.
Nickname: Rod.
Other sporting activities: Football, snooker.

RANDALL, Derek William.
County: Nottinghamshire.
Role: Right-hand bat, right arm medium bowler.
Date and place of birth: 24 February 1951, Retford, Nottinghamshire.
Height: 5′ 8½″. *Weight:* 10 st 7 lbs.
Parents: Frederick and Mavis Randall.
Wife: Elizabeth.
Married: September 1973.
Children: Simon, June 1977.
Education and qualifications: Sir Frederick Milner Secondary Modern School, Retford.
Occupation outside cricket: Contracted to Messrs. Gunn & Moore, Nottingham.
Family links with cricket: Father played local cricket, "tried to bowl fast off a long run and off the wrong foot too!"
County debut: 1972. *County cap:* 1973.
Off-season 1979–80: Touring Australi with England. Played for North Perth before joining tour party.
Outside interests: Listening to varied selection of tapes. Family man.
Nickname: Arkle.
Other sporting activities: Football, squash.
General: Played in one John Player League match in 1971 for Notts. Before joining Notts staff, played for Retford Cricket Club in the Bassetlaw League, and helped in Championship win of 1964–68. "Very nervous character". Sings and talks to himself when batting. Earned praise from England tour

RATCLIFFE, Robert Malcolm.
County: Lancashire.
Role: Right-hand bat, right arm medium bowler.

Currently playing with Middlesbrough F.C. at centre-half.
Address and telephone number: c/o Yorkshire County Cricket Club, Headingley Cricket Ground, Leeds LS6 3BN.
Personal best: Batting f/class 19 Yorkshire v Cambridge University, Cambridge 1979; jpl 8* Yorkshire v Northants, Milton Keynes 1977; 8* Yorkshire v Hants, Leeds, 1979; b&h 17* Yorkshire v Combined Universities, Barnsley 1976. Bowling f/class 3–24 Yorkshire v Cambridge University, Cambridge 1979; jpl 3–51 Yorkshire v Kent, Canterbury 1977.

manager Alec Bedser for walking after an appeal for caught at the wicket v Queensland in December 1979, although appeal turned down by umpire.
Address and telephone number: c/o Nottinghamshire County Cricket Club, Trent Bridge, Nottingham.
Personal best: Batting Tests 174 England v Australia, Melbourne 1976–77; other f/class 209 Notts v Middlesex, Trent Bridge 1979; jpl 107* Notts v Middlesex, Lord's 1976; b&h 103* Notts v Minor Counties North, Trent Bridge 1979; gillette 75 Notts v Sussex, Hove 1979.

Date and place of birth: 29 October 1951, Accrington.
Height: 6′ 0″. *Weight:* 13 st 2 lbs.

continued overleaf

Parents: Jim and Mavis Ratcliffe.
Wife: Susan.
Married: 15 September 1973.
Children: Lee-James, 18 November 1976.
Education and qualifications: Hollins County. Advanced cricket coach.
Occupation outside cricket: School cricket coach, Queen Elizabeth Grammar School, Blackburn. Has own private coaching school.
County debut: 1972. *County cap:* 1976.
Outside interests: Music.
Nickname: Ratters.
Other sporting activities: Football, golf, running.
Address and telephone number: c/o Lancashire County Cricket Club, Old Trafford, Manchester M16 0PX.
Personal best: Batting f/class 101* Lancs v Warwicks, Old Trafford 1979; jpl 28 Lancs v Essex, Old Trafford 1976; b&h 14 Lancs v Derby, Southport 1976; gillette 17 Lancs v Cornwall, Truro 1977. Bowling f/class 7–58 Lancs v Hants, Bournemouth 1978; jpl 4–19

Lancs v Somerset, Old Trafford 1975; b&h 3–33 Lancs v Warwicks, Edgbaston 1976; gillette 4–25 Lancs v Hants, Old Trafford 1975.

REIDY, Bernard Wilfrid.
County: Lancashire.
Role: Left-hand bat, left arm medium bowler.
Date and place of birth: 18 September 1953, Bramley Meade, Whalley, Lancashire.
Height: 5′ 11½″. *Weight:* 13 st.
Parents: Wilfrid and Ann Reidy.
Wife: Unmarried.
Education and qualifications: St Mary's College, Blackburn, Lancashire.
Occupation outside cricket: Heating engineer.
Family links with cricket: Brother, David, has played in one of the leagues in Lancashire and is also a cricket coach.
County debut: 1973.
Off-season 1979–80: Playing in Tasmania for South Launceston C.C.
Outside interests: Reading.
Other sporting activities: Squash, running, swimming, snooker, badminton, football.
General: Toured West Indies with England Young Cricketers in 1972. Played for Lancashire 2nd XI since 1971.
Address and telephone number: 3 Cleveleys Road, Accrington, Lancashire BB5 5ET. Telephone: Accrington 33719.
Personal best: Batting f/class 131* Lancs v

Derby, Chesterfield 1979; jpl 58* Lancs v Somerset, Old Trafford 1975; 58 Lancs v Worcs, Old Trafford 1979; b&h 65* Lancs v Leics, Leicester 1979; gillette 18 Lancs v Gloucs, Old Trafford 1975. Bowling f/class 5–61 Lancs v Worcs, Worcester 1979; jpl 3–33 Lancs v Surrey, Old Trafford 1978; gillette 2–46 Lancs v Middlesex, Old Trafford 1978.

124

RICE, Clive Edward Butler.
County: Nottinghamshire.
Role: Right-hand bat, right arm fast medium
bowler.
Date and place of birth: 23 July 1949, Johan-
nesburg, South Africa.
Height: 6' 0". *Weight:* 13 st 3 lbs.
Parents: Patrick and Angela Rice.
Wife: Susan Elizabeth.
Married: 28 February 1975.
Education and qualifications: Sandringham
Primary School, St John's College and
Damelin College, Johannesburg, Natal Uni-
versity, Pietermaritzburg.
Occupation outside cricket: Director of
family companies.
Family links with cricket: Grandfather,
Phillip Syndercombe Bower, played for
Oxford University. Brother, Richard Patrick
Butler Rice, selected for Transvaal B, but
unavailable because of university exams.
Brother, John Cromwell Rice, captain of
school first eleven.
County debut: 1975. *County cap:* 1975.
Outside interests: Reading, listening to
music, studying stockmarkets.
Nickname: Ricie.
Other sporting activities: Hockey, South
African Country Districts 1972, water-skiing,
diving, tennis, squash, golf.
General: Writes for local South African
newspapers. Endorses Stuart Surridge sports
equipment, captain of Nottinghamshire
County Cricket Club, captain Bedfordview
Cricket Club, Johannesburg. Contracted to
World Series Cricket until 1980-81 season.
Runner-up in World Series Cricket, Man of
the Series Competition 1978-79. Debut for
Transvaal 1969. Professional for Rams-

bottom in Lancashire League 1973.
Originally appointed county captain in 1978,
but was at first relieved of appointment after
signing for World Series Cricket. Re-
appointed 1979. Has scored most runs in
J.P.L. in one season: 814.
Address and telephone number: c/o
Nottinghamshire County Cricket Club, Trent
Bridge, Nottingham NG2 6AG.
Personal best: Batting f/class 246 Notts v
Sussex, Hove 1976; jpl 120* Notts v
Glamorgan, Swansea 1978; b&h 94 Notts v
Middlesex, Newark 1976; gillette 71 Notts v
Yorkshire, Bradford 1978. Bowling f/class
7-62 Transvaal v Western Province,
Johannesburg 1975-76; jpl 4-23 Notts v
Glamorgan, Trent Bridge 1975; b&h 4-9
Notts v Combined Universities, Trent Bridge
1977; gillette 3-29 Notts v Sussex, Trent
Bridge 1975.

RICE, John Michael.
County: Hampshire.
Role: Right-hand bat, right arm medium
bowler.
Date and place of birth: 23 October 1949,
Chandler's Ford, Hampshire.
Height: 6' 3". *Weight:* 13 st.
Parents: Henry John and Sheila Phyllis Fry
Rice.
Wife: Susan Ann.
Married: 31 March 1973.
Children: Matthew John, 20 January 1977;
and Daniel John, 19 February 1979.
Education and qualifications: Brockley
County Grammar School, Ladywell,

London.
Occupation outside cricket: Office clerk,
cricket coach at Crystal Palace Sports Centre,
assembly line worker with Ford Motor
Company, engraver of trophies.
Family links with cricket: Father played high
grade club cricket in London.
County debut: 1971. *County cap:* 1975.
Outside interests: Do-it-yourself carpentry,
car mechanics, walking, running, music.
Nickname: Dicey.
Other sporting activities: Football.
General: On Surrey staff 1970 but not re-
engaged. Holds record for most catches in

continued overleaf

John Player League in one season: 16 in
1978. Also, most in one J.P.L. match: 5 v
Warwicks in 1978.
Address and telephone number: c/o
Hampshire County Cricket Club, Northlands
Road, Southampton SG9 2TY.
Personal best: Batting f/class 96* Hants v
Somerset, Weston 1975; jpl 91 Hants v
Yorkshire, Leeds 1979; b&h 43 Hants v
Lancs, Southampton 1977; gillette 40 Hants v
Gloucs, Bristol 1979. Bowling f/class 7–48
Hants v Worcs, Worcester 1977; jpl 5–14
Hants v Northants, Southampton 1975; b&h
3–20 Hants v Somerset, Bournemouth 1975;
gillette 5–35 Hants v Yorkshire, Bourne-
mouth 1977.

RICHARDS, Clifton James.
County: Surrey.
Role: Right-hand bat, wicket-keeper.
Date and place of birth: 10 August 1958,
Penzance.
Height: 5′ 10″. *Weight:* 11 st 8 lbs.
Parents: Clifton and Elizabeth June
Richards.
Wife: Unmarried.
Education and qualifications: Humphry
Davy Grammar School, Penzance.
Occupation outside cricket: Trainee electrical
engineer, apprentice draughtsman.
Family links with cricket: Father a member of
Penzance C.C. and Surrey County Cricket
Club.
County debut: 1976. *County cap:* 1978.
Off-season 1979–80: Touring Australia with
Derrick Robin's Under-23 XI.
Outside interests: Reading, television,
driving.
Nickname: Jack.
Other sporting activities: Golf, squash,
rugby, soccer, snooker.
General: Toured Far East with Surrey C.C.C.
1978–79. Toured Australasia with Derrick
Robins Under-23 team, February and March
1980. Lord's Taverners/Schweppes Award

for Best Young Wicket-keeper of 1979.
Address and telephone number: 50 Parc-an-
Creet, St Ives, Cornwall. Telephone: St Ives
5131.
Personal best: Batting f/class 50 Surrey v
Notts, The Oval 1978; jpl 18* Surrey v
Gloucs, Cheltenham 1977; b&h 25* Surrey v
Derby, Derby 1979; gillette 14 Surrey v Essex,
Colchester 1978.

RICHARDS, Gwyn.
County: Glamorgan.
Role: Right-hand bat, off-break bowler.
Date and place of birth: 29 November 1951,
Maesteg.

County debut: 1971. *County cap:* 1976.
General: Formerly on M.C.C. staff. Played
for Maesteg Town in South Wales League in
1979.
Address and telephone number: c/o

Glamorgan County Cricket Club, 6 High Street, Cardiff. Telephone: Cardiff 29956.
Personal best: Batting f/class 102* Glamorgan v Yorkshire, Middlesbrough 1976; jpl 73 Glamorgan v Gloucs, Cardiff 1978; b&h 52 Glamorgan v Hants, Swansea 1975; gillette 18 Glamorgan v Surrey, Cardiff 1977; 18 Glamorgan v Kent, Swansea 1979. Bowling f/class 5–55 Glamorgan v Somerset, Taunton 1978; jpl 5–29 Glamorgan v Lancs, Swansea 1977; b&h 2–24 Glamorgan v Minor Counties West, Amersham 1977; gillette 2–17 Glamorgan v Leics, Swansea 1977.

RICHARDS, Ian Michael.
County: Northamptonshire.
Role: Left-hand bat, right-arm medium bowler.
Date and place of birth: 9 December 1957, Stockton-on-Tees, County Durham.
Height: 5′ 11″. *Weight:* 11 st.
Parents: Colin and Marion Richards.
Wife: Unmarried.
Education and qualifications: Grangefield Grammar School and Stockton Sixth Form College, five O-levels.
Occupation outside cricket: Clerk.
Family links with cricket: Father played for and captained Stockton Cricket Club in North Yorkshire and South Durham Cricket League.
County debut: 1976.
Outside interests: Travelling, listening to popular music, "especially Rolling Stones and Beatles".
Other sporting activities: Rugby, swimming, squash, most other sports.
General: Played grade cricket in New South Wales 1978–79.
Address and telephone number: c/o 5 Castleton Road, Stockton-on-Tees, Cleveland.

Personal best: Batting f/class 50 Northants v Notts, Northampton 1976; jpl 18 Northants v Worcs, Milton Keynes 1978; gillette 1* Northants v Kent, Northampton 1978. Bowling f/class 4–57 Northants v Warwicks, Edgbaston 1978; jpl 1–57 Northants v Yorkshire, Scarborough 1978; gillette 1–22 Northants v Kent, Northampton 1978.

RICHARDS, Isaac Vivien Alexander.
County: Somerset.
Role: Right-hand bat, off-break bowler.
Date and place of birth: 7 March 1952, St John's, Antigua.

Education and qualifications: Antigua Grammar School.
County debut: 1974. *County cap:* 1974.
General: Debut 1971–72 for Leeward
continued overleaf

Islands. One of Wisden's Cricketers of the Year 1977. Played for Queensland in 1976–77 Sheffield Shield Competition. Toured with West Indies to India, Sri Lanka and Pakistan 1974–75; Australia 1975–76 and 1979–80; England 1976. Has scored 1,000 runs in a season six times. Also scored 2,161 runs at an average of 65.48 in 1977. Shared in fourth wicket partnership record for Somerset of 251 with P. M. Roebuck v Surrey at Weston-super-Mare in 1977. Holds records for most sixes hit in John Player League in one season: 26 in 1977. Has written autobiography with David Foot, entitled *Viv Richards*.

Address and telephone number: c/o Somerset County Cricket Club, St James's Street, Taunton TA1 1JT.

Personal best: Batting Tests 291 West Indies v England, The Oval 1976; other f/class 241* Somerset v Gloucs, Bristol 1977; jpl 126* Somerset v Gloucs, Bristol (I.S.) 1975; b&h 85 Somerset v Glamorgan, Cardiff 1978; gillette 139* Somerset v Warwicks, Taunton 1978. Bowling Tests 2–34 West Indies v Pakistan, Port-of-Spain 1976–77; other

f/class 3–15 Somerset v Surrey, Weston 1977; jpl 3–32 Somerset v Gloucs, Bristol 1978; b&h 1–24 Somerset v Hants, Bournemouth 1975; gillette 1–40 Somerset v Glamorgan, Cardiff 1978.

ROBINSON, Paul Andrew.
County: Lancashire.
Role: Right-hand bat, right arm fast medium bowler.
Date and place of birth: 16 July 1956, Boksburgh, South Africa.
Height: 6′ 8″.
County debut: 1979.
General: Debut for Northern Transvaal 1977–78 Currie Cup Competition. Played for Cheshire 1978.
Address and telephone number: c/o Lancashire County Cricket Club, Old Trafford, Manchester M16 0PX.
Personal best: Batting f/class 25* Northern Transvaal v Griqualand West, Pretoria 1977–78; jpl 1* Lancs v Kent, Maidstone 1979. Bowling f/class 3–33 Northern Transvaal v Border, East London 1977–78; jpl 3–49 Lancs v Kent, Maidstone 1979.

ROBINSON, Robert Timothy.
County: Nottinghamshire.
Role: Right-hand bat, right arm medium bowler.
Date and place of birth: 21 November 1958, Sutton-in-Ashfield, Nottinghamshire.

Height: 6′ 0″. *Weight:* 12 st 3 lbs.
Parents: Eddy and Christine Verley Robinson.
Wife: Unmarried.
Education and qualifications: Dunstable Grammar School, High Pavement College,

Sheffield University, three A-levels, one S-level, degree in accountancy and financial management.
Family links with cricket: Father, uncle, cousin, all played local cricket.
County debut: 1978.
Outside interests: Driving, music.
Nickname: Robbo.
Other sporting activities: Golf, squash, football.
General: Played for Northants 2nd XI in 1974–75 and for Nottinghamshire 2nd XI 1977.
Address and telephone number: 103 Ribblesdale Road, Sherwood, Nottingham. Telephone: Nottingham 265215.
Personal best: Batting f/class 40 Notts v Middlesex, Trent Bridge 1979; jpl 35 Notts v Somerset, Trent Bridge 1979.

ROCK, David John.
County: Hampshire.
Role: Right-hand bat, right arm medium bowler.
Date and place of birth: 20 April 1957, Southsea, Portsmouth.
Height: 6′ 2″. *Weight:* 12 st 7 lbs.
Parents: Donald and Peggy Rock.
Wife: Unmarried.
Education and qualifications: Front Lawn Infants and Front Lawn Junior School, Leigh Park, Portsmouth Grammar School. Nine O-levels, three A-levels, English, French and German.
Occupation outside cricket: Working for Corralls Ltd (fuel merchants) as a trainee accountant.
Family links with cricket: "No first-class cricketers in the family. My grandfather and father were both very capable local cricketers and both played representative cricket at Portsmouth."
County debut: 1976.
Outside interests: "Enjoys reading the works of Thomas Hardy, listening to a wide range of music, keen visitor to discotheques, and partial to an alcoholic drink from time to time. Also enjoys a round on a pitch-and-putt course occasionally but have never played a full round of 'proper' golf."
Nickname: Jungle, or Rocky.
Other sporting activities: 1st XV Rugby at

School. Played football in FA Youth Cup for Bognor F.C. and plays regularly on Saturdays now. Likes all ball games, specially table tennis, tennis and badminton.
Address and telephone number: 4 Luard Court, Warblington, Havant, Hampshire. Telephone: Havant 477479.
Personal best: Batting f/class 114 Hants v Leics, Leicester 1977; jpl 68 Hants v Gloucs, Portsmouth 1977; b&h 49 Hants v Leics, Southampton 1979; gillette 50 Hants v Middlesex, Lord's 1977.

129

ROEBUCK, Peter Michael.
County: Somerset.
Role: Right-hand bat, leg break bowler.
Date and place of birth: 6 March 1956, Oxford, Oxfordshire.
Height: 6' 0". *Weight:* 13 st.
Parents: James and Elizabeth Roebuck.
Wife: Unmarried.
Education and qualifications: Park School, Bath. Millfield School. Cambridge University. First Class honours degree in law.
Occupation outside cricket: Taught English, Athens and Sydney.
Family links with cricket: Mother and sister both played for Oxford University Ladies. Young brother, Paul, played for E.S.C.A. Under-15.
County debut: 1974. *County cap:* 1978.
Off-season 1979–80: Playing in Perth, Australia. Touring in Australia with Combined Oxford and Cambridge XI.
Outside interests: Reading, writing, "music (of many hues)."
Nickname: Roger, Professor.
Other sporting activities: "Vague efforts at golf and tennis".
General: Played for Somerset Second XI at the age of 13. Cambridge Blue 1975, 1976, 1977. Shared in fourth wicket partnership record for county of 251 with I. V. A. Richards v Surrey (Weston-Super-Mare)

1977. Plays in spectacles.
Address and telephone number: 5 Vesty Road, Street, Somerset, Telephone: Somerset County Cricket Club, Taunton 2946.
Personal best: Batting f/class 158 Cambridge University v Oxford University, Lord's 1975; jpl 50 Somerset v Notts, Trent Bridge 1979; b&h 48 Combined Universities v Kent, Oxford 1976; gillette 57 Somerset v Essex, Taunton 1978. Bowling f/class 6–50 Cambridge University v Kent, Canterbury 1977.

ROOPE, Graham Richard James.
County: Surrey.
Role: Right-hand bat, right arm medium bowler.
Date and place of birth: 12 July 1946, Fareham, Hampshire.
Height: 6' 1". *Weight:* 12 st 10 lbs.
Parents: William and Sylvia Roope.
Wife: Susan.
Married: 21 March 1974.
Children: Charlotte Louise, 15 September 1975; Fiona Claire, 27 January 1979.
Education and qualifications: Bradfield College, Berkshire.
Occupation outside cricket: Coaching abroad, print firm representative, has worked for Selfridges sports department.
Family links with cricket: Father played for Basingstoke and North Hampshire. Greatuncle, Alfred Watson, played for Yorkshire 2nd XI.
County debut: 1964. *County cap:* 1969.

Benefit: 1980.
Outside interests: Records, watching television.

Nickname: Cyril.
Other sporting activities: Plays soccer for Kingstonians. Has played for Corinthian Casuals, Wimbledon, Hayes, Guildford, Ramsgate, Margate, Ashford, Addlestone and Slough. Plays as goalkeeper.
General: Endorses cricket equipment for Slazengers Ltd. Played for Public Schools XI v Combined Service at Lord's 1963 and 1964. Played for Berkshire 1963. Played for Griqualand West in 1973–74 Currie Cup Competition. Toured India, Pakistan and Sri Lanka 1972–73, Pakistan and New Zealand 1977–78. "Inveterate talker in the field".

Address and telephone number: c/o Surrey County Cricket Club, Kennington Oval, London SE11 5SS.
Personal best: Batting Tests 77 England v Australia, The Oval 1975; other f/class 171 Surrey v Yorkshire, The Oval 1971; jpl 120* Surrey v Worcs, Byfleet 1973; b&h 115* Surrey v Essex, Chelmsford 1973; gillette 66 Surrey v Somerset, The Oval 1975. Bowling f/class 5–14 Surrey v West Indies, The Oval 1969; jpl 4–31 Surrey v Glamorgan, The Oval 1974; b&h 3–31 Surrey v Essex, Chelmsford 1978; gillette 5–23 Surrey v Derbyshire, The Oval 1967.

ROSE, Brian Charles.
County: Somerset.
Role: Left-hand bat, left arm medium bowler.
Date and place of birth: 4 June 1950, Dartford, Kent.
Education and qualifications: Weston-Super—Mare Grammar School; Borough Road College, Isleworth.
County debut: 1969.   *County cap:* 1975.
Off-season 1979–80: Playing for Claremont-Cottesloe in West Australia.
General: Played for English schools Cricket Association at Lord's in 1968. Appointed County Captain 1978. Toured Pakistan, New Zealand 1977–78. Has scored 1,000 runs in a season five times.
Address and telephone number: c/o Somerset County Cricket Club, St. James's Street, Taunton TA1 1JT.
Personal best: Batting Tests 27 England v Pakistan, Hyderabad, 1977–78; other f/class 205 Somerset v Northants, Weston 1977; jpl 81* Somerset v Yorkshire, Scarborough

1979; b&h 68 Somerset v Gloucs, Street 1975; gillette 128 Somerset v Derby, Ilkeston 1977. Bowling f/class 3–9 Somerset v Gloucs, Taunton 1975; jpl 3–25 Somerset v Lancs, Old Trafford 1975.

ROUSE, Stephen John.
County: Warwickshire.
Role: Left-hand bat, left arm medium bowler.
Date and place of birth: 20 January 1949, Merthyr Tydfil.
Height: 6' 1½".   *Weight:* 12 st 12 lbs.
Parents: Ruth and Dennis Rouse.
Wife: Judith.
Married: 12 February 1972.
Children: James and Natasha.
Education and qualifications: Moseley C. of

E. Junior School; Moseley County Secondary.
Occupation outside cricket: Sports ground contracting groundsman. Coaching in Rhodesia.
County debut: 1970.   *County cap:* 1974.
Outside interests: Gardening, cine films, home movies, opera, likes cooking curries. "Even my wife lets me get on with it."
Nickname: Rebel.
Other sporting activities: Golf, squash,

continued overleaf

hockey, rugby, basketball, swimming, table tennis, weightlifting, karate.
General: Has suffered regularly from knee injuries.
Address and telephone number: 15 Windermere Road, Moseley, Birmingham. Telephone 021–449–3572.
Personal best: Batting f/class 93 Warwicks v Hants, Bournemouth 1976; jpl 36 Warwicks v Somerset, Weston 1978; b&h 34* Warwicks v Glamorgan, Edgbaston 1978; gillette 34 Warwicks v Middlesex, Lord's 1977. Bowling f/class 6–34 Warwicks v Leics, Leicester 1976; jpl 5–20 Warwicks v Kent, Canterbury 1976; b&h 5–21 Warwicks v Worcs, Worcester 1974; gillette 4–27 Warwicks v Sussex, Hove 1976.

ROWE, Charles James Castell.
County: Kent.
Role: Right-hand bat, off-break bowler.
Date and place of birth: 27 November 1951, Hong Kong.
Height: 5′ 9½″. *Weight:* 11 st 10 lbs.
Parents: George and Betty Rowe.
Wife: Susan.
Married: 12 March 1977.
Children: Lucy, 25 September 1977; James 5 July 1979.
Education and qualifications: Hawkhurst Court Prep School, King's School, Canterbury, four A-levels, six O-levels.
Occupation outside cricket: Worked two years for Hong Kong and Shanghai Banking Corporation in London before making cricket a career.
Family links with cricket: Father and two of father's brothers played for Manchester Grammar School. Both he and father represented Hong Kong, although at different times. Father captained Hong Kong.
County debut: 1974. *County cap:* 1977.
Outside interests: Reading, "historical novels, sci-fi novels, particularly, but read most things." Cars, cinema, travel, "I enjoy going for a drive in the country on days off." Photography and music, mainly non-classical, "but it's not easy with two young children these days."
Nickname: Charlie, Chas.
Other sporting activities: Played rugby, hockey, tennis, squash and soccer at school,

also table tennis. Plays squash in the winter for Beckenham to keep fit. Also swimming.
General: Used to be on the committee of the Stragglers of Asia Cricket Club. Married into a "sporty" family. Wife, Susie, played tennis for Kent, getting to the finals of Junior Wimbledon, being part of the Junior Wightman Cup squad. Her father, George Morgan, represented Kent at rugby and her brother, Guy Morgan, has captained Kent at squash for several years, and was at one time ranked number 18 in UK. At school used to bowl with both hands, i.e. right arm spin and left arm chinaman. Known in the dressing-room for being absent-minded.
Address and telephone number: 38 Oakwood

Avenue, Beckenham, Kent. Telephone: 01-650-0823.
Personal best: Batting f/class 147* Kent v Sussex, Canterbury 1979; jpl 78* Kent v Notts, Canterbury 1977; b&h 40 Kent v

Combined Universities, Canterbury 1977; gillette 18* Kent v Somerset, Canterbury 1978. Bowling f/class 6-46 Kent v Derby, Dover 1976; jpl 5-32 Kent v Worcester, Worcester 1976.

RUSSELL, Philip Edgar.
County: Derbyshire.
Role: Right-hand bat, right arm medium and off-break bowler.
Date and place of birth: 9 May 1944, Ilkeston.
Education and qualifications: Ilkeston Grammar School.
Occupation outside cricket: Works full-time for Derbyshire C.C.C.
County debut: 1965. *County cap:* 1975.
General: Not re-engaged after 1972 season, but re-joined County in 1974 and is now County Coach.
Address and telephone number: c/o Derbyshire County Cricket Club, Nottingham Road, Derby DE2 6DA.
Personal best: Batting f/class 72 Derby v Glamorgan, Swansea 1970; jpl 47* Derby v Glamorgan, Buxton 1975; b&h 22* Derby v Lancs, Southport 1976; gillette 27* Derby v Middlesex, Derby 1978. Bowling f/class 7-46 Derby v Yorkshire, Sheffield 1976; jpl 6-10

Derby v Northants, Buxton 1976; b&h 3-28 Derby v Kent, Lord's 1978; gillette 3-44 Derby v Somerset, Taunton 1975.

MOHAMMAD, Sadiq.
County: Gloucestershire.
Role: Left-hand bat, leg-break and googly bowler.
Date and place of birth: 3 May 1945, Junagadh.
Family links with cricket: Member of famous Mohammad family 3 of whose brothers, including Hanif and Mushtaq Mohammad, have all played for Pakistan.
County debut: 1972. *County cap:* 1973.
Off-season 1979-80: Playing for Pakistan in India.
General: Debut in Pakistan 1959-60 at age of 14yrs 9mths. Played for Northants. 2nd XI in 1967 and 1968. Played for Nelson in Lancashire League in 1968, and subsequently for Poloc in Scottish Western Union. Played for Derrick Robins XI v Oxford University in 1969, and for Essex v Jamaica XI in 1970. Played for Tasmania v M.C.C. 1974-75. Toured with Pakistan to England 1971, 1974 and 1978; Australia, New Zealand in 1972-73; Australia and West Indies 1976-77.

Scored four centuries in four consecutive innings in 1976 including two centuries in one match (163 not out and 150) v Derbyshire at Bristol.

continued overleaf

Address and telephone number: c/o Gloucestershire County Cricket Club, Neville Road, Bristol BS7 9EJ.
Personal best: Batting Tests 166 Pakistan v New Zealand, Wellington 1972–73; other f/class 184* Gloucs v New Zealand, Bristol 1973; jpl 131 Gloucs v Somerset, Bristol 1975; b&h 128 Gloucs v Minor Counties South Bristol 1974; gillette 122 Gloucs v Lancs, Old Trafford 1975. Bowling f/class 5–29 P.I.A. v Dacca, Dacca 1964–65; 5–29 Karachi B v Lahore Greens, Karachi 1970–71; jpl 3–27 Gloucs v Hants, Bristol 1972; b&h 3–20 Gloucs v Minor Counties South Bristol 1972; gillette 3–19 Gloucs v Oxfordshire, Bristol 1975.

SAINSBURY, Gary Edward.
County: Essex.
Role: Left arm medium bowler.
Date and place of birth: 17 January 1958, Wanstead, London E11.
Height: 6′ 3″. *Weight:* 12 st 9 lbs.
Parents: Gordan and Muriel Sainsbury.
Wife: Unmarried.
Education and qualifications: Beal Grammar School; Bath University; B.Sc. Hons Statistics; 11 O-levels, 3 A-levels.
Occupation outside cricket: Computer programmer.
County debut: 1979.
Outside interests: Listening to records, reading books.
Other sporting activities: Badminton, squash, football, golf, tennis, table tennis.
Address and telephone number: 50 Widecombe Gardens, Ilford, Essex.
Personal best : Bowling f/class 1–38 Essex v Northants, Northampton 1979.

NAWAZ, Malik Sarfraz.
County: Northamptonshire.
Role: Right-hand bat, right arm fast medium bowler.
Date and place of birth: 1 December 1948, Lahore, Pakistan.
Height: 6′ 3″. *Weight:* 14 st 4 lbs.
Parents: Malik Mohammad Nawaz.
Education and qualifications: Government College, Lahore; B.A. graduate.
Occupation outside cricket: Banker.
Family links with cricket: Asif Ali Malik (played university match and state matches).
County debut: 1969. (not re-engaged after 1971 season but rejoined staff in 1974).
County cap: 1975.
Outside interests: Listening to music; horse-racing; kite-flying; dancing.
Nickname: Saf.
Other sporting activities: Hockey, swimming, badminton, squash.
General: Debut 1967–68 for West Pakistan Governor's XI v Punjab University; played in 26 tests for Pakistan between 1968–69 and 1978. Toured with Pakistan to England in 1971, 1974 and 1978; Australia and New Zealand 1972–73; Australia and West Indies, 1976–77. Took 101 wickets (average of 20.30) in 1975.
Address and telephone number: c/o Northamptonshire County Cricket Club, Wantage Road, Northampton MN1 4TJ. Telephone: Northampton 32917.

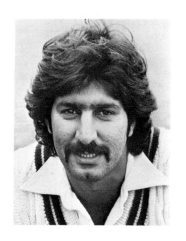

Personal best: Batting Tests 53 Pakistan v England, Leeds 1974; other f/class 86 Northants v Essex, Chelmsford 1975; jpl 43* Northants v Lancs, Old Trafford 1975; b&h 50 Northants v Kent, Northampton 1977; gillette 22 Northants v Cambridge, March 1975. Bowling Tests 9–86 Pakistan v Australia, Melbourne 1978–79; other f/class 8–27 Pakistan v Notts, Nottingham 1974; jpl 5–15 Northants v Yorkshire, Northampton 1975; b&h 3–11 Northants v Minor Counties East, Horton 1977; gillette 4–17 Northants v Herts, Northampton 1976.

SAVAGE, Richard LeQuesne.
County: Warwickshire.
Role: Right-hand bat, right arm medium and off-break bowler.
Date and place of birth: 10 December 1955, London.
Height: 5' 10". *Weight:* 11 st.
Parents: Christopher Roland and Wendy Savage.
Wife: Unmarried.
Education and qualifications: Marlborough College; Pembroke College, Oxford; B.A. Hons History.
Occupation outside cricket: Has been part-time teacher at British School in Florence.
County debut: 1976.
Outside interests: Reading novels (Tolstoy, Jane Austen), listening to music (Vivaldi, Elgar, Rolling Stones, Dire Straits), history of art, "speaking Italian ineptly."
Nickname: Fred.
General: Played for County 2nd XI since 1974. Oxford Blue 1976–77–78. Toured with Crocodiles to South Africa 1974–75. Toured with Derrick Robins XI to Canada 1976. Took three wickets in one over for Oxford v Cambridge 1976 to enforce the follow-on.
Address and telephone number: c/o Warwickshire County Cricket Club,

Edgbaston, Birmingham.
Personal best: Batting f/class 22* Oxford University v Worcs, Oxford 1977; jpl 1* Warwicks v Northants, Wellingborough 1976; b&h 9* Combined Universities v Surrey, Cambridge 1977. Bowling f/class 7-50 Warwicks v Glamorgan, Nuneaton 1977; jpl 3-19 Warwicks v Worcs, Edgbaston 1979; b&h 2-22 Combined Universities v Surrey, Cambridge 1977.

SCHEPENS, Martin.
County: Leicestershire.
Role: Right-hand bat, leg-break bowler.
Date and place of birth: 12 August 1955, Barrow-upon-Soar, Leicestershire.
Education and qualifications: Rawlins School, Quorn.
County debut: 1973, aged 17yrs 8mths.
Nickname: Skep.
General: Played for Leicestershire 2nd XI since 1971.
Address and telephone number: c/o Leicestershire County Cricket Club, Grace Road, Leicester LE2 8AD. Telephone: Leicester 832128.
Personal best: Batting f/class 57 Leics v Glamorgan, Leicester 1979; jpl 24 Leics v Warwicks, Edgbaston 1979; gillette 3 Leics v Essex, Leicester 1978.

SCOTT, Christopher John.
County: Lancashire.
Role: Left-hand bat, wicket-keeper.
Date and place of birth: 16 September 1959,

Swinton, Manchester.
Height: 6' 0". *Weight:* 11 st 12 lbs.
Parents: John and Joan Scott.

continued overleaf

Wife: Laura.
Married: 15 March 1980.
Education and qualifications: Mossfield Junior School; Eccles Grammar School, six O-levels.
Occupation outside cricket: Milkman, driver for a timber firm.
County debut: 1977.
Outside interests: Watching and playing other sports, greyhound racing, reading.
Nickname: Rock.

Other sporting activities: Had trials with Birmingham City F.C. in 1974.
General: Part-owner of a greyhound. Made debut at age of 17yrs 8mths.
Address and telephone number: 55 Brindlehurst Avenue, Astley, Leigh, Lancashire.
Personal best: Batting f/class 16 Lancs v Cambridge University, Cambridge 1979; jpl 6 Lancs v Glamorgan, Swansea.

SELVEY, Michael Walter William.
County: Middlesex.
Role: Right-hand bat, right arm fast medium bowler.
Date and place of birth: 25 April 1948, Chiswick.
Height: 6′ 2″. *Weight:* 14 st.
Parents: Walter and Edith Selvey.
Wife: Mary.
Married: 29 August 1970.
Children: Nichola, 12 May 1975.
Education and qualifications: Battersea Grammar School, Manchester University, Cambridge University. B.Sc. Certificate of Education.
Occupation outside cricket: Various teaching posts, also overseas coaching and playing.
Family links with cricket: Gandfather, Bill Hull, "was connected with Warwickshire but there has been no other competitive cricket played in the family."
County debut: 1972. *County cap:* 1973.
Outside interests: Reading, crosswords, "visiting my village local."
Nickname: Walter or Walt.
Other sporting activities: Played soccer for Cambridge but now only plays golf.
General: Debut for Surrey, 1968. Cambridge Blue 1971. Played for Orange Free State 1973-74 in Currie Cup Competition. Took 101 wickets at average of 19.09 in 1978. Wife was a model. Spent 1979-80 off-season coaching and playing in Auckland, New Zealand. Has decided opinions on cricket. Took four West Indies wickets in Test debut at Manchester 1976. Known for very

informal dress. Bearded.
Address and telephone number: Matmakers, Park Road, Sherington, Buckinghamshire.
Personal best: Batting Tests 5* England v India, Bombay 1976-77; other f/class 45 Middlesex v Essex, Colchester 1979; jpl 38* Middlesex v Essex, Chelmsford 1979; 38 Middlesex v Essex, Southend 1977; b&h 27* Middlesex v Surrey, Lord's 1973; gillette 14 Middlesex v Derby, Derby 1978. Bowling Tests 4-41 England v West Indies, Old Trafford 1976; other f/class 7-20 Middlesex v Gloucs, Gloucester 1976; 5-18 Middlesex v Glamorgan, Cardiff 1975; b&h 5-39 Middlesex v Gloucs, Lord's 1972; gillette 3-32 Middlesex v Somerset, Lord's 1977.

SHANTRY, Brian Keith.
County: Gloucestershire.
Role: Left-hand bat, left arm fast medium bowler.
Date and place of birth: 26 May 1955,

Bristol.
Height: 6′ 3″. *Weight:* 12 st.
Parents: Leonard John and Lillian Martha Shantry.
Wife: Unmarried.

Education and qualifications: Rose Green High, Whitefield Comprehensive School.
Occupation outside cricket: Senior data processing officer (computer operator).
County debut: 1978.
Outside interests: Astronomy, reading (non-fiction).
Nickname: Shants.
Other sporting activities: Fishing, football, golf.
General: First wicket in first over of first championship game v Somerset. Played for Warwickshire 2nd XI in between spells with Gloucester.
Address and telephone number: 24 Avon Park, Redfield, Bristol. Telephone Bristol 559306.
Personal best: f/class 2-63 Gloucs v Somerset, Bristol 1978; jpl 1-33 Gloucs v Warwicks, Edgbaston 1978.

SHARP, George.
County: Northamptonshire.
Role: Right-hand bat, wicket-keeper, can also bowl left arm medium.
Date and place of birth: 12 March 1950, Hartlepool, County Durham.
Height: 6′ 0″. *Weight:* 14 st.
Parents: George and Grace Sharp.
Wife: Audrey,
Married: 14 September 1974.
Education and qualifications: Elwick Road Secondary Modern, Hartlepool.
Occupation outside cricket: Sports turf adviser for Mommersteeg Int.
County debut: 1968. *County cap:* 1973.
Outside interests: Watching all sports.
Nickname: Sharpie or Blunt.
Other sporting activities: Football.
Address and telephone number: c/o Northamptonshire County Cricket Club, Wantage Road, Northampton NN1 4TJ.
Personal best: Batting f/class 85 Northants v Warwicks, Edgbaston 1976; jpl 47* Northants v Worcs, Milton Keynes 1978; 47

Northants v Sussex, Hove 1974. Bowling b&h 43 Northants v Surrey, Northampton 1979; gillette 35* Northants v Durham, Northampton 1977.

Family links with cricket: "Father played with Woodhouse in Leeds League for many years. Young brother, David (age 14), now playing local cricket."
County debut: 1976.
Off-season 1979–80: Touring Australasia with Derrick Robins Under-23 XI.
Outside interests: "Travelling, going to pub.

SHARP, Kevin.
County: Yorkshire.
Role: Left-hand bat, off-break bowler.
Date and place of birth: 6 April 1959, Leeds.
Height: 5′ 10″. *Weight:* 12 st.
Parents: Gordon and Joyce Sharp.
Education and qualifications: Abbey Grange C. of E. High School, Leeds. C.S.E. Grade 1 in Religious Education.

continued overleaf

Favourite relaxation sleeping".
Nickname: Action Man. Razor.
Other sporting activities: Golf, soccer.
General: Captain England Under-19 v West Indies Under-19 1978 at Worcester.
Address and telephone number: 136, Church Lane, Meanwood, Leeds, 6. Telephone: Leeds 758218.
Personal best: Batting f/class 91 Yorkshire v Middlesex, Bradford 1978; jpl 40 Yorkshire v Surrey, The Oval 1978; b&h 41 Yorkshire v Notts, Bradford 1979; gillette 25 Yorkshire v Middlesex, Lord's 1979.

SHEPHERD, David Robert.
County: Gloucestershire.
Role: Right-hand bat, right arm medium bowler.
Date and place of birth: 27 December 1940, Bideford, Devon.
Height: 5' 10". *Weight:* 15 st 7 lbs.
Parents: Herbert (deceased) and Doris Shepherd.
Wife: Unmarried.
Education and qualifications: Barnstaple Grammar School and St. Luke's College, Exeter.
Occupation outside cricket: Teacher.
Family links with cricket: "Brother, Bill, good cricketer with M.C.C. Young Professionals at Lord's, 1957–60. (Played for Devon.) Played against brother at Lord's, M.C.C. Young Professionals v English Schools 1959.
County debut: 1965. *County cap:* 1969.
Benefit: Jointly with J. Davey in 1978.
Off-season 1979–80: Touring West Indies, helping in family sub-post office/newsagent in home village of Instow, Devon.
Outside interests: All sports. Stamp collecting. Enjoys his beer.
Nickname: Shep.
Other sporting activities: Played local rugby for South Molton, Devon. Represented Devon Public and Grammar XV at scrum half ("honest!!!").
General: Played for Devonshire from

1959–64. Played for Minor Counties v Australians, 1964. Scored 108 in first match v Oxford University. Retired at end of 1979 season. Was burliest first-class cricketer.
Address and telephone number: 6 Linnet Close, Patchway, Bristol. Telephone Bristol 698325.
Personal best: Batting, f/class 153 Gloucs v Middlesex, Bristol 1968; jpl 100 Gloucs v Glamorgan, Cardiff 1978; b&h 81 Gloucs v Hants, Bristol 1974; gillette 72* Gloucs v Surrey, Bristol 1973. Bowling f/class 1–1 Gloucs v Northants, Gloucester 1968.

SHEPHERD, John Neil.
County: Kent.
Role: Right-hand bat, right arm medium bowler.
Date and place of birth: 9 November 1943, St Andrew, Barbados.
Height: 5′ 10½″. *Weight:* 13 st.
Parents: Ollie and Kathleen Shepherd.
Wife: Terry.
Married: 14 December 1968.
Children: Caroline, 31 May 1976; Jacqueline, 21 September 1978.
Education and qualifications: St Andrew's Boys (Primary); Alleyne School, Barbados.
Family links with cricket: Grandfather and two younger brothers all played.
County debut: 1966. *County cap:* 1967.
Benefit: 1979.
Outside interests: Music, golf.
Nickname: Shep, Walter.
Other sporting activities: Golf.
General: Debut 1964–65 in one match for Barbados. Played for Rhodesia in 1975–76 Currie Cup Competition. One of Wisden's Cricketers of the Year 1978. Five tests for the West Indies 1969 and 1970–71, but never played again after playing in Rhodesia. "One of the most cheerful characters in cricket". Introduced to Kent by Colin Cowdrey. Toured South Africa in 1973 with Derrick Robins XI, being first black cricketer to tour there.
Address and telephone number: c/o Kent County Cricket Club, St. Lawrence Ground, Canterbury CT1 3NZ.
Personal best: Batting, Tests 32 West Indies v England, Lord's 1969; other f/class 170 Kent v Northants, Folkestone 1968; jpl 94 Kent v Hants, Southampton 1978; b&h 96 Kent v

Middlesex, Lord's 1975; gillette 101 Kent v Middlesex, Canterbury 1977. Bowling, Tests 5–104 West Indies v England, Old Trafford 1969; other f/class 8–83 Kent v Lancs, Tunbridge Wells 1977, jpl 4–17 Kent v Middlesex, Lord's 1978; b&h 4–25 Kent v Derby, Lord's 1978; gillette 4–23 Kent v Essex, Leyton 1972.
Personal best: Batting, Tests 32 West Indies v England, Lord's 1969; other f/class 170 Kent v Northants, Folkestone 1968; jpl 94 Kent v Hants, Southampton 1978; b&h 96 Kent v Middlesex, Lord's 1975; gillette 101 Kent v Middlesex, Canterbury 1977. Bowling Tests 5–104 West Indies v England, Old Trafford 1969; other f/class 8–83 Kent v Lancs, Tunbridge Wells 1977; jpl 4–17 Kent v Middlesex, Lord's 1978; b&h 4–25 Kent v Derby, Lord's 1978; gillette 4–23 Kent v Essex, Leyton 1972.

SHUTTLEWORTH, Kenneth.
County: Leicestershire.
Role: Right-hand bat, right arm fast medium bowler.
Date and place of birth: 13 November 1944, St. Helen's, Lancashire.
County debut: 1977. *County cap:* 1977.
Testimonial: £12,500 jointly with J. Sullivan while playing for Lancashire C.C.C. in 1975.
Nickname: Shut.

General: Made debut for Lancashire in 1964 and was awarded Lancashire cap in 1968. Did not play for Lancashire in 1976 and not re-engaged at the end of the season, joining Leicestershire in 1977. Played one match for England v Rest of the World 1970. Toured Australia, New Zealand 1970–71.
Address and telephone number: c/o Leicestershire County Cricket Club, Grace

continued overleaf

Road, Leicester LE2 8AD. Telephone: Leicester 832128.

Personal best: Batting, Tests 21 England v Pakistan, Edgbaston 1971; other f/class 71 Lancs v Gloucs, Cheltenham 1967; jpl 24* Leics v Hants, Portsmouth 1979; b&h 12* Lancs v Derby, Old Trafford 1974; gillette 23 Lancs v Somerset, Old Trafford 1967. Bowling, Tests 5–47 England v Australia, Brisbane 1970–71; other f/class 7–41 Lancs v Essex, Leyton 1968; jpl 5–13 Lancs v Notts, Trent Bridge 1972; b&h 3–15 Lancs v Notts, Old Trafford 1972; gillette 4–26 Lancs v Essex, Clemsford 1971.

SIDEBOTTOM, Arnold.
County: Yorkshire.
Role: Right-hand bat, right arm fast medium bowler.
Date and place of birth: 1 April 1954, Barnsley, Yorkshire.
Height: 6′ 2″. *Weight:* 13 st 6 lbs.
Parents: Jack and Florence Sidebottom.
Wife: Gillian.
Married: 17 June 1977.
Children: Ryan Jay, 15 January 1978.
Education and qualifications: Barnsley Broadway Grammar School.
Occupation outside cricket: Professional footballer, Manchester United, five years; Huddersfield Town, two years; Halifax Town one year;
Family links with cricket: "Father good cricketer."
County debut: 1973.
Outside interests: Horse-racing, watching television, "taking my son on outings."
Nickname: Woofer Thanold. Arnie.
Other sporting activities: Football, tennis, table tennis, badminton.
General: Played for Yorkshire 2nd XI since 1971.
Address and telephone number: 40 Meadow Park, Kirkheaton, Huddersfield. Telephone: Huddersfield 46167.

Personal best: Batting, f/class 124 Yorkshire v Glamorgan, Cardiff 1977; jpl 31 Yorkshire v Sussex, Hove 1975; b&h 15 Yorkshire v Notts, Bradford 1979; gillette 45 Yorkshire v Hants, Bournemouth 1977. Bowling, f/class 4–47 Yorkshire v Derby, Chesterfield 1975; jpl 4–24 Yorkshire v Surrey, Scarborough 1975; b&h 3–21 Yorkshire v Minor Counties North, Jesmond 1979; gillette 4–36 Yorkshire v Hants, Bournemouth 1977.

SIMMONS, Jack.
County: Lancashire.
Role: Right-hand bat, off-break bowler.
Date and place of birth: 28 March 1941,

Clayton-le-Moors, near Accrington.
Height: 6′ 1¾″. *Weight:* 14 st 7 lbs.
Parents: Ada and Robert Simmons.
Wife: Jacqueline.

140

Married: 23 March 1963.
Education and qualifications: Accrington Technical School, Accrington until 16 years old. Blackburn Technical College until 21 years old. Five O-levels, O.N.C., City & Guilds in Quantities.
Occupation outside cricket: Draughtsman with Accrington Brick & Tile Co Ltd., and Lancashire County Surveyors' Dept.
Family links with cricket: Father, Robert, played with Enfield, Lancashire League: grandfather, Robert, also played for Enfield since 1887, "giving 92 years association with the same club."
County debut: 1968. *County cap:* 1971.
Benefit: 1980.
Outside interests: Soccer, golf, horse-racing. "Plus eating. Playing cards. Relaxation: watching television and going on holiday."
Nickname: Simmo, Flat Jack.

Other sporting activities: Was semi-pro with Great Harwood in Lancs. Combination and Northern Premier League. Plus golf.
General: "I didn't play for a couple of years because I broke my leg three times in ten months and the previous year broke my arm quite badly. All playing soccer, except one broken leg, which was broken going down to the football ground just after I had it out of plaster from the first time." Made debut for 2nd XI in 1959. Played for Blackpool in Northern League as professional. Played for Tasmania from 1972–73 to 1978–79—where he is "a bit of a folk hero". Captained Tas-

mania to Gillette Cup for first time ever in 1979.
Address and telephone number: Jacmar, 16 Southcliffe, Great Harwood, near Blackburn. Telephone: 0254–884697.
Personal best: Batting f/class 112 Lancs v Sussex, Hove 1970; jpl 54 Lancs v Leics, Old Trafford 1979; b&h 64 Lancs v Derby, Old Trafford 1978; gillette 37* Lancs v Cornwall, Truro 1977. Bowling f/class 7–59 Tasmania v Queensland, Brisbane 1978–79; jpl 5–28 Lancs v Northants, Peterborough 1972; b&h 4–31 Lancs v Yorks, Old Trafford 1975; gillette 5–49 Lancs v Worcs, Worcester 1974.

SLACK, Wilfred Norris.
County: Middlesex.
Role: Left-hand bat, right arm medium bowler.
Date and place of birth: 12 December 1954, Troumaca, St. Vincent.
County debut: 1977.
Nickname: Wilf, Slacky.
General: Played for Buckinghamshire in 1976. Spent off-season 1979–80 playing in Auckland, New Zealand.
Address and telephone number: c/o Middlesex County Cricket Club, Lord's Cricket Ground, St John's Wood Road, London NW8 8QN. Telephone: 01–289–1300.
Personal best: Batting f/class 66 Middlesex v Notts, Trent Bridge 1979; jpl 57 Middlesex v Kent, Lord's 1978. Bowling jpl 2–36 Middlesex v Worcs, Lord's 1979.

SLOCOMBE, Philip Anthony.
County: Somerset.
Role: Right-hand bat, right arm medium bowler.
Date and place of birth: 6 September 1954, Weston-Super-Mare.
Height: 5' 9¾". *Weight:* 11 st 7 lbs.
Parents: Anthony William and Margaret Amelia Slocombe.
Wife: Unmarried.
Education and qualifications: Weston-Super-Mare Grammar School and Millfield School.
Occupation outside cricket: Owns his own sports shop in Taunton.
Family links with cricket: Father played club cricket with Weston-Super-Mare Cricket Club. Brother played once for Somerset 2nd XI, and now plays club cricket in Weston-Super-Mare.
County debut: 1975. *County cap:* 1978.
Outside interest: Favourite relaxation is listening to music, classical and contemporary. Fashion and travel.
Nickname: Slocs or Sir Len.
Other sporting activities: Enjoys playing soccer when at home in the winter, golf, and tennis.
General: Played for Somerset 2nd XI in 1969 at the age of 14. Plays soccer for Weston-Super-Mare in Western League. "As a major

national sport, I am surprised how much the game of cricket is still under-selling itself."
Address and telephone number: c/o Somerset County Cricket Club, St. James's Street, Taunton TA1 1JT.
Personal best: Batting f/class 132 Somerset v Notts, Taunton 1975; jpl 39 Somerset v Glamorgan, Yeovil 1977; b&h 11 Somerset v Minor Counties West, Chippenham 1976; gillette 42 Somerset v Surrey, The Oval 1975.

SMEDLEY, Michael John.
County: Nottinghamshire.
Role: Right-hand bat, off-break bowler.
Date and place of birth: 28 October 1941, Maltby, Yorkshire.
Education and qualifications: Woodhouse Grammar School, Sheffield.
County debut: 1964. *County cap:* 1966.
Benefit: £8,500 in 1975.
General: Played for Yorkshire 2nd XI 1960–62. Nottinghamshire C.C.C. County Captain from 1975–79. Scored 1,000 runs in a season nine times. Scored two centuries in a match, 119 and 109, v Lancashire at Manchester in 1971. Shared in seventh wicket partnership record for county, 204 with R. A. White, v Surrey at the Oval in 1976. Left county 1979.
Address and telephone number: c/o Nottinghamshire County Cricket Club, Trent Bridge, Nottingham NG2 6AG.
Personal best: Batting f/class 149 Notts v Glamorgan, Cardiff 1970; jpl 69 Notts v

Kent, Dover 1975; b&h 66 Notts v Minor Counties North, Trent Bridge 1973; gillette 75 Notts v Gloucs, Trent Bridge 1968.

SMITH, Christopher Lyall.
County: Glamorgan.
Role: Right-hand bat.
Date and place of birth: 15 October 1958, Durban, South Africa.
Height: 5' 11". *Weight:* 11 st 12 lbs.
Parents: John Arnold and Elaine Jessie Smith.
Wife: Unmarried.
Education and qualifications: Northaland High School Durban, matriculation pass.
Occupation outside cricket: Sales representative for horse-racing company.
Family links with cricket: Grandfather, Vernon Lyall Shearer, played for Natal.
County debut: 1979.
Outside interests: "Bathing on Durban beaches in free time."
Nickname: Kippy.
Other sporting activities: Plays league squash; golf.
General: Played for Natal Schools 1975, South African Schools 1976, Natal B debut 1978. toured U.K. with Kingsmead Mynahs (Natal Under-25s under another name) 1976. Has been engaged by Hampshire for 1980

season. Played for Gorscinon in South Wales League, 1979.
Address and telephone number: 9 Cherron Avenue, La-Lucia, Durban, Natal, South Africa. Telephone: 031–522925.
Personal best: Batting f/class 67 Glamorgan v Sri Lanka, Swansea 1979.

SMITH, David Mark.
County: Surrey.
Role: Left-hand bat, right arm medium bowler.
Date and place of birth: 9 January 1956, Balham.
Height: 6' 4". *Weight:* 14 st.
Parents: Dennis Henry and Tina Smith.
Wife: Jacqui.
Married: 7 January 1977, Salisbury, Rhodesia.
Education and qualifications: Battersea Grammar School, O-level in Maths, French and English.
Occupation outside cricket: Two years with insurance company, one year with Harrods, one year spent in Rhodesia, two years with building firm. Coaching cricket.
Family links with cricket: Father plays cricket for B.B.C.
County debut: 1973, aged 17 years 4 months while still at school.
Outside interests: Reading biographies and historical novels, watching motor racing, collecting LPs, making video recordings and cine films.
Nickname: Smudger or Smurf.

Other sporting activities: Football, kart racing, table tennis.
General: Contract with Gray Nicholls to use their cricket equipment. "Has a cocker spaniel called Winston". Played for Surrey 2nd XI in 1972. Was not retained after 1977 but was re-instated in 1978.

continued overleaf

Address and telephone number: 96 Hydethorpe Road, Balham, London SW12.
Personal best: Batting f/class 115 Surrey v Hants, Portsmouth 1978; jpl 45 Surrey v Middlesex, The Oval 1979; b&h 45* Surrey v Northants, Northampton 1979; gillette 61

Surrey v Northants, Northampton 1979. Bowling f/class 3-40 Surrey v Sussex, The Oval 1976; jpl 2-21 Surrey v Worcs, Byfleet 1973; b&h 1-24 Surrey v Combined Universities, The Oval 1979; gillette 3-39 Surrey v Derby, Ilkeston 1976.

SMITH, Kenneth David.
County: Warwickshire.
Role: Right-hand bat.
Date and place of birth: 9 July 1956, Newcastle-on-Tyne.
Height: 6' 2". *Weight:* 14 st.
Parents: Kenneth Desmond and Joy Smith.
Wife: Unmarried.
Education and qualifications: Heaton Grammar School, Newcastle.
Occupation outside cricket: Coaching in Capetown, South Africa.
Family links with cricket: Father played for Northumberland and Leicestershire.
County debut: 1973. *County cap:* 1978.
Nickname: Smithy.
Off-season 1979-80: Coaching in South Africa.
Other sporting activities: Squash, tennis.
General: Played for 2nd XI in 1972.
Address and telephone number: 64 Geraldine Road, Yardley, Birmingham. Telephone: 021-706-8725.
Personal best: Batting f/class 135 Warwicks v

Lancs, Old Trafford 1977; jpl 60 Warwicks v Glamorgan, Swansea 1979; b&h 68 Warwicks v Hants, Bournemouth 1979; gillette 28 Warwicks v Somerset, Taunton 1978.

SMITH, Michael John.
County: Middlesex.
Role: Right-hand bat, slow left arm orthodox bowler.
Date and place of birth: 4 January 1942, Enfield, Middlesex.
Height: 6' 2". *Weight:* 12 st 12 lbs.
Parents: John Alfred Smith, deceased, and Eileen Mary Smith.
Wife: Eli Foosnaes.
Married: 9 March 1979.
Children: Deborah Jane and Elizabeth Ann from first marriage to Christine Lucy.
Education and qualifications: Enfield Grammar School.
Occupation outside cricket: Representative for fund-raising printers.
Family links with cricket: Father, Jack, played 45 years for North Enfield Cricket Club. Uncle, Tom Smith, captained North Enfield C.C. in the 1950s. Brother, Rod, plays for Enfield C.C. in Middlesex League.

County debut: 1959. *County cap:* 1967.
Benefit: £20,000 in 1976.
Outside interests: Golf.

Nickname: Smudger.
Other sporting activities: Played soccer for Middlesex Schools. Enfield Old Grammarians in Old Boys' League until 1964. Was junior tennis champion at school.
General: Played for Middlesex v India and Lancashire while still a schoolboy. Cricket Society Schoolboy Cricketer of the Year in 1959. Played for Public Schools XI in 1959 (as a grammar school boy). Has played for and is still a member of both North Enfield C.C. and Enfield C.C. Almost retired after 1978 season, but was persuaded to stay on, and scored 5 centuries in 1979.
Address and telephone number: 41 Lancaster Grove, Swiss Cottage, London NW3. Telephone: 01-794-3753.
Personal best: Batting f/class 181 Middlesex v Lancs, Old Trafford 1967; jpl 110 Middlesex v Lancs, Lord's 1971; b&h 105 Middlesex v Minor Counties East, Lord's 1976; gillette 123 Middlesex v Hants, Lord's 1977. Bowling f/class 4-13 Middlesex v Gloucs, Lord's 1961; jpl 1-5 Middlesex v Sussex, Lord's 1970.

SMITH, Neil.
County: Essex.
Role: Right-hand bat, wicket-keeper.
Date and place of birth: 1 April 1949, Dewsbury, Yorkshire.
Height: 6′ 0″. *Weight:* 14 st.
Parents: Clifford and Dorothy Smith.
Wife: Unmarried.
Education and qualifications: Ossett Grammar School.
Occupation outside cricket: Representative for Bulldog Petroleum.
County debut: 1973. *County cap:* 1975.
Outside interests: Listening to music, e.g. "ELO, Supertramp, Jerry Rafferty, Neil Diamond."
Nickname: Sam. Smudger.
Other sporting activities: Golf, snooker and cross-country running.
General: Debut for Yorkshire 1970.
Address and telephone number: Wethersfield, Essex.
Personal best: Batting f/class 126 Essex v

Somerset, Leyton 1976; jpl 32 Essex v Glamorgan, Chelmsford 1979; b&h 61 Essex v Northants, Chelmsford 1977; gillette 12 Essex v Leics, Southend 1977.

SOUTHERN, John William.
County: Hampshire.
Role: Right-hand bat, slow left arm orthodox bowler.
Date and place of birth: 2 September 1952, King's Cross, London.
Height: 6′ 4″. *Weight:* 13 st 7 lbs.
Parents: Stanley and Sandy Southern.
Wife: Unmarried.
Education and qualifications: Tetherdown Primary (Hornsey), William Ellis School, London, University of Southampton. Hon B.Sc. Chemistry. Advanced cricket coaching certificate.
Family links with cricket: My two brothers, and father, have all played or still play cricket at club level.
County debut: 1975. *County cap:* 1978.
Outside interests: Any sports, "devoted Tottenham supporter. Collecting second-hand books on history, drinking home-made wine. Relaxation: not thinking about cricket."
Other sporting activities: Squash, football.
General: Uses Duncan Fearnley equipment. "Ambition: to score 100." Feels that "with ever-increasing costs, all county cricket clubs should enter into money-making schemes in order to secure their financial future."

continued overleaf

Address and telephone number: c/o Hampshire County Cricket Club, Northlands Road, Southampton SO9 2TY.
Personal best: Batting f/class 61* Hants v Yorkshire, Leeds 1979; jpl 2* Hants v Derby, Darley Dale 1975; 2* Hants v Gloucs, Bristol 1976; b&h 1 Hants v Lancs, Old Trafford 1979; gillette 0*. Bowling f/class 6–46 Hants v Gloucs, Bournemouth 1975; jpl 2–36 Hants v Kent, Canterbury 1976; b&h 2–38 Hants v Lancs, Old Trafford 1979; gillette 2–34 Hants v Northants, Southampton 1976.

SPENCER, John.
County: Sussex.
Role: Right-hand bat, right arm medium bowler.
Date and place of birth: 6 October 1949, Brighton.
Height: 6′ 2½″.   *Weight:* 12 st 7 lbs.
Parents: Henry Arthur and Marie Patricia Spencer.
Wife: Catherine.
Married: 15 September 1973.
Children: Nicola Sarah Brooke.
Education and qualifications: Brighton Hove and Sussex Grammar School. Cambridge University, M.A. Cantab.
Occupation outside cricket: Coaching cricket at Diocesan College, Capetown 1972–76. Teaching geography and coaching cricket at Cranbrook School, Sydney 1976–78. Director of coaching for World Series Cricket 1977–79. Teaching geography at Brighton College.
Family links with cricket: Elder brother represented Sussex Schools.
County debut: 1969.   *County cap:* 1973.
Outside interests: Photography, gardening, travel.
Nickname: Spud.
Other sporting activities: Squash. Previously soccer but this was ended by winters abroad.
General: Cambridge Blue 1970–71–72.
Address and telephone number: c/o Sussex

County Cricket Club, Eaton Road, Hove BN3 3AN.
Personal best: Batting f/class 79 Sussex v Hants, Southampton 1975; jpl 35 Sussex v Northants, Northampton 1977; b&h 18 Cambridge University v Warwicks, Edgbaston 1972; gillette 14 Sussex v Gloucester, Hove 1971. Bowling f/class 6–19 Sussex v Gloucs, Gloucester 1974; jpl 4–16 Sussex v Somerset, Bath 1973; b&h 4–19 Sussex v Minor Counties South, Hove 1975; gillette 4–25 Sussex v Derby, Chesterfield 1973.

STEELE, David Stanley.
County: Derbyshire.
Role: Right-hand bat, slow left arm orthodox bowler.
Date and place of birth: 29 September 1941, Stoke-on-Trent.
Wife: Carol.
Children: Son, Arran.
Education and qualifications: Enden Secondary Modern, Stoke-on-Trent. 6-year apprenticeship with printers.
Occupation outside cricket: Sales representative for printing company.
Family links with cricket: Younger brother, J. F. Steele, plays for Leicestershire C.C.C. Cousin, B. S. Crump, played for Northamptonshire C.C.C. Uncle, Stan Crump, played as professional in Lancashire League.
County debut: 1979.
Benefit: £25,000 in 1975, while at Northamptonshire.
Nickname: Stainless.
General: Played for Staffordshire 1958-62. Was one of Wisden's Cricketers of the Year 1976. Debut for Northamptonshire C.C.C. in 1963, cap 1965. Joined Derbyshire as County Captain in 1979, but gave up captaincy to Geoff Miller half-way through the season. Had match double of 100 runs and ten wickets (130, 6 for 36, 5 for 39) v Derbyshire at Northampton in 1978. Cricket was not played at his school. Wears spectacles. Admits to being amongst the worst car-drivers in cricket. Got a steak from a local butcher for every run he made for England in

1975.
Address and telephone number: c/o Derbyshire County Cricket Club, Nottingham Road, Derby DE2 6DA.
Personal best: Batting Tests 106 England v West Indies, Trent Bridge 1976; other f/class 140* Northants v Worcs, Worcester 1971; jpl 74 Northants v Sussex, Hove 1974; b&h 69 Northants v Warwicks, Northampton 1974; gillette 109 Northants v Cambridgeshire, March 1975. Bowling Tests 1-1 England v Australia, Lord's 1975; other f/class 8-29 Northants v Lancs, Northampton 1966; jpl 4-21 Derby v Notts, Derby 1979; b&h 2-29 Derby v Glamorgan, Cardiff 1979; gillette 2-54 Northants v Glamorgan, Northampton 1972.

STEELE, John Frederick.
County: Leicestershire.
Role: Right-hand bat, slow left arm orthodox bowler.
Date and place of birth: 23 July 1946, Stafford.
Family links with cricket: Younger brother of David Steele of Derbyshire and England, and cousin of former Northants player, B. S. Crump. Uncle, Stan Crump, played as professional in Lancashire League.
County debut: 1970. *County cap:* 1971.
Nickname: Steeley.
General: Was 12th man for England v Rest of the World at Lord's in 1970, only a month after making debut. Played for Natal in

continued overleaf

1973–74 and 1977–78 Currie Cup Competitions. Scored 1,000 runs in a season six times.
Address and telephone number: c/o Leicestershire County Cricket Club, Grace Road, Leicester LE2 8AD. Telephone: Leicester 832128.
Personal best: Batting f/class 195 Leics v Derby, Leicester 1971; jpl 92 Leics v Essex, Leicester 1973; b&h 91 Leics v Somerset, Leicester 1974; gillette 108* Leics v Staffs, Longton 1975. Bowling f/class 7–29 Natal B v Griqualand West, Umzinto 1973–74; jpl 5–22 Leics v Glamorgan, Leicester 1979; b&h 3–17 Leics v Cambridge University, Leicester 1972; gillette 5–19 Leics v Essex, Southend 1977.

STEPHENSON, George Robert.
County: Hampshire.
Role: Right-hand bat, wicket-keeper.
Date and place of birth: 9 November 1942, Derby.
Height: 5′ 7½″. *Weight:* 11 st.
Parents: George Ternent and Phyllis Edna Stephenson.
Wife: Maureen.
Married: 7 March 1967.
Education and qualifications: Derby School.
Occupation outside cricket: Has coached cricket and football, worked as a representative, and run his own business repairing sports gear.
County debut: 1969. *County cap:* 1969.
Benefit: 1979.
Outside interests: Watching television.
Nickname: Bob.
Other sporting activities: Playing football and golf. Played professional football for Derby County, Shrewsbury and Rochdale.
General: Writes for *Southern Evening Echo* and *Imprint Magazine.* Hampshire representative on the Cricketers' Association, and also on the executive committee. Debut for Derbyshire 1967, following injury to R. W. Taylor. Hampshire County Captain 1979.

Relinquished captaincy at end of 1979.
Address and telephone number: 26 Gurney Road, Shirley, Southampton. Telephone: Southampton 776888.
Personal best: Batting f/class 100* Hants v Somerset, Taunton 1976; jpl 30 Hants v Worcs, Worcester 1979; b&h 29* Hants v Somerset, Taunton 1974; gillette 29 Hants v Notts, Trent Bridge 1972.

STEVENSON, Graham Barry.
County: Yorkshire.
Role: Right-hand bat, right arm fast medium bowler.
Date and place of birth: 16 December 1955, Hemsworth, Yorkshire.
Height: 6′ 0″. *Weight:* 13 st.
Wife: Angela.
Married: 29 October 1977.
Education and qualifications: Minsthorpe High School.
Occupation outside cricket: Has worked as clerk at Foster Wheeler Power Products Ltd., Snaith, near Goole.
Family links with cricket: Two uncles, Keith and Jack Stevenson, both played local league cricket. Keith currently umpiring Yorkshire.
County debut: 1973. *County cap:* 1978.
Off-season 1979–80: Touring Australia with England.
Outside interests: Watching Sheffield Wednesday F.C.
Nickname: "Several—unprintable!" Moonbeam.
Other sporting activities: Member of local club snooker team.
General: Under agreement with Slazengers Ltd. Vice-President Townville C.C. Toured

Australia with England 1979-80, being called in after return to England through injury of Mike Hendrick. Played for Yorkshire 2nd in 1972.

Address and telephone number: c/o Yorkshire County Cricket Club, Headingley Cricket Ground, Leeds LB6 3BU.

Personal best: Batting f/class 83 Yorkshire v Derby, Chesterfield 1976; jpl 33* Yorkshire v Derby, Huddersfield 1978; b&h 16 Yorkshire v Middlesex, Lord's 1977; gillette 27 Yorkshire v Gloucs, Leeds 1976. Bowling f/class 8-65 Yorkshire v Lancs, Leeds 1978; jpl 5-41 Yorkshire v Leics, Leicester 1976; b&h 5-28 Yorkshire v Kent, Canterbury 1978; gillette 4-57 Yorkshire v Lancs, Leeds 1974.

STEVENSON, Keith.

County: Hampshire.

Role: Right-hand bat, right arm fast medium bowler.

Date and place of birth: 6 October 1950, Derby, Derbyshire.

Height: 5' 11". *Weight:* 13 st 7 lbs.

Parents: E. W. Stevenson, deceased and Mrs. A. Dolman.

Wife: Frances Mary.

Married: 25 March 1978.

Children: Richard William, 18 November 1979.

Education and qualifications: Bemrose Grammar School, Derby. O-levels: mathematics, English, book-keeping.

Occupation outside cricket: 1968-73, budget and forecast officer with Rolls-Royce, Derby, obtaining qualifications within the Rolls-Royce system.

Family links with cricket: Father and two brothers played club cricket in Derbyshire.

County debut: 1978.

Off-season 1979-80: Working for estate agents.

Outside interests: Gardening, watching sport and films on television.

Nickname: Stevo.

Other sporting activities: Football, squash.

General: Left Derbyshire of his own free will after 1977 season and moved to Hampshire.

Address and telephone number: c/o Hampshire County Cricket Club, Northlands Road, Southampton SO9 2TY.

Personal best: Batting f/class 33 Derby v Northants, Chesterfield 1974; jpl 6* Derby v Kent, Folkestone 1976; gillette 14 Derby v Surrey, Ilkeston 1976; b&h 2 Derby v Lancs, Old Trafford 1974; Bowling f/class 7-22 Hants v Oxford University, Oxford 1979; jpl 3-29 Derby v Surrey, Chesterfield 1975; b&h 1-18 Hants v Derby, Derby 1979; gillette 4-21 Derby v Surrey, Ilkeston 1976.

STOVOLD, Andrew Willis-.
County: Gloucestershire.
Role: Right-hand bat, wicket-keeper.
Date and place of birth: 19 March 1953, Bristol.
Height: 5' 7". *Weight:* 12 st 4 lbs.
Parents: Lancelot Walter and Dorothy Patricia Willis-Stovold.
Wife: Kay Elizabeth,.
Married: 30 September 1978.
Education and qualifications: Olveston Primary; Filton High School; Loughborough College of Education, Certificate of Education.
Occupation outside cricket: Coaching posts 1974–78. Master at Tockington Manor Prep School, Bristol.
Family links with cricket: Father played local club cricket for Old Down Cricket Club and is now chairman. Brother, Martin, plays county cricket for Gloucestershire.
County debut: 1973. *County cap:* 1976.
Outside interests: Hunting, horse-racing.
Nickname: Stovers, Stov, or Squeak.
Other sporting activities: Golf, football, cross-country running, squash.
General: Organizer of Gloucestershire C.C.C. football team for charity fixtures. Responsible for local clubs fitness and training.

Address and telephone number: c/o Gloucestershire County Cricket Club, Neville Road, Bristol BS7 9EJ.
Personal best: Batting f/class 196 Gloucs v Notts, Trent Bridge 1977; jpl 98* Gloucs v Kent, Cheltenham 1977; b&h 104 Gloucs v Leics, Leicester 1977; gillette 45 Gloucs v Lancs, Old Trafford 1978. Bowling f/class 1–0 Gloucs v Derby, Bristol 1976.

STOVOLD, Martin Willis-.
County: Gloucestershire.
Role: Left-hand batsman.
Date and place of birth: 28 December 1955, Almondsbury, Bristol.
Height: 5' 10". *Weight:* 12 st.
Parents: Lancelot and Patricia Willis-Stovold.
Wife: Unmarried.
Education and qualifications: Olveston and Elberton C. of E. Primary School, Thornbury Grammar School, Marlwood School, Loughborough College of Physical Education.
Occupation outside cricket: P.E. teacher at Cotham Grammar School, Bristol. Cricket coach at Wynberg Boys' High School, Capetown, South Africa.
Family links with cricket: Brother, Andrew, also plays for Gloucestershire.
County debut: 1979.
Outside interests: Racing, watching television, listening to music.

Nickname: Bubble.
Other sporting activities: Football, squash, "any sport".

General: Plays club cricket for Almondsbury C.C. Played in one John Player League match v Essex at Gloucester 1978.
Address and telephone number: The Laurels, Church Hill, Olveston, Bristol.
Personal best: Batting f/class 27 Gloucs v Worcs, Worcester 1979; jpl 5 Gloucs v Kent, Gloucester 1979.

SWARBROOK, Frederick William.

County: Derbyshire.
Role: Left-hand bat, slow left arm orthodox bowler.
Date and place of birth: 17 December 1950, Derby.
County debut: 1967, *County cap:* 1975.
Nickname: Swarby.
Other sporting activities: Played soccer for Derby County F.C. Juniors.
General: Youngest ever player to appear for Derbyshire C.C.C. at 16 years, 196 days v Cambridge in 1967. Played for Griqualand West, South Africa, in Currie Cup Competition 1972-73 and 1976-77 and Orange Free State 1979-80. Not re-engaged by county for 1980 season.
Address and telephone number: c/o Derbyshire County Cricket Club, Nottingham Road, Derby DE2 6DA.
Personal best: Batting f/class 90 Derby v Essex, Leyton 1970; jpl 42* Derby v Glamorgan, Ilkeston 1977; 42* Derby v Notts, Ilkeston, 1977; b&h 20* Derby v Hants, Southampton 1976; gillette 58* Derby v

Surrey, Ilkeston 1976. Bowling f/class 9-20 Derby v Sussex, Hove 1975; jpl 4-15 Derby v Gloucs, Bristol 1976; b&h 4-33 Derby v Warwicks, Ilkeston 1978; gillette 3-53 Derby v Middlesex, Chesterfield 1975.

SWART, Peter Douglas.

County: Glamorgan.
Date and place of birth: 27 April 1946, Bulawayo, Rhodesia.
Height: 6′ 0″. *Weight:* 11 st 6 lbs.
Parents: Peter and Rene Swart.
Education and qualifications: Jameson High School, Gatooma, Rhodesia.
Family links with cricket: "Outstanding help from my father when young. He played at league level."
County debut: 1978.
Outside interests: Vegetable gardening, beach swimming.
Other sporting activities: Tennis, golf.
General: Made debut 1965-66 for Rhodesia in Currie Cup Competition. Played for Western Province in 1967-68. Played for International Cavaliers v Barbados at Scarborough in 1969 and for Derrick Robins XI v Pakistanis at Eastbourne in 1974. Professional for Accrington in 1969, and for

Haslingden from 1974-77 in Lancashire League. Scored 1,078 runs for county in 1978

continued overleaf

151

(average 31.70). Left county of own free will after 1979 season. Has joined East Lancashire in Lancashire League on one year contract.
Address and telephone number: Alexandra Cottage, Spaanschemat River Road, Constantia, Cape, South Africa. Telephone: 741620.
Personal best: Batting f/class 122 Glamorgan v Worcs, Swansea 1979; jpl 85* Glamorgan v

Surrey, The Oval 1978; b&h 83* Glamorgan v Combined Universities, Oxford 1978; gillette 44 Glamorgan v Somerset, Cardiff 1978. Bowling f/class 6-85 Western Province v Natal, Pietermaritzburg 1971-72; jpl 4-35 Glamorgan v Essex, Chelmsford 1978; b&h 3-36 Glamorgan v Gloucs, Swansea 1979; gillette 2-71 Glamorgan v Somerset, Cardiff 1978.

TAVARÉ, Christopher James.
County: Kent.
Role: Right-hand bat, right arm medium bowler.
Date and place of birth: 27 October 1954, Orpington, Kent.
Height: 6′ 1½″. *Weight:* "11 st 7 lbs 12 st".
Parents: Andrew and June Tavaré.
Wife: Vanessa.
Married: 22 March 1979.
Education and qualifications: Riverhead Primary; Sevenoaks School; Oxford University, studied zoology.
Occupation outside cricket: Off-season work for Save and Prosper Ltd., London, investment company.
Family links with cricket: Father, uncle, Jack Tavaré, and uncle, Derrick Attwood, all played school and club cricket. Father and Uncle Jack at Chatham House. Father and Derrick at Bickley Park C.C.
County debut: 1974. *County cap:* 1978.
Off-season 1979-80: Playing cricket in Melbourne, Australia.
Outside interests: Music, zoology, playing backgammon and cards, seeing occasional films.
Nickname: Chris.
Other sporting activities: "Play squash, take an interest in most sports."
General: Played for England Schools v All-India Schools at Birmingham in 1973, scoring

124 not out. Oxford University cricket blue 1975-76-77. Whitbread Scholarship to Perth, Australia, 1978-79.
Address and telephone number: c/o Kent County Cricket Club, St. Lawrence Ground, Canterbury CT1 3NZ.
Personal best: Batting f/class 150* Kent v Essex, Tunbridge Wells 1979; jpl 136* Kent v Gloucs, Canterbury 1978; b&h 89 Combined Universities v Surrey, The Oval 1976; gillette 87 Kent v Lancs, Canterbury 1979. Bowling f/class 1-20 Kent v Northants, Dartford 1978.

TAYLOR, Derek John Somerset.
County: Somerset.
Role: Right-hand bat, wicket-keeper.
Date and place of birth: 12 November 1942, Amersham, Buckinghamshire.
Education and qualifications: Amersham College.

Family links with cricket: Twin brother of M. N. S. Taylor of Hampshire C.C.C.
County debut: 1970. *County cap:* 1971.
Benefit: 1978.
Other sporting activities: Has played football for Corinthian Casuals.
General: Debut for Surrey 1966, cap 1969.

Left staff after 1969 season to make debut for Somerset 1970. Played for Griqualand West in Currie Cup Competition 1970-71 and 1971-72. Scored 1,000 runs in a season once.

Address and telephone number: c/o Somerset County Cricket Club, St. James's Street, Taunton TA1 1JT.

Personal best: Batting f/class 179 Somerset v Glamorgan, Swansea 1974; jpl 93 Somerset v Surrey, Guildford 1975; b&h 83* Somerset v Gloucs, Street 1975; gillette 49 Somerset v Kent, Canterbury 1974.

TAYLOR, Leslie Brian.

County: Leicestershire.

Role: Right-hand bat, right arm fast medium bowler.

Date and place of birth: 25 October 1953, Earl Shilton, Leicestershire.

Height: 6′ 3½″. *Weight:* 14 st 7 lbs.

Parents: Peggy and Cyril Taylor.

Wife: Susan.

Married: 12 July 1973.

Children: Jamie, 24 June 1976; Donna 10 November 1978.

Education and qualifications: Heathfield High School, Earl Shilton.

Occupation outside cricket: Qualified carpenter and joiner, also machine driver underground.

Family links with cricket: Relation of the late Sam Coe, holder of highest individual score for Leicestershire, 252 not out v Northants at Leicester in 1914.

County debut: 1977.

Outside interests: Game-shooting and fox-hunting with the Atherstone Hunt.

Nickname: Les.

Other sporting activities: Swimming and football.

General: Toured South America with Derrick Robins XI in 1978-79 off-season. Once a coal-miner. Lord's Taverners/Schweppes Award 1979 for Best Young Bowler.

Address and telephone number: c/o Leicestershire County Cricket Club, Grace Road, Leicestershire LE2 8AD.

Personal best: Batting f/class 15 Leics v Kent, Canterbury 1978; jpl 9 Leics v Somerset, Glastonbury 1978; b&h 2 Leics v Derby, Leicester 1979; gillette 2* Leics v Northants, Northampton 1979. Bowling f/class 6-61 Leics v Essex, Chelmsford 1979; jpl 5-23 Leics v Notts, Trent Bridge 1978; b&h 1-35 Leics v Hants, Southampton 1979; gillette 3-11 Leics v Hants, Leicester 1978.

TAYLOR, Michael Norman Somerset.
County: Hampshire.
Role: Right-hand bat, right arm medium bowler.
Date and place of birth: 12 November 1942, Amersham, Buckinghamshire.
Height: 5′ 11″. *Weight:* 12 st 12 lbs.
Parents: Charles Norman and Isabel Kathleen Taylor.
Wife: Carol Lynne.
Married: 12 November 1976.
Education and qualifications: Amersham College, three O-levels.
Occupation outside cricket: Sales clerk for 2½ years prior to signing for Notts County Cricket Club in 1962. Life assurance consultant winter months 1969–70–71. Currently employed as assistant secretary of Hants C.C.C.
Family links with cricket: None, apart from twin brother, D. J. S. Taylor, the Somerset wicket-keeper.
County debut: 1973. *County cap:* 1973.
Outside interests: Southern Africa, television, golf, travel and gardening.
Nickname: Tay.
Other sporting activities: Golf.
General: Played for Buckinghamshire 1961–62. Debut for Notts 1964, cap 1967. Not re-engaged after 1972 season. Hat trick for Notts v Kent (Dover) in 1965. Took 99 wickets (average 21.00) 1968. Had strong influence in Cricketers' Association move to cut down number of overseas players, but

now says he has changed his views.
Address and telephone number: c/o Hampshire County Cricket Club, Northlands Road, Southampton SO9 2TY, Telephone Southampton 24155.
Personal best: Batting f/class 105 Notts v Lancs, Trent Bridge 1967; jpl 57* Hants v Notts, Trent Bridge 1978; b&h 41 Hants v Minor Counties South, Portsmouth 1974; gillette 58 Notts v Hants, Trent Bridge 1972. Bowling f/class 7–23 Hants v Notts, Basingstoke 1977; jpl 4–20 Notts v Surrey, Trent Bridge 1969; b&h 3–15 Hants v Somerset, Taunton 1974; gillette 4–31 Notts v Lancs, Trent Bridge 1968.

TAYLOR, Neil Royston.
County: Kent.
Role: Right-hand bat.
Date and place of birth: 21 July 1959, Farnborough, Kent.
Height: 6′ 0″. *Weight:* 13 st 3 lbs.
Parents: Leonard and Audrey Taylor.
Wife: Unmarried.
Education and qualifications: Cray Valley Technical High School; eight O-levels, two A-levels.
Occupation outside cricket: Clerk for Inland Revenue. Has worked for insurance brokers.

Family links with cricket: Brother, Colin, played for Kent Young Cricketers. Father and Colin play local club cricket for Sennocke.
County debut: 1979.
Outside interests: Listening to records.
Other sporting activities: Rugby (played for Kent Under-19s), golf.
Address and telephone number: c/o Kent County Cricket Club, St. Lawrence Ground, Canterbury CT1 3NZ.
Personal best: Batting f/class 110 Kent v Sri Lanka, Canterbury 1979 on debut.

TAYLOR, Robert William.
County: Derbyshire.
Role: Right-hand bat, wicket-keeper, occasional right arm medium bowler.

Date and place of birth: 17 July 1941, Stoke-on-Trent.
County debut: 1961. *County cap:* 1962.
Testimonial: £6,672 in 1973.

Off-season 1979-80: Playing for England in Australia.
Outside interests: Pipe-smoker. Golf.
Nickname: Chat.
Other sporting activities: Played professional football for Port Vale F.C.
General: Appointed County Captain during 1975 season, but relinquished post during 1976 season. One of Wisden's Cricketers of the Year 1977. Toured Australia, New Zealand 1970-71 and 1974-75; Australia with Rest of the World team 1971-72; West Indies 1973-74 with England; also Pakistan, New Zealand 1977-78; Australia 1978-79 and 1979-80. Withdrew from India, Sri Lanka, Pakistan tour 1972-73. Dismissed ten batsmen in a match, all caught, v Hampshire at Chesterfield in 1963, and seven in one innings, all caught, v Glamorgan at Derby in 1966. Played for Bignall End (North Staffordshire and South Cheshire League) when only 15, and for Staffordshire 1958-60. Debut for Minor Counties v South Africans at Stoke-on-Trent in 1960. First wicket-keeper to 100 dismissals, and to 100 catches, in John Player League. Has written *Anyone for Cricket* jointly with David Gower about the 1978-79 Australia Tour. Also *Wicket-Keeping.*

Address and telephone number: c/o Derbyshire County Cricket Club, Nottingham Road, Derby DE2 6DA.
Personal best: Batting Tests 97 England v Australia, Adelaide 1978-79; other f/class 97 International Wanderers v South African XI, Johannesburg 1975-76; jpl 43* Derby v Gloucs, Buxton 1969; b&h 31* Derby v Hants, Southampton 1976; gillette 53* Derby v Middlesex, Lord's 1965.

TERRY, Vivian Paul.
County: Hampshire.
Role: Right-hand bat, right arm medium bowler.
Date and place of birth: 14 January 1959, Osnabruck, West Germany.
Height: 6′ 0″. *Weight:* 12 st 4 lbs.
Parents: Michael and Patricia Terry.
Wife: Unmarried.
Education and qualifications: Durlston Court, Barton-on-Sea, Hampshire. Millfield School, Street, Somerset.
County debut: 1978.
Other sporting activities: Golf, squash, soccer.
General: Played for Hampshire 2nd XI since 1976.
Address and telephone number: Thatchover Lodge, Winchester Road, Shedfield, Hampshire. Telephone: Wickham 833142.
Personal best: Batting f/class 21 Hants v Warwicks, Nuneaton 1979; jpl 33 Hants v

Gloucs, Basingstoke 1979; gillette 11 Hants v Middlesex, Lord's 1979.

THOMAS, David John.
County: Surrey.
Role: Left-hand bat, left arm medium bowler.
Date and place of birth: 30 June 1959, Solihull, Warwickshire.
Height: 6' 1". *Weight:* 13 st.
Parents: Howard James and Heather Thomas.
Wife: Unmarried.
Education and qualifications: Eversfield Prep School, Solihull; Licensed Victuallers' School, Slough.
Occupation outside cricket: Has been sales representative in Durban, South Africa, playing cricket at weekends.
Family links with cricket: "Father very keen club cricketer and committee man, working all his life for the furtherance of cricket in many areas. Played representative cricket for the Royal Air Force during the war." Brother, Howard Michael Thomas, very keen cricketer also. Played junior county team.
County debut: 1977.
Nickname: Teddy.
Other sporting activities: Golf, squash, football and general interest in all sports.
Address and telephone number: Chiltern View, Red House Close, Knotty Green,

Beaconsfield, Buckinghamshire. Telephone: Beaconsfield 5618.
Personal best: Batting f/class 15* Surrey v Worcs, The Oval 1979; jpl 5 Surrey v Kent, Maidstone 1979; gillette 8* Surrey v Northants, Northampton 1979. Bowling f/class 6–84 Surrey v Derby, The Oval 1979; jpl 4–13 Surrey v Sussex, The Oval 1978; gillette 1–28 Surrey v Shropshire, Wellington 1978.

THOMAS, Gary Philip.
County: Warwickshire.
Role: Right-hand bat, right arm medium bowler.
Date and place of birth: 8 November 1958, Birmingham.
Height: 5' 8½". *Weight:* 12 st.
Parents: Derek and Noreen Thomas.
Wife: Unmarried.
Education and qualifications: George Dixon Grammar School, Birmingham.
Occupation outside cricket: Despatch clerk.
County debut: 1978.

Outside interests: Racing (betting).
Nickname: Tight Lines.
Other sporting activities: Golf, football.
General: Played for 2nd XI since 1975. Took catch v Gloucestershire 2nd XI to give Warwickshire 2nd XI the championship in 1979.
Address and telephone number: 865 Walsall Road, Great Barr, Birmingham B42 1ER. Telephone: 021-358-6928.
Personal best: Batting, f/class 9 Warwicks v Derby, Chesterfield 1979; jpl 16 Warwicks v Lancs, Old Trafford 1978.

THOMAS, John Gregory.
County: Glamorgan.
Date and place of birth: 12 August 1960, Pontardawe.
Height: 6' 2½". *Weight:* 13 st.
Parents: Illtyd and Margaret Thomas.
Wife: Unmarried.
Education and qualifications: Pontardawe Comprehensive School, Cyncoed College, Cardiff.

Family links with cricket: Father played for Pontardawe Cricket Club.
County debut: 1979.
Outside interests: Listening to music.
Nickname: Greg.
Other sporting activities: Trialist Under-19 Schools rugby at No. 8 or flanker. Playing any sport.
General: Captain of secondary school cricket team. Invited but declined due to exams to

captain rugby team. Represented Wales Under-19 Schools for three consecutive years. Representative game with Glamorgan 1st XI at 14 years. Played for Colts, 2nd XI and Under-25.
Address and telephone number: 228 Swansea

Road, Trebanos, Pontardawe, Swansea, West Glamorgan SA8 4BX. Telephone: Clydach 842984.
Personal best: Batting f/class 34 Glamorgan v Sri Lanka, Swansea 1979. bowling f/class 1–65 Glamorgan v Sri Lanka, Swansea 1979.

TITMUS, Frederick John.
County: Middlesex.
Role: Right-hand bat, Off-break bowler.
Date and place of birth: 24 November 1932. St. Pancras, London.
Education and qualifications: William Ellis School, Highgate.
Occupation outside cricket: Runs a Post Office in Hertfordshire.
County debut: 1949. *County cap:* 1953.
Benefit: £6,833 in 1963. £6,196 in 1973.
Nickname: Fred.
Other sporting activities: Golf. Was good amateur footballer.
General: Lost three toes in boating accident in West Indies. Went to Surrey as coach in 1978. Tours: Pakistan in 1955–56. Australia and New Zealand in 1962–63, 1965–66, 1974–75. India in 1963–64. South Africa in 1964–65. West Indies in 1967–68, as vice-captain. Played for Orange Free State in 1975–76 Currie Cup. Achieved double of 1,000 runs and 100 wickets in a season 8 times. Youngest ever player for Middlesex C.C.C. at 16 years, 213 days, v Somerset 1949.
Address and telephone number: c/o Middlesex County Cricket Club, Lord's Cricket Ground, St. John's Wood Road, London NW8 8QN. Telephone: 01–289–1300.
Personal best: Batting Tests 84* England v

India, Bombay, 1963–64; other f/class 137* M.C.C. v South Australia, Adelaide 1962–63; jpl 28 Middlesex v Warwicks, Lord's 1973; b&h 17* Middlesex v Worcs, Lord's 1974; gillette 41 Middlesex v Sussex, Lord's 1973. Bowling Tests 7–79 England v Australia, Sydney 1962–63; other f/class 9–52 Middlesex v Cambridge University, Cambridge 1962; jpl 5–25 Middlesex v Essex, Lord's 1971; b&h 3–21 Middlesex v Northants, Lord's 1976; gillette 5–26 Middlesex v Derby, Lord's 1970.

TODD, Paul Adrian.
County: Nottinghamshire.
Role: Right-hand bat, right arm medium bowler.
Date and place of birth: 12 March 1953, Nottingham.
Height: 6'. 1". *Weight:* 14 st.
Parents: Tom and Joan Todd.
Wife: Jennifer.
Married: 15 September 1979.

Education and qualifications: Edward Cludd, Southwell.
Occupation outside cricket: Mostly playing cricket abroad, or working for R. Lee & Son making race course fences.
Family links with cricket: Father played for local club side. Brother played for Notts Colts and Notts 2nd XI.
County debut: 1972. *County cap:* 1977.

continued overleaf

Outside interests: Darts, watching football, stamp collecting.
Nickname: Tubs.
Other sporting activities: Football, golf, squash, tennis, badminton.
Address and telephone number: 6 Fisher Close, Swinderby Road, Collingham, Newark, Nottinghamshire.
Personal best: Batting f/class 178 Notts v Gloucs, Trent Bridge 1975; jpl 79 Notts v Hants, Trent Bridge 1978; b&h 59 Notts v Kent, Canterbury 1979; gillette 105 Notts v Warwicks, Edgbaston 1979.

TOLCHARD, Roger William.
County: Leicestershire.
Role: Right-hand bat, wicket-keeper.
Date and place of birth: 15 June 1946, Torquay.
Height: 5' 9". Weight: 11 st 6 lbs.
Parents: Tom and Dorothy Elliott Tolchard.
Wife: Unmarried.
Education and qualifications: Firswood, Torquay, Wolborough Hill Prep School, Malvern College.
Family links with cricket: Father, brothers and brothers-in-law, all play. Brother, Jeff, played for Leicestershire C.C.C. Two brothers now play for Devon.
County debut: 1965. *County cap:* 1966.
Benefit: 1979.
Outside interests: Riding and fox-hunting.
Nickname: "Tolly is the only one I'll admit to!"
Other sporting activities: All sports. Had soccer trial for Leicester City. Golf.
General: Played for Devon in 1963 and 1964, also played for Hampshire 2nd XI in 1964. Public Schools v Combined Services at Lord's in 1964. Vice-Captain of Leicestershire in 1970–73. First wicket-keeper in John Player League to score 1,000 runs and get 100 dismisals in 1974 after 86 matches.

TOMLINS, Keith Patrick.
County: Middlesex.
Role: Right-hand bat, right arm medium bowler.
Date and place of birth: 23 October 1957,

Address and telephone number: 18 Ratcliffe Court, Ratcliffe Road, Leicester. Telephone: Leicester 708235.
Personal best: Batting Tests 67 England v India, Calcutta 1976–77; other f/class 126* Leics v Cambridge University, Cambridge 1970; jpl 103 Leics v Middlesex, Lord's 1972; b&h 92* Leics v Worcs, Worcester 1976, gillette 86* Leics v Gloucs, Leicester 1975. Bowling f/class 1–4 Leics v Northants, Leicester 1972.

Kinsgton-upon-Thames.
Height: 5' 9½". Weight: 11 st 10 lbs.
Parents: Royston John and Joan Murial Tomlins.

158

Wife: Unmarried.
Education and qualifications: St. Mary Magdalen's Primary School, Mortlake; St. Benedict's School, Ealing; College of St. Hild and St. Hild and St. Bede, Durham University.
Family links with cricket: Father and eldest brother play for Wycombe House C.C. in Osterley, Middlesex.
County debut: 1977.
Outside interests: Reading, listening to live music (jazz, rock), fishing.
Nickname: Tommo.
Other sporting activities: Playing member of Richmond Rugby Club.
General: Toured South America with Derrick Robins XI, February and March 1979.
Address and telephone number: 34 Montrose Avenue, Whitton, Middlesex. Telephone: 01-894-4002.
Personal best: Batting f/class 94 Middlesex v Worcs, Worcester 1978; jpl 15 Middlesex v

Sussex, Hove 1978. Bowling jpl 4-24 Middlesex v Notts, Trent Bridge 1978.

TREMLETT, Timothy Maurice.
County: Hampshire.
Role: Right-hand bat, right arm medium bowler.
Date and place of birth: 26 July 1956, Wellington, Somerset.
Height: 6' 2". *Weight:* 13 st.
Parents: Maurice Fletcher and Melina May Tremlett.
Wife: Carolyn Patricia.
Married: 18 September 1979.
Education and qualifications: Shirley Infants School, Bellemor Secondary Modern, Richard Taunton Sixth Form College.
Occupation outside cricket: Furrier, cricket coach.
Family links with cricket: Father played for Somerset and England 1947-48 against West Indies in the West Indies. Captained Somerset 1958-60.
County debut: 1976.
Outside interests: Collecting cricket books, record collecting, gardening, cinema. "N.B.—my new wife".
Nickname: Hurricane, Tremers.
Other sporting activities: Golf, handicap 9, table tennis, squash, swimming and badminton.
General: Member of local cricket club, Deanery, uses Gray Nicholls cricket equipment. Batted in almost every position in batting order from 1 to 11, in 1979.

Address and telephone number: 16 King's Road, Chandler's Ford, Eastleigh, near Southampton, Hampshire.
Personal best: Batting f/class 50 Hants v Gloucs, Basingstoke 1978; jpl 5* Hants v Middlesex, Lord's 1979; b&h 15* Hants v Derby, Derby 1979; gillette 3 Hants v Leics, Leicester 1978. Bowling f/class 2-9 Hants v Surrey, The Oval 1979; jpl 3-19 Hants v Kent, Canterbury 1979; b&h 3-21 Hants v Combined Universities, Cambridge 1978; gillette 1-20 Hants v Leics, Leicester 1978.

159

TRIM, Geoffrey Edward.
County: Lancashire.
Role: Right-hand bat, leg-break bowler.
Date and place of birth: 6 April 1956, Openshaw.
Height: 5' 6". *Weight:* 9 st.
Parents: Edward and Hilda Trim.
Wife: Unmarried.
Education and qualifications: Secondary school, followed by college. OND in technology.
Family links with cricket: Father and grandfather played club cricket. My brother played for Lancashire Federation (Lancs Under-19), and Lancs Schoolboys (Under-15).

County debut: 1976.
Outside interests: Renovating vintage cars.
Nickname: Trimy.
Other sporting activities: A lot of cricket coaching.
General: Played in last John Player League match of 1975 season. Did not play in 1977, 1978.
Address and telephone number: c/o Lancashire County Cricket Club, Old Trafford, Manchester M16 0PX.
Personal best: Batting f/class 91 Lancs v Derby, Chesterfield 1979; jpl 18 Lancs v Middlesex, Old Trafford 1979.

TUNNICLIFFE, Colin John.
County: Derbyshire.
Role: Right-hand bat, left arm fast medium bowler.
Date and place of birth: 11 August 1951, Derby.
County debut: 1973. *County cap:* 1977.
Nickname: Tunners.
General: Left staff after 1974 season but re-appeared in 1976.
Address and telephone number: c/o Derbyshire County Cricket Club, Nottingham Road, Derby DE2 6DA.
Personal best: Batting f/class 82* Derby v Middlesex, Ilkeston 1977; jpl 42 Derby v Yorkshire, Huddersfield 1978; b&h 28 Derby v Warwicks, Edgbaston 1979; gillette 13 Derby v Somerset, Ilkeston 1977. Bowling f/class 4–22 Derby v Middlesex, Ilkeston 1977; jpl 3–12 Derby v Essex, Chesterfield 1974; b&h 3–16 Derby v Lancs, Old Trafford

1978; gillette 2–44 Derby v Sussex, Hove 1977.

TUNNICLIFFE, Howard Trevor.
County: Nottinghamshire.
Role: Right-hand bat, right arm medium bowler.
Date and place of birth: 4 March 1950, Derby.
Height: 6' 0". *Weight:* 12 st 5 lbs.
Parents: Walter Arthur and Pauline Ann Tunnicliffe.
Wife: Susan Margaret Tunnicliffe.

Married: 3 June 1978.
Education and qualifications: Malvern College; Loughborough Colleges. B.Ed. degree, physical education teaching certificate.
County debut: 1973.
Outside interests: Snooker; music (listening only), cinema fanatic, "darts (and a pint)", "will eat prawns anywhere, any time", yoga, as relaxation and stimulation.

Nickname: Pally.
Other sporting activities: Squash, football, swimming, tennis.
Address and telephone number: 36 Kendal Road, Cropwell Bishop, Notts.
Personal best: Batting f/class 97 Notts v Glamorgan, Trent Bridge 1979; jpl 52* Notts v Somerset, Trent Bridge 1978; b&h 32 Notts v Kent, Canterbury 1976; gillette 53* Notts v Yorkshire, Bradford 1978. Bowling f/class 4-30 Notts v Sri Lanka, Trent Bridge; jpl 3-17 Notts v Sussex, Trent Bridge 1975; b&h 2-35 Notts v Kent, Canterbury 1976; gillette 2-40 Notts v Kent, Trent Bridge 1975.

TURNER, David Roy.
County: Hampshire.
Role: Left-hand bat, right arm medium bowler.
Date and place of birth: 5 February 1949, Corsham, near Chippenham, Wiltshire.
Height: 5' 6". *Weight:* 11 st 4 lbs.
Parents: Robert Edward and Evelyn Peggy Turner.
Wife: Henriette.
Married: 18 February 1977.
Education and qualifications: Chippenham Boys' High School, O-levels in Maths, History, Science, Woodwork, five C.S.E.s.
Occupation outside cricket: Player-coach for the Paarl Cricket Club, South Africa.
Family links with cricket: Brother played for Southern Schools.
County debut: 1966. *County cap:* 1970.
Outside interests: Chess, gardening, reading, television, watching war films.
Nickname: Birdy.
Other sporting activities: Golf.
General: Toured with Derrick Robins XI to South Africa 1972-73. Played for Western Province in the 1977-78 Currie Cup Competition. Played for Wiltshire in 1965.
Address and telephone number: 16 Firgrove

Close, North Baddesley, near Southampton, Hampshire. Telephone: Rownhams 732781.
Personal best: Batting f/class 181* Hants v Surrey, The Oval 1969; jpl 99* Hants v Gloucs, Bristol 1972; b&h 123* Hants v Minor Counties South, Amersham 1973; gillette 86 Hants v Northants, Southampton 1976. Bowling f/class 1-1 Hants v India, Southampton 1979.

TURNER, Glenn Maitland.
County: Worcestershire.
Role: Right-hand bat, off-break bowler.
Date and place of birth: 26 May 1947, Dunedin, New Zealand.

Height: 5' 9½". *Weight:* 11 st 7 lbs.
Married: 1 daughter.
Education and qualifications: Otago Boys' High School.

continued overleaf

County debut: 1967. *County cap:* 1968.
Benefit: 1978.
Off-season 1979–80; Playing in New Zealand.
Outside interests: Music, fishing.
Other sporting activities: Hockey. Has played hockey for Worcestershire and had trial for Midlands.
General: Debut for Otago in Plunket Shield Competition 1964–65 while still at school. One of Wisden's Cricketers of the Year 1971. Toured with New Zealand to England 1969 and 1973, Vice-Captain; India, Pakistan 1969–70; Australia 1969–70 and 1973–74 as Vice-Captain; West Indies 1971–72; Pakistan and India 1976–77, as Captain. Has scored 1,000 runs in a season twelve times. Best season 2,416 runs at an average of 67.11 in 1973, including 1,018 runs before the end of May. Scored ten centuries in 1970, a county record. Scored two centuries in a match four times: 122 and 128 not out v Warwickshire at Birmingham in 1972; 101 and 110 not out New Zealand v Australia at Christchurch 1973–74; 135 and 108 for Otago v Northern Districts at Gisborne in 1974–75; and 105 and 186 not out Otago v Central Districts at Dunedin 1974–75. Scored 141 not out, out of Worcestershire's total of 149 v Glamorgan at Swansea in 1977, namely 83.4% of the total, a record for first-class cricket. Has scored highest ever aggregate in John Player League: 4,948. Also holds J.P.L. record of 41 innings

over 50. Scored 100 runs before lunch v Warwickshire, at Worcester, 1979.
Address and telephone number: c/o Worcestershire County Cricket Club, New Road, Worcester WR2 4QQ.
Personal best: Batting Tests 259 New Zealand v West Indies, Georgetown 1971–72; other f/class 259 New Zealand v Guyana, Georgetown 1971–72; jpl 129* Worcs v Glamorgan, Worcester 1973; b&h 143* Worcs v Warwicks, Edgbaston 1976; gillette 117* Worcs v Lancs, Worcester 1971. Bowling f/class 3–18 Worcs v Pakistan, Worcester 1967; jpl 2–25 Worcs v Yorkshire, Leeds 1969.

TURNER, Stuart.
County: Essex.
Role: Right-hand bat, right arm fast medium bowler.
Date and place of birth: 18 July 1943, Chester.
Height: 6′ 0½″. *Weight:* 12 st 6 lbs.
Parents: Arthur Leonard and Alice Turner.
Wife: Jacqueline Linda.
Children: Jeremy Paul, 8 February 1968; Emma Louise, 21 January 1970.
Education and qualifications: Epping Junior and Epping Secondary Modern. Qualified as advanced cricket coach.
Occupation outside cricket: Insurance broking; coaching, both in South Africa and in England during off-season.
Family links with cricket: None, but "father planted the first seeds of interest at an early age and taught me all he knew."

County debut: 1965. *County cap:* 1970.
Benefit: 1979.
Outside interests: Reading, playing records, "doing anything that takes my interest and just enjoying life."
Other sporting activities: Squash, occasional football, "enjoy trying as many sports as possible. Not a great deal of time when one makes a living at sport."
General: Played for Natal in 1976–77 and 1977–78 Currie Cup Competition. First bowler to reach 200 wickets in John Player League. Has missed only one John Player match since competition began in 1969.

Address and telephone number: c/o Essex County Cricket Club, New Writtle Street, Chelmsford CM2 0RW.
Personal best: Batting f/class 121 Essex v Somerset, Taunton 1970; jpl 87 Essex v Worcs, Chelmsford 1975; b&h 41* Essex v Minor Counties East, Chelmsford 1977; gillette 50 Essex v Lancs, Chelmsford 1971. Bowling f/class 6–26 Essex v Northants, Northampton 1977; jpl 5–35 Essex v Hants, Chelmsford 1978; b&h 4–22 Essex v Minor Counties South, Bedford 1975; gillette 3–16 Essex v Glamorgan, Ilford 1971.

UNDERWOOD, Derek Leslie.
County: Kent.
Role: Right-hand bat, left arm medium bowler.
Date and place of birth: 8 June 1945, Bromley, Kent.
Height: 5′ 11″. *Weight:* 12 st.
Parents: Leslie Underwood, deceased, and Evelyn Underwood.
Wife: Dawn.
Married: 6 October 1973.
Children: Heather, 7 February 1976.
Education and qualifications: Dulwich College Prep School, Beckenham and Penge Grammar School.
Occupation outside cricket: Company representative, cricket coach, P.E. schoolmaster.
Family links with cricket: "I played with my father and brother for a local village team, Farnborough. I played for Beckenham with my brother until I played for the Kent 1st XI. My brother now plays for Poloc C.C. in Glasgow."
County debut: 1963. *County cap:* 1964.
Benefit: £24,114 in 1975.
Outside interests: Photography, philately, coarse fishing, gardening.
Nickname: Deadly.
Other sporting activities: Occasional golf.
General: President of Fledglings C.C. Took 100 wickets in debut season of 1963, being youngest player ever to do so in debut season. Second youngest player to receive county cap. Elected Best Young Cricketer of the Year in 1966 by Cricket Writers' Club, was

one of Wisden's Cricketers of the Year in 1968. Played World Series Cricket 1978–79.
Address and telephone number: c/o Kent County Cricket Club, St. Lawrence Ground, Canterbury CT1 3NZ.
Personal best: Batting Tests 45* England v Australia, Leeds 1968; other f/class 80 Kent v Lancs, Old Trafford 1969; jpl 22 Kent v Worcs, Dudley 1969; b&h 17 Kent v Essex, Canterbury 1973; gillette 28 Kent v Sussex, Tunbridge Wells 1963. Bowling Tests 8–51 England v Pakistan, Lord's 1974; other f/class 9–28 Kent v Sussex, Hastings 1964; jpl 5–19 Kent v Gloucs, Maidstone 1972; b&h 5–35 Kent v Surrey, The Oval 1976; gillette 4–57 Kent v Leics, Canterbury 1974.

WALLER, Christopher Edward.
County: Sussex.
Role: Right-hand bat, slow left arm orthodox.
Date and place of birth: 3 October 1948, Guildford, Surrey.
Height: 5' 10¼". *Weight:* 11 st 7 lbs.
Parents: Frederick Edward and Iris Waller.
Wife: Lesley Deborah.
Married: 25 March 1972.
Children: Alexandra Lois, 21 August 1975; Stephanie Kate, 16 May 1977; Adrian Paul, 5 August 1979.
Education and qualifications: St. Bede's C. of E. Secondary School, Send, Woking, Surrey. N.C.A. advanced coach.
Occupation outside cricket: Coaching at Alf Gover's Cricket School, Wandsworth; Crystal Palace National Sports Centre, and Sussex C.C.C. Indoor School.
Family links with cricket: Father played for Horsley C.C. for 47 years as an opening batsman and off-spin bowler. "I first played for Horsley C.C. at the age of 11."
County debut: 1974. *County cap:* 1976.
Outside interests: Listening to records and reading books on any sport. "Spending free time with my wife and children."
Nickname: Wal.
Other sporting activities: Squash, football, "Sussex C.C.C. have formed their own team."
General: Debut for Surrey, 1967, cap 1972. Left after 1973 season. Coached 1977–78 in

New South Wales, Australia, for World Series Cricket.
Address and telephone number: c/o Sussex County Cricket Club, Eaton Road, Hove BN3 3AN.
Personal best: Batting f/class 47 Surrey v Pakistan, The Oval 1971; jpl 18* Sussex v Glamorgan, Hove 1975; b&h 11* Sussex v Essex, Chelmsford 1975; gillette 14* Sussex v Notts, Trent Bridge 1975. Bowling f/class 7–64 Surrey v Sussex, The Oval 1971; jpl 4–28 Sussex v Essex, Hove 1976; b&h 4–25 Sussex v Minor Counties South, Hove 1975; gillette 1–41 Sussex v Notts, Trent Bridge 1975.

WALTERS, John.
County: Derbyshire.
Role: Left-hand bat, right arm fast medium bowler.
Date and place of birth: 7 August 1949, Brampton, Yorkshire.
Occupation outside cricket: Works in a garage. Worked as a bouncer in a night-club.
County debut: 1977.
Nickname: Welder.
General: Has played in Huddersfield League. Has his own Fan Club at Derby.
Address and telephone number: c/o Derbyshire County Cricket Club, Nottingham Road, Derby DE2 6DA.
Personal best: Batting f/class 90 Derby v Warwicks, Edgbaston 1978; jpl 55* Derby v Worcs, Worcester 1978; b&h 12 Derby v Warwicks, Edgbaston 1979; gillette 3 Derby v Middlesex, Derby 1978. Bowling f/class 4–100 Derby v Worcs, Derby 1979; jpl 4–14

Derby v Glamorgan, Swansea 1979; b&h 2–28 Derby v Surrey, Derby 1979.

WATSON, Gregory George.
County: Worcestershire.
Role: Right-hand bat, right arm fast medium bowler.
Date and place of birth: 29 January 1955, Gulgong, New South Wales, Australia.
Education and qualifications: Mudgee High School; University of New South Wales.
County debut: 1978.
Nickname: Greg.
General: Toured England with Old Collegians team in 1977 and played for Smethwick in Birmingham League. Debut for New South Wales 1977-78.
Address and telephone number: c/o Worcestershire County Cricket Club, New Road, Worcester WR2 4QQ.
Personal best: Batting f/class 38 Worcs v Somerset, Taunton 1978; jpl 2 Worcs v Warwicks, Worcester 1978; b&h 5* Worcs v Somerset, Taunton 1978. Bowling f/class 6-45 Worcs v Sussex, Eastbourne 1978; jpl

4-30 Worcs v Somerset, Taunton 1978; b&h 5-22 Worcs v Combined Universities, Worcester 1978.

WATSON, William Kenneth.
County: Nottinghamshire.
Role: Right-hand bat, right arm fast medium bowler.
Date and place of birth: 21 May 1955, Port Elizabeth, South Africa.
Height: 6' 3". *Weight:* 13 st 3 lbs.
Parents: Mr. and Mrs. E. V. Gilbert, "Erik and Em".
Education and qualifications: Dale College, Kingwilliamstown, South Africa.
County debut: 1976 (played only in John Player League matches in 1977).
Nickname: Ken.
Outside interests: "Sunbathing."
Other sporting activities: Rugby, soccer.
General: Debut for Border 1974-75. Played for Northern Transvaal 1975-76 and for Eastern Province 1976-77.
Address and telephone number: South Africa: 46 5th Avenue, Walmer 6065, Port Elizabeth, South Africa. Telephone: 041-511713. England: 65 Stratford Road, Westbridgford, Nottingham. Telephone: Nottingham 813152.
Personal best: Batting f/class 28* Notts v

Cambridge University, Cambridge 1978; jpl 5 Notts v Somerset, Trent Bridge 1979; gillette 5 Notts v Yorkshire, Bradford 1978. Bowling f/class 6-51 Notts v Derby, Trent Bridge 1979; jpl 3-20 Notts v Hants, Bournemouth 1977; gillette 1-22 Notts v Sussex, Hove 1979.

WATTS, Patrick James.
County: Northamptonshire.
Role: Left-hand bat, right arm medium bowler.

Date and place of birth: 16 June 1940, Henlow, Bedfordshire.
Height: 193 cm. *Weight:* 176 lbs.

continued overleaf

Parents: Arthur and Ethel Mary Watts, both deceased.
Wife: (1) Rosalie Anne, September 1961, died of Hodgkin's Disease 1978. (2) Elaine, March 1979.
Children: Carol Mary, 30 June 1962; David James, 5 December 1964; Stepdaughter: Amelia Elizabeth Stevenson, 3 March 1969.
Education and qualifications: Stratton Grammar School, Biggleswade, Bedfordshire; Nene College, Northampton, B.Ed.
Occupation outside cricket: Teacher, Spratton Hall Prep School, Spratton, Northants.
Family links with cricket: Brother, P. D. Watts, played first-class cricket with Northamptonshire and Nottinghamshire; Northants staff 1956–66. Notts 1967. Other brother, Christopher John, now in Canada, very good cricketer at club level. "Father just very keen."
County debut: 1959. *County cap:* 1962.
Benefit: £6,351 in 1974.
Outside interests: Family life, walking, "particularly in out of the way places".
Nickname: Jim.
Other sporting activities: Coaching rugby, football, and cricket at school. "Very keen on football in early years."
General: Having made debut in 1959, left staff after 1966 season but rejoined in 1970. County captain from 1971–74. Left staff after 1974 season to train as a teacher. Played occasionally in 1975 but not at all in 1976 and 1977. Reappointed County Captain in 1978. Member Northants C.C.C. general cricket committee, member T.C.C.B. umpire's

committee, member T.C.C.B. cricket committee. Always uses Gray Nicholls sports gear.
Address and telephone number: 74 Doddington Road, Earls Barton, Northampton. Telephone: Northampton 810293.
Personal best: Batting f/class 145 Northants v Hants, Bournemouth 1964; jpl 83 Northants v Lancs, Bedford 1971; b&h 40 Northants v Middlesex, Lord's 1974; gillette 40 Northants v Glamorgan, Northampton 1972. Bowling f/class 6–18 Northants v Somerset, Taunton 1965; jpl 5–24 Northants v Notts, Peterborough 1971; b&h 4–11 Northants v Middlesex, Lord's 1974; gillette 4–48 Northants v Warwicks, Northampton 1964.

WELLS, Colin Mark.
County: Sussex.
Role: Right-hand bat, right arm medium bowler.
Date and place of birth: 3 March 1960, Newhaven, Sussex.
Height: 6′ 0″. *Weight:* 12 st 7 lbs.
Parents: Ernest William Charles and Eunice Mae Wells.
Wife: Unmarried.
Education and qualifications: Tideway Comprehensive School, Newhaven. Two

C.S.E.s, nine O-levels, one A-level.
Occupation outside cricket: Laboratory assistant.
Family links with cricket: Father had trials for Sussex and played for Sussex Cricket Association. Both brothers play cricket and youngest brother, Alan, played for England Schools and toured Canada with N.C.A. 1979.
County debut: 1979.
Outside interests: Sea-angling.
Other sporting activities: Football, rugby,

hockey, basketball, tennis, table tennis.
General: Played in three John Player League matches in 1978.
Address and telephone number: 33 Northdown Road, Newhaven, Sussex.
Personal best: Batting f/class 29 Sussex v Hants, Bournemouth 1979; jpl 27 Sussex v Middlesex, Lord's 1979; gillette 7 Sussex v Suffolk, Hove 1979. Bowling f/class 4-23 Sussex v Oxford University, Pagham 1979; jpl 2-21 Sussex v Middlesex, Hove 1978; gillette 2-20 Sussex v Suffolk, Hove 1979.

WESSELS, Kepler Christoffel.
County: Sussex.
Role: Left-hand bat, off-break bowler.
Date and place of birth: 14 September 1957, Bloemfontein, South Africa.
Education and qualifications: Grey's College, Bloemfontein.
County debut: 1976. *County cap:* 1977.
Off-season 1979-80: Playing cricket in Brisbane.
General: Debut for Orange Free State in 1973-74 Currie Cup Competition, aged 16 years 4 months. Played for Northern Transvaal 1977-78. Played for World Series Cricket. Top run-getter in England in 1979 with 1,800 runs.
Address and telephone number: c/o Sussex County Cricket Club, Eaton Road, Hove BN3 3AN. Telephone: Brighton 732161.
Personal best: Batting f/class 187 Sussex v Kent, Eastbourne 1979; jpl 88 Sussex v Notts, Trent Bridge 1977; b&h 106 Sussex v Notts,

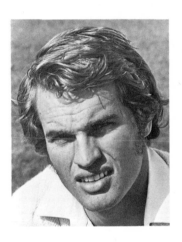

Hove 1977; gillette 43 Sussex v Staffs, Stone 1978. Bowling f/class 1-4 Northern Transvaal v Western Province B, Pretoria 1977-78.

WESTON, Martin John.
County: Worcestershire.
Date and place of birth: 8 April 1959, Worcester.
Height: 6' 1". *Weight:* 14 st 7 lbs.
Parents: John Franklyn and Sheila Margaret Weston.
Education and qualifications: St. George's C. of E. Junior, Samuel Southall Secondary Modern. City & Guilds and Advance Crafts in Bricklaying.
County debut: 1979.
Outside interests: Horse-racing.
Other sporting activities: Golf. Football.
General: Is on Committee of Worcester City Cricket Club.
Address and telephone number: 39 Lansdowne Street, Barbourne, Worcester, WR1 1QE. Telephone Worcester 22797.

WHITEHOUSE, John.
County: Warwickshire.
Role: Right-hand bat, off break bowler.
Date and place of birth: 8 April 1949, Nuneaton.
Height: 5' 9½". *Weight:* 12 st.
Married: with one son, two daughters.
Education and qualifications: King Edward VI School, Nuneaton; Bristol University.
Occupation outside cricket: Accountant.
Family links with cricket: Father played for Nuneaton C.C.
County debut: 1971. *County cap:* 1973.
Nickname: Flight.
Other sporting activities: Rugby union.
General: Played for county v Scotland in 1970, a match no longer regarded as first-class. Scored 173 v Oxford University at Oxford in 167 minutes in first innings of debut match 1971. Elected Best Young Cricketer of the Year 1971 by Cricket Writers' Club. County Captain 1978 and 1979, but now relinquished it.
Address and telephone number: c/o Warwickshire County Cricket Club, Edgbaston, Birmingham.
Personal best: Batting f/class 173 Warwicks v

Oxford University, Oxford 1971; jpl 92 Warwicks v Surrey, Edgbaston 1976; b&h 71* Warwicks v Lancs, Edgbaston 1976; gillette 109 Warwicks v Glamorgan, Edgbaston 1976. Bowling f/class 2–55 Warwicks v Yorkshire, Edgbaston 1977; jpl 1–36 Warwicks v Lancs, Old Trafford 1978.

WHITELEY, John Peter.
County: Yorkshire.
Role: Right-hand bat, off-break bowler.
Date and place of birth: 22 February 1955, Otley, Yorkshire.
Height: 6' 2". *Weight:* 12 st 7 lbs.
Parents: John and Mavis Whiteley.
Wife: Carol.
Married: 22 October 1977.
Education and qualifications: Ashfield College, Harrogate. Bristol University, B.Sc. Chemistry.
Occupation outside cricket: Has worked in accounts department of Vallance's electrical retailers.
Family links with cricket: Father, Chairman, Dales Council Cricket League. Mother, Secretary, Harrogate Ladies Cricket Club. Two brothers play for Harrogate Cricket Club. Sister, Harrogate Ladies and North Yorks Under-19 Ladies teams. Wife, Harrogate Ladies team.
County debut: 1978.
Off-season 1979–80: Coaching in South Africa.
Outside interests: Gardening and reading.

Nickname: Nimmo.
Other sporting activities: Rugby Union, tennis, golf.
General: Played for Yorkshire Second XI since 1972.
Address and telephone number: c/o

168

Yorkshire County Cricket Club, Headingley Cricket Ground, Leeds LS6 3BU.
Personal best: Batting f/class 20 Yorkshire v

Northants, Northampton 1979. Bowling f/class 4–14 Yorkshire v Notts, Scarborough 1978.

WILKINS, Alan Haydn.
County: Glamorgan.
Role: Right-hand bat, left arm medium bowler.
Date and place of birth: 22 August 1953, Cardiff.
Height: 5′ 10″.   *Weight:* 11 st 10 lbs.
Parents: William Haydn and Anne Elizabeth Wilkins.
Wife: Dot.
Married: 22 September 1979.
Education and qualification: Whitchurch Grammar School, Cardiff. Loughborough College of Education/University. B.Ed. in physical education and history, Cert. Ed. Loughborough.
Family links with cricket: Father, Haydn Wilkins, Captain, Cardiff Cricket Club, played for Royal Engineers and Glamorgan C.C.C. Colts, club and ground Second XI.
County debut: 1976.
Off-season 1979–80: Coaching and playing for Springs High School, near Johannesburg. South Africa.
Outside interests: Reading—physical education aspects, psychology, philosophy, history, novels, *Daily Telegraph* crosswords, photography, music and sophisticated hi-fi equipment, films, "Favourite beer, draught Guinness or Brains dark. Favourite dressing-room magazine, *Playboy.*
Nickname: Wilki.
Other sporting activities: Rugby (Loughborough Colleges R.F.C., Cardiff R.F.C., Glamorgan Wanderers R.F.C.), golf.

General: Would like to contribute to sports writing, especially to a cricket magazine. Feels the T.C.C.B. should relax its laws governing advertising on cricket gear. Would like to qualify in physiotherapy.
Address and telephone number: c/o Glamorgan County Cricket Club.
Personal best: Batting f/class 70 Glamorgan v Notts, Worksop 1977; jpl 3 Glamorgan v Sussex, Swansea 1979; b&h 5* Glamorgan v Worcs, Worcester 1978; 5 Glamorgan v Somerset, Taunton 1979. Bowling f/class 6–79 Glamorgan v Hants, Southampton 1979; jpl 5–23 Glamorgan v Warwicks, Edgbaston 1978; b&h 5–17 Glamorgan v Worcs, Worcester 1978; gillette 2–33 Glamorgan v Surrey, Cardiff 1977.

WILLEY, Peter.
County: Northamptonshire.
Role: Right-hand bat, off-break bowler.
Date and place of birth: 6 December 1949, Sedgefield, County Durham.
Height: 6′ 1″.   *Weight:* 13 st.
Parents: Oswald and Maisie Willey.
Wife: Charmaine.
Married: 23 September 1971.
Education and qualifications: Secondary modern (Seaham, County Durham).
Occupation outside cricket: Has worked as a

groundsman, labourer and in a shoe factory. Has coached in South Africa 1978–79.
Family links with cricket: Father played local club cricket in County Durham.
County debut: 1966, aged 16 years 5 months.   *County cap:* 1971.
Outside interests: "Spending time with my two dogs, Irish Setter and cross Labrador-Setter."
Nickname: Chin. Will.
Other sporting activities: Golf.

continued overleaf

General: Endorses Slazengers sporting goods.
Shared in fourth wicket partnership record
for county, 370 with R. T. Virgin v Somerset
at Northampton in 1976. Toured Australia
with England 1979-80. Three hundreds in
one season (1976) equals record for a season
with Barry Richards (Hampshire). Youngest
player ever to play for Northants C.C.C. at
16 years, 180 days v Cambridge in 1966.
Address and telephone number: 36
Sandringham Road, Northampton.
Personal best: Batting Tests 52 England v
India, The Oval 1979; other f/class 227
Northants v Somerset, Northampton 1976;
jpl 107 Northants v Warwicks, Edgbaston
1975; 107 Northants v Hants, Tring 1976;
b&h 58 Northants v Warwicks, Northampton
1974; gillette 89 Northants v Sussex, Hove
1979. Bowling Tests 2-96 England v India,
The Oval 1979; other f/class 7-37 Northants
v Oxford University, Oxford 1975; jpl 4-59
Northants v Kent, Northampton 1971; b&h

3-12 Northants v Minor Counties East,
Horton 1977; gillette 3-37 Northants v
Cambridge University, March 1975.

WILLIAMS, Richard Grenville.

County: Northamptonshire.
Role: Right-hand bat, off-break bowler.
Date and place of birth: 10 August 1957,
Bangor, Caernarvonshire.
Height: 5′ 6″.
Education and qualifications: Ellesmere Port
Grammar School.
County debut: 1974, aged 16 years 10
months.
Off-season 1979-80: Playing club cricket in
Sydney, Australia on Whitebread
Scholarship. Touring Australasia in February
and March 1980 with Derrick Robins Under-
23 XI.
General: Debut for 2nd XI in 1972 aged 14
years 11 months. Toured West Indies with
England Young Cricketers 1976. Made
maiden century in 1979, and then scored four
centuries in 5 innings. Spent off-season
1979-80 playing grade cricket in Sydney,
N.S.W.
Address and telephone number: c/o
Northamptonshire County Cricket Club,
Wantage Road, Northampton NN1 4TJ.
Telephone: Northampton 32917.
Personal best: Batting f/class 151* Northants
v Warwicks, Northampton 1979; jpl 65*
Northants v Glamorgan, Cardiff 1976; b&h

10* Northants v Minor Counties East,
Longton 1976; gillette 51 Northants v
Durham, Northampton 1977. Bowling
f/class 5-57 Northants v Sussex,
Northampton 1979; jpl 4-32 Northants v
Derby, Long Eaton 1979; b&h 2-26
Northants v Combined Universities,
Cambridge 1979; gillette 3-15 Northants v
Leics, Northampton 1979.

WILLIS, Robert George Dylan.
County: Warwickshire.
Role: Right-hand bat, right arm fast bowler.
Date and place of birth: 30 May 1949,
Sunderland.
Height: 6′ 6″. *Weight:* 14 st.
Parents: Edward and Anne Willis.
Wife: Juliet Smail.
Married: 19 March 1980.
Education and qualifications: Guildford
Royal Grammar School.
Family links with cricket: Brother, David,
keeps wicket for Blackheath C.C.
County debut: 1972. *County cap:* 1972.
Outside interests: Music, classical and
popular, especially Bob Dylan.
Nickname: Dylan, Goose, Harold,
Swordfish.
Other sporting activities: Soccer, tennis,
badminton.
General: Appointed Captain of
Warwickshire for 1980. Debut for Surrey
1969. Left staff after 1971 season, to make
debut for Warwickshire in 1972. Was one of
Wisden's Cricketers of the Year in 1978.
Added third name, Dylan, by deed poll,
because of admiration for songwriter and
singer, Bob Dylan. Operations on both knees
during 1975 threatened to end his career, but
he re-established his England place in 1976.
Toured Australia, New Zealand 1970–71 and
1974–75; West Indies 73–74; India, Sri
Lanka and Australia 1976–77; Pakistan and
New Zealand 1977–78; Australia 1978–79
and 1979–80, as Vice-Captain. Has played
soccer, goalkeeper, for Guildford City.
Published *Diary of a Cricket Season* in 1979.
Went through hypnotism courses to improve
mental attitude.

Address and telephone number: c/o
Warwickshire County Cricket Club,
Edgbaston, Birmingham.
Personal best: Batting Tests 24 England v
India, Old Trafford 1974; 24* England v
Australia, The Oval 1977; other f/class 43
Warwicks v Middlesex, Edgbaston 1976; jpl
52* Warwicks v Derby, Edgbaston 1975; b&h
25* Warwicks v Northants, Northampton
1977; gillette 12* Surrey v Sussex, The Oval
1970. Bowling Tests 7–78 England v
Australia, Lord's 1977; other f/class 8–32
Warwicks v Gloucs, Bristol 1977; jpl 4–12
Warwicks v Middlesex, Lord's 1973; b&h
5–27 Warwicks v Lancs, Edgbaston 1976;
gillette 6–49 Surrey v Middlesex, The Oval
1970.

WILSON, Peter Hugh L'Estrange.
County: Surrey.
Role: Right-hand bat, right arm fast medium
bowler.
Date and place of birth: 17 August 1958,
Guildford, Surrey.
Height: 6′ 5″. *Weight:* 14 st 7 lbs.
Parents: Peter Sydney (Lt-Cdr, R.N.) and
Heather Margaret Wilson.
Education and qualifications: Wellington

College.
County debut: 1978.
Outside interests: Photography.
Nickname: Flea.
Other sporting activities: Golf, squash,
hockey.
General: Played for Hampshire Second XI
1976–77. Action is often compared with Bob
Willis, and Willis did in fact coach him.
continued overleaf

Spent 1979–80 off-season in South Africa.
Address and telephone number: The Old
Mill, Bramshott, Liphook, Hampshire.
Personal best: Batting f/class 15 Surrey v
Worcs, The Oval 1979; jpl 18* Surrey v
Worcs, The Oval 1979; gillette 8* Surrey v
Essex, Colchester 1978. Bowling f/class 4–39
Surrey v Warwicks, The Oval 1979; jpl 4–32
Surrey v Middlesex, The Oval 1979; b&h
5–21 Surrey v Combined Universities, The
Oval 1979; gillette 3–59 Surrey v Essex,
Colchester 1978.

WINCER, Robert Colin.
County: Derbyshire.
Role: Left-hand bat, right arm fast medium
bowler.
Date and place of birth: 2 April 1952,
Portsmouth.
Education and qualifications: Hemsworth
Grammar School, Yorkshire.
County debut: 1978.
Nickname: Bob.
Address and telephone number: c/o
Derbyshire County Cricket Club,
Nottingham Road, Derby DE2 6DA.
Personal best: Batting f/class 26 Derby v
Kent, Chesterfield 1979; jpl 11 Derby v Kent,
Chesterfield 1979; b&h 6* Derby v Kent,
Lord's 1978. Bowling f/class 4–42 Derby v
Leics, Derby 1978; jpl 2–28 Derby v Kent,
Chesterfield 1979.

WOOLMER, Robert Andrew.
County: Kent.
Role: Right-hand bat, right arm medium
bowler.
Date and place of birth: 14 May 1948,
Kanpur, India.
Height: 6′ 0″. *Weight:* 13 st 5 lbs.
Parents: Clarence (Charles) and Stella
Katherine Woolmer.
Wife: Gillian Shirley.
Married: 9 November 1974.
Children: Dale Robert Woolmer, 21 March
1979.
Education and qualifications: Yardley Court
Prep School and Skinner's School. Five O-

levels. Three years in school XI.
Occupation outside cricket: Director of
sports goods firm, cricket coach, P.R.O. for
catering company, Thwaites and Matthews,
sports coach Holmewood House School.
Coach in Durban, South Africa.
Family links with cricket: Father played in
Ranji Trophy, Utah Pradesh, against
Maharashtra in 1947–48. Also played club
cricket for Calcutta, Colombo and Tonbridge
Cricket Club.
County debut: 1968. *County cap:* 1970.
Outside interests: Photography, theatre.
Enjoys indoor games.
Nickname: Bob, Woolly.

Other sporting activities: Hockey for Tonbridge Hockey Club and represented Kent A 1969-70. Golf handicap 19.
General: Uses County Sports bats and endorses Grade A English-made cricket ball. Was one of Wisden's Cricketers of the Year in 1975. Played for Natal 1973-74 and 1975-76 Currie Cup Competition. First bowler to take 50 John Player League wickets, in 1970. Only person to bowl more than 8 overs in a John Player League match: 8-1 v Hants in 1972. When he was a baby, his father placed a bat in his hands and said "I hope this will be your life."
Address and telephone number: 63 Sandown Park, Tunbridge Wells, Kent. Business telephone, Tunbridge Wells 36405.
Personal best: Batting Tests 149 England v Australia, The Oval 1975; other f/class 169 Kent v Yorkshire, Canterbury 1979; jpl 64 Kent v Lancs, Old Trafford 1976; b&h 79 Kent v Derby, Lord's 1978; gillette 78 Kent v Notts, Trent Bridge 1975. Bowling Tests 1-8 England v Australia, Leeds 1977; other

f/class 7-47 Kent v Sussex, Canterbury 1969; jpl 6-9 Kent v Derby, Chesterfield 1979; b&h 4-14 Kent v Sussex, Tunbridge Wells 1972; gillette 4-28 Kent v Somerset, Taunton 1979.

WRIGHT, John Geoffrey.

County: Derbyshire.
Role: Left-hand bat, right arm medium bowler.
Date and place of birth: 5 July 1954, Darfield, New Zealand.
Education and qualifications: Christ's College, Christchurch, and Otago University, New Zealand.
County debut: 1977. *County cap:* 1977.
Off-season 1979-80: Playing in New Zealand.
Nickname: Wrighty.
Other sporting activities: Golf.
General: Toured England with New Zealand 1978.
Address and telephone number: c/o Derbyshire County Cricket Club, Nottingham Road, Derby DE2 6DA.
Personal best: Batting Tests: 88 New Zealand v Pakistan, Napier 1978-79; other f/class 164 Derby v Pakistan, Chesterfield 1978; jpl 75

Derby v Gloucs, Heanor 1977; b&h 102 Derby v Worcs, Chesterfield 1977; Gillette 87* Derby v Sussex, Hove 1977.

WINDAYBANK, Stephen James.

County: Gloucestershire.
Date and place of birth: 10 October 1956, Pinner, Middlesex.
Height: 6′ 2″. *Weight:* 12 st.

Parents: Barbara and James Windaybank.
Education and qualifications: Cotham Grammar School, Bristol, Bristol Polytechnic. H.N.D. in Business Studies.

continued overleaf

Family links with cricket: Father, Grandfather and Uncle were very keen local cricketers "in London before we moved to Bristol, and encouraged me a great deal."
County debut: 1979.
Off-season 1979–80: Playing cricket in Melbourne, Australia.
Outside interests: "Going to concerts, listening to music, a good film."
Nickname: Windy.
Other sporting activities: Golf, swimming.
Address and telephone number: 53 Druid Hill, Stoke Bishop, Bristol, Avon.
Personal best: Batting f/class 53 Gloucs v Cambridge University, Cambridge 1979.

WOOD, Barry.
County: Derbyshire.
Role: Right-hand bat, right arm medium bowler.
Date and place of birth: 26 December 1942, Ossett, Yorkshire.
Height: 5′ 7″. *Weight:* 11 st.
Parents: Herman and Ethel Wood.
Wife: Janet.
Children: Fiona Jane, 12 February 1967; Nathan Theodore, 4 October 1974.
Education and qualifications: Secondary.
Occupation outside cricket: Semi-professional footballer.
Family links with cricket: Brother, Ron, played for Yorkshire C.C.C. as slow left arm bowler.
County debut: 1966. County cap: 1968.
Testimonial: 1979.
Outside interests: Horse-riding and animals in general.
Nickname: Sawdust.
Other sporting activities': Football.
General: Debut for Yorkshire County Cricket Club 1964. Played for Eastern Province in Currie Cup 1971–72 and 1973–74. Scored centuries in both Roses matches in 1970 against his native Yorkshire. Rejected Lancs. offer for 1980 season.
Address and telephone number: c/o Lancashire County Cricket Club, Old Trafford, Manchester M16 0PX.

Personal best: Batting Tests 90 England v Australia, The Oval 1972; other f/class 198 Lancs v Glamorgan, Liverpool 1976; jpl 90* Lancs v Notts, Old Trafford 1977; b&h 79 Lancs v Minor Counties North, Longton 1975; gillette 116 Lancs v Kent, Canterbury 1979. Bowling f/class 7–52 Lancs v Middlesex, Old Trafford 1968; jpl 5–19 Lancs v Kent, Old Trafford 1971; b&h 5–12 Lancs v Derby, Southport 1976; gillette 4–17 Lancs v Hants, Old Trafford 1975.

YARDLEY, Thomas James.
County: Northamptonshire.
Role: Left-hand bat, right arm medium bowler, occasional wicket-keeper.
Date and place of birth: 27 October 1946, Chaddesley Corbett, Worcestershire.
Height: 6′ 1″. *Weight:* 13 st 3 lbs.
Parents: John and Sarah Yardley
Wife: Ruth.
Married: 3 April 1969.
Children: Alison, 5 November 1971; Elizabeth, 29 April 1976.
Education and qualifications: King Charles I Grammar School.
Occupation outside cricket: Sales administrator for carpet manufacturer in Kidderminster. Now, promotions for Northamptonshire C.C.C.
Family links with cricket: Two brothers play club cricket in Worcestershire.
County debut: 1976. *County cap:* 1978.
Outside interests: National Hunt and point-to-point racing, pop music, gardening.
Nickname: Jim.
Other sporting activities: "Used to play soccer quite seriously years ago and had chance to play professional soccer."
General: Debut for Worcestershire 1967, cap 1972. Not re-engaged after 1975 season. Debut for Northants 1976. "I have been fortunate enough in the 14 years that I have played to have gained a championship medal

in 1974, John Player winners 1971, runners-up 1975, Gillette winners 1976, runners-up 1979, Benson & Hedges runners-up 1973."
Address and telephone number: c/o Northamptonshire County Cricket Club, Wantage Road, Northampton NN1 4TJ.
Personal best: Batting f/class 135 Worcs v Notts, Worcester 1973; jpl 66* Northants v Middlesex, Lord's 1977; b&h 75* Worcs v Warwicks, Worcester 1972; Gillette 52 Worcs v Warwicks, Edgbaston 1972; 52* Worcs v Warwicks, Edgbaston 1973.

AHMED, Younis.
County: Worcestershire.
Role: Left-hand bat, left arm medium bowler.
Date and place of birth: 20 October 1947 in Jullundur, Pakistan.
Education and qualifications: Moslem High School, Lahore.
Occupation outside cricket: Has coached in Rhodesia and South Africa which led to ban from playing for Pakistan.
Family links with cricket: Younger half-brother of Saeed Ahmed who played for Pakistan.
County debut: 1979. *County cap:* 1979.
Off-season 1979–80: Playing in Australia.
General: Highest scoring left-hander in John Player League: 4,231 runs. Debut in 1962 at age of 14 years and 4 months for Pakistan School v South Zone (counts as first-class). Debut for Surrey in 1965. Cap 1969. Played for South Australia in 1972–73 Sheffield

Shield. Is now eligible to play for England.
Address and telephone number: c/o
continued overleaf

Worcestershire County Cricket Club, New Road, Worcester WR2 4QQ.
Personal best: Batting Tests 62 Pakistan v New Zealand, Karachi 1969-70; other f/class 221* Worcs v Notts, Newark 1979; jpl 113 Surrey v Middlesex, Lord's 1979; 113 Surrey v Warwicks, Edgbaston 1976; b&h 107* Worcs v Surrey, Worcester 1979; gillette 87 Surrey v Middlesex, The Oval 1970. Bowling f/class 4-10 Surrey v Cambridge University, Cambridge 1975; jpl 3-26 Worcs v Surrey, The Oval 1979; b&h 2-44 Worcs v Gloucs, Worcester 1979; gillette 2-54 Worcs v Leics, Leicester 1979.

ABBAS, Syed Zaheer.
County: Gloucestershire.
Role: Right-hand bat, off-break bowler.
Date and place of birth: 24 July 1947, Sialkot, Pakistan.
County debut: 1972. *County cap:* 1975.
Off-season 1979-80: Touring India with Pakistan.
Nickname: Zed.
General: Debut for Karachi Whites 1965-66. Subsequently played for Pakistan International Airways. Was one of Wisden's Cricketers of the Year in 1972. Played for Rest of the World v Australia 1971-72. Toured with Pakistan to Australia and West Indies, 1976-77. Wears spectacles. Scored two centuries in a match twice in 1976, 216 not out and 156 not out, v Surrey at the Oval; and 230 not out and 104 not out, v Kent at Canterbury; scored two centuries in a match once in 1977, 205 not out and 108 not out, v Sussex at Cheltenham. Was dismissed for hitting the ball twice for Pakistan International Airways v Karachi Blues at Karachi in 1969-70. Shared in second wicket record partnership for Pakistan, 291 with Mushtaq Mohammed v England at Birmingham in 1971.
Address and telephone number: c/o

Gloucestershire County Cricket Club, Neville Road, Bristol BS7 9EJ.
Personal best: Batting Tests 274 Pakistan v England, Edgbaston 1971; other f/class 230* Gloucs v Kent, Canterbury 1977; jpl 114* Gloucs v Hants, Bristol 1976; b&h 98 Gloucs v Surrey, The Oval 1975; gillette 131* Gloucs v Leics, Leicester 1975. Bowling f/class 5-15 Dawood v Railways, Lahore 1975-76; gillette 1-11 Gloucs v Oxfordshire, Bristol 1975.

DEBRETT

The English Gentleman

BY DOUGLAS SUTHERLAND
FOREWORD BY SIR IAIN MONCREIFFE OF THAT ILK, BART.

Is the "English Gentleman" a disappearing species? Douglas Sutherland examines the creature's habits and habitats in a light-hearted but penetrating way, and provides an amusing insight into the world of this endangered species.

£3.50

DEBRETT'S PEERAGE LIMITED
73-77 Britannia Road, London S.W.6. Tel: 01-736 6524

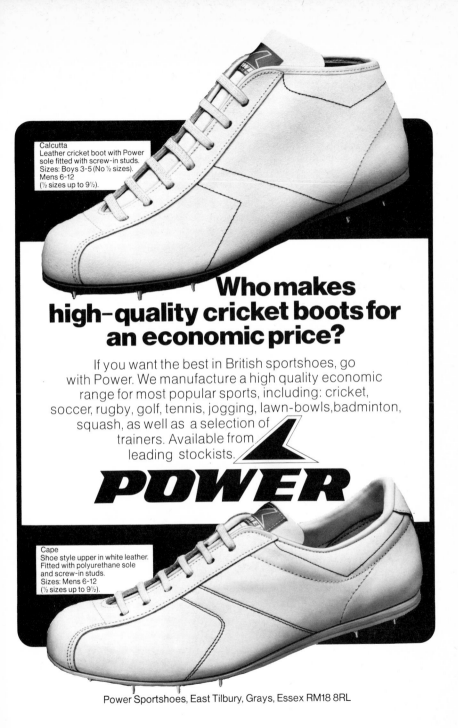

BY APPOINTMENT TO
H.R.H. THE DUKE OF EDINBURGH
BOOKSELLERS

BY APPOINTMENT TO
HER MAJESTY THE QUEEN
BOOKSELLERS

BY APPOINTMENT TO
H.M. QUEEN ELIZABETH
THE QUEEN MOTHER
BOOKSELLERS

Hatchards

For all Cricket Books and Sports Books generally

ESTABLISHED 1797

187 PICCADILLY LONDON W1V 9DA

TELEPHONE 01-439 9921 (10 lines)

*Books posted to any address. All books Reviewed or Advertised
on any subject can be ordered from Hatchards.*

Scores well in tests.

The Audi 100 five cylinder. Audi

The Malcolm Sargent Cancer Fund for Children

It is not usual to associate cricket with cancer but many of the children helped by the Malcolm Sargent Cancer Fund for Children can.

The Sargent XI has raised hundreds of pounds so that these children could benefit from grants that otherwise may not have been possible. A specially adapted car for a boy with spinal cancer, convalescent holidays (often the child's last), a longed for pet — these are just some of the many ways in which the money raised by the team has been spent.

The side is captained by well-known actor, William Franklyn, who has a long list of stage, film and TV appearances to his credit, but who for many is associated with TV commercials for a famous soft drink. In 1980 he celebrates fifty years of playing cricket having played his first match in Melbourne, Australia at the age of 5. His regular team includes Leonard Rossiter, Ed Stewart, Julian Holloway, Robert Powell, Brian Moore and other stars who make up the team when engagements permit — not least Mr Robert Morley who supports each match by just being himself!

This year three major matches are scheduled. At the Essex County ground on 1st June, against the Tom Pearce XI, at Amersham on a date in August to be announced, against the Hit or Miss XI and in September at Lords against The Cross Arrows. These matches will raise more money to help the children who look to the Fund for help.

The Malcolm Sargent Cancer Fund for Children is very proud of its cricket team and what is has achieved.

The Fund was launched in March, 1968 as a lasting and practical memorial to the much-loved British musician whose name it bears. Last year £9,400 (more than double the previous year) was spent providing convalescent holidays. A further £61 per day was spent during the winter months for essential home heating.

A minimum of £143,000 is estimated for these and other services for the ensuing year. Modern methods of treatment ensure longer survival for the young patient, consequently demands on the Fund's resources are for ever increasing.

For further information, Deed of Covenant forms, etc, please contact the Fund's administrative offices:

The Malcolm Sargent Cancer Fund for Children
Department DC, 6 Sydney Street, London, SW3 6PP.
Telephone: 01-352 6884

All donations will be gratefully acknowledged

MARIE CURIE 1867–1934

The Marie Curie Memorial Foundation

A unique independent organisation
dedicated to the welfare of those
with cancer, supported by voluntary
contributions, interest-free loans
and bequests.
This worthy cause needs your help -
to the extent of nearly £5 million
annually simply to maintain,
for those in need,
its vital humanitarian services.

These include, within the United Kingdom, eleven residential
Nursing Homes, nationwide Home Nurses, Welfare Needs
in kind, an Enquiry and Advice Bureau
together with specialised Research Laboratories
contributing to the understanding of the cancer problem.
Will you please help?

**If you require further details or wish now to respond
to this appeal, or perhaps interest others,
please write to the Secretary at:-**

THE MARIE CURIE MEMORIAL FOUNDATION
124 Sloane Street, LONDON SW1X 9BP
Tel: 01 730 9157
PATRON: Her Majesty Queen Elizabeth The Queen Mother

No genuine call
for help remains unanswered

ARTHUR WOOLLACOTT LIMITED

THE
PACKAGING SPECIALISTS

11 Fitzroy Square
London W1

Telephone 01 388 9591
Telex 22237

DEBRETT'S
Fine Books

We are proud to announce the long awaited new edition of **Debrett's Peerage & Baronetage** (£45),
which is the oldest established reference book on British titles and contains much invaluable information.
Correct Form (£5.95) is the definitive work on forms of address, precedence and protocol.
Kenneth Snowman's new exquisite book on **Carl Fabergé** (£12.95) is the ultimate collection of the best of Fabergé's work.
The Big Shots (£6.95) has become a bestselling book on the strength of its combination
of fascinating information and humorous anecdotes about shooting in the Edwardian era.
Maldwin Drummond's latest book **Salt-Water Palaces** (£8.95), with the introduction by the late Lord Mountbatten,
will enthrall any sailing enthusiast as well as any of those interested in living in the grand style.
The English Gentleman Series (£3.50 each) by Douglas Sutherland, which describes the strange customs and habits of
the Gentleman, his Wife and Child, has established itself as a popular bestseller and all of these books make ideal gifts.
I'll Never be Asked Again (£3.50) amusingly describes the pitfalls of a grouse party as experienced by a "foreigner",
U and Non-U Revisited (£3.75) has become famous as the successor to Nancy Mitford's Noblesse Oblige.
And finally **In & Out** (£3.95) which is a very light-hearted guide to contemporary society.

Debrett's Peerage Limited, 73/77 Britannia Road, London SW6 2JR. Telephone: 01-736 6524

Run Out.